THE SCIENCE OF BASKETBALL

The Science of Basketball is the only book to examine the scientific principles underpinning preparation and performance in basketball, applied to both individual and team contexts.

Drawing on the very latest scientific evidence, and including contributions from leading international coaches and scientists involved in the sport, the book explores every aspect of physical and mental preparation and performance, including:

- strength and conditioning, and training strategies
- physiological aspects of performance
- nutrition and supplementation
- psychological preparation
- skill acquisition
- biomechanical aspects of performance
- performance analysis
- injury epidemiology, prevention and rehabilitation
- coach education

Incorporating case studies at the end of each chapter to demonstrate how scientific principles can be applied to practice, the book bridges the gap between theory and applied practice in basketball better than any other. It is essential reading for any student, researcher, sport scientist, coach, physiotherapist or clinician with an interest in the game, and illuminative supplementary reading for students of sport science and sports coaching.

Alexandru Radu is a Senior Lecturer who has a vast teaching experience in the field of sports coaching, sports development and sport management. Currently he is lecturing at the University of Worcester, UK.

THE SCIENCE OF BASKETBALL

Edited by Alexandru Radu

LONDON AND NEW YORK

First published 2019
by Routledge
2 Park Square, Milton Park, Abingdon, Oxon OX14 4RN

and by Routledge
711 Third Avenue, New York, NY 10017

Routledge is an imprint of the Taylor & Francis Group, an informa business

© 2019 selection and editorial matter, Alexandru Radu; individual chapters, the contributors

The right of Alexandru Radu to be identified as the author of the editorial material, and of the authors for their individual chapters, has been asserted in accordance with sections 77 and 78 of the Copyright, Designs and Patents Act 1988.

All rights reserved. No part of this book may be reprinted or reproduced or utilised in any form or by any electronic, mechanical, or other means, now known or hereafter invented, including photocopying and recording, or in any information storage or retrieval system, without permission in writing from the publishers.

Trademark notice: Product or corporate names may be trademarks or registered trademarks, and are used only for identification and explanation without intent to infringe.

British Library Cataloguing-in-Publication Data
A catalogue record for this book is available from the British Library

Library of Congress Cataloging-in-Publication Data
Names: Radu, Alexandru, editor.
Title: Science of basketball / edited by Alexandru Radu.
Description: First edition. | New York : Routledge, 2018. | Includes bibliographical references and index.
Identifiers: LCCN 2018013688 | ISBN 9781138701533 (hardback) | ISBN 9781138701540 (paperback) | ISBN 9781315204000 (ebook)
Subjects: LCSH: Basketball. | Sports sciences.
Classification: LCC GV885 .S374 2018 | DDC 796.323—dc23
LC record available at https://lccn.loc.gov/2018013688

ISBN: 978-1-138-70153-3 (hbk)
ISBN: 978-1-138-70154-0 (pbk)
ISBN: 978-1-315-20400-0 (ebk)

Typeset in Bembo
by Apex CoVantage, LLC

This book is dedicated to my wife and my two boys, who fully supported me through the process of getting this project to completion.

CONTENTS

List of figures   x
List of tables   xii
About the authors   xiv

1 Strength and conditioning for basketball players and teams   1
   Alejandro Vaquera and Alexandru Radu

   1.1 Introduction 1
   1.2 Training principles and training methods 5
   1.3 Overview of physical abilities relevant to basketball training and coaching: integrated training 8
   1.4 Key stages and age groups when to develop the physical abilities in basketball players 25
   1.5 Physical preparation for basketball players – periodisation and training plans for basketball players 27
   1.6 Summary 29
   References 29

2 Physiology of basketball players and teams   33
   Christopher Holland

   2.1 Introduction 33
   2.2 Physiological requirements for basketball players 33
   2.3 Principles of physiological testing 44
   2.4 Summary 46
   References 46

viii Contents

3 Nutrition for basketball players and teams 51
   Juan Mielgo Ayuso and Ainhoa Prieto

   3.1 Introduction 51
   3.2 Nutritional limiting factors 52
   3.3 Summary 75
   Appendix 3.1 Match-oriented diet of a 90 kg basketball player competing on Sunday at 18:00 77
   References 81

4 Psychology for basketball players and teams 85
   Alexandru V. Stewart Mardan

   4.1 Introduction 85
   4.2 Rationale for psychological preparation in basketball 86
   4.3 Psychological preparation for competition in basketball 88
   4.4 Psychological preparation content for basketball players 89
   4.5 Summary 97
   References 97

5 Wheelchair basketball 101
   Miles Thompson and Haj Bhania

   5.1 Introduction 101
   5.2 Basic rules and offensive skills/actions: players' classification 102
   5.3 The sports wheelchair: player positional play 107
   5.4 Preparation for competition 108
   5.5 Defence 112
   5.6 Summary 118
   Appendix 5.1 Training and game schedule for the 2017 European Championships Tenerife (Spain) 119
   Appendix 5.2 Competition schedule from the 2016 Rio Paralympic Games 124
   References 126

6 Women's basketball 127
   Alexandru Radu and Florin Nini

   6.1 Introduction 127
   6.2 Training aspects specific to female junior and senior players 127
   6.3 Women as coaches 137
   6.4 Summary 138
   References 139

7   Medical issues in basketball   143
    Darren Cooper

    7.1 Introduction 143
    *7.2 Common injuries in basketball: injury prevention and
        treatment 143*
    7.3 Rehabilitation after injuries 151
    7.4 Means of recovery for basketball players 152
    7.5 Summary 154
    References 154

8   Coaching and basketball coach education   156
    Alexandru Radu

    8.1 Introduction 156
    8.2 Development of basketball coaches 157
    *8.3 Coaches role in the development and performance of
        basketball players 162*
    8.4 Summary 163
    References 164

9   Youth basketball   167
    Rutenis Paulauskas and Alexandru Radu

    9.1 Introduction 167
    *9.2 Selection and identification of young players: stages in the
        talent identification process 167*
    *9.3 Potential predictors of talent in basketball/selection
        criteria 179*
    9.4 Summary 180
    References 181

Index   *184*

FIGURES

1.1	Example of integrated training (strength)	13
1.2	Examples of integrated training (plyometrics)	14
1.3	Example of integrated training (aerobic endurance)	17
1.4	Example of integrated training (anaerobic-alactic endurance)	18
1.5	Example of integrated training (anaerobic-lactic endurance)	19
1.6	Example of integrated training (speed reaction)	21
1.7	Example of integrated training (speed)	22
1.8	Example of integrated training (drill speed)	23
3.1	Variation of vitamin D levels in blood after 8 months of season in the NBA	68
3.2	Modification of iron metabolism (ferritin and serum iron) throughout a basketball season	69
3.3	Ascorbic acid levels in the supplemented and placebo groups in pre-supplementation (PS), pre-training (PT), after training (AT) and 24 hours after training (24h-AT)	70
3.4	Changes in CK after 10 days of supplementation after exercise	72
3.5	Plasma levels of IL-2, TNF-α, MDA, and Catalase after 6 weeks of supplementation	74
6.1	Heart rate and time spent in various effort zones during training for a guard	131
6.2	Heart rate and time spent in various effort zones during training for a forward	132
6.3	Heart rate and time spent in various effort zones during training for a centre	133
8.1	Learning situations which lead to coach learning and development	157
9.1	Basketball players' evaluation and selection methods	169

9.2	Characteristic features of basketball players in the course of specialized selection	169
9.3	Correlation between average height of 6-year-old children who started attending basketball training sessions and their parents' average height	170
9.4	Parameters of competitive activities applied in the selection of players	176
9.5	Standardized indicator profiles of physical development and physical fitness for Women's Euroleague 2010 top scoring player C. L.	178
9.6	Standardized indicator profiles of physical development and physical fitness for Men's Euroleague 2008 MVP R. Š.	178
9.7	Athlete's mental characteristics and personality traits of maturity	179

TABLES

1.1	Most frequent actions performed by basketball players during game time	2
1.2	Distance covered during game time by players playing different positions	4
1.3	Strength training for basketball	11
1.4	Windows of opportunity to train physical abilities for young players	25
1.5	Suitable ages to teach technical and tactical concepts to young players	26
1.6	Recommended participation guidelines for basketball at various ages	26
1.7	Rest guidelines for various age groups	26
2.1	Normative physiological test data for elite male basketball players (PG – Point Guard, SG – Shooting Guard, SF – Small Forward, PF – Power Forward)	35
2.2	Example test battery for basketball	46
3.1	Example of annual distribution of basketball training	53
3.2	General planning of a basketball season	54
3.3	Zones and characteristics of basketball training	55
3.4	Food sources rich in CHO	56
3.5	Examples of breakfast substitution	57
3.6	Moment of CHO intake in competition	57
3.7	Protein-rich food sources	58
3.8	Fat-rich food sources	59
3.9	Things to consider when a basketball player is keen to consume supplements	60
3.10	Some combinations of electrolyte rich food sources to take post-exercises	61
3.11	Pre-match meal examples	62
3.12	Pre-match and during-match snack examples	62

3.13	Examples of foods to take during basketball games	63
3.14	Post-match meals	63
3.15	Possible nutritional strategies to promote an adequate training and match adaptation	64
3.16	Example of a weekly plan in a competitive period with 2 matches during the same week	66
3.17	Nutritional strategies for each training phase including supplements with potential benefits for basketball players	67
5.1	IWBF classification system – 2004 Classification Commission	106
5.2	Preparation calendar over a 12 month period for a GB Team	109
5.3	Factors to consider during the preparation process	110
5.4	Example of a training session with offensive emphasis	111
6.1	Height, weight and percentage of body fat in women's basketball at junior and senior level	129
6.2	Weekly training plan for a national team (senior women) during preparation period	135
6.3	Game load for elite female basketball players	135
9.1	Percentile scale of Lithuanian 6-year-old children's (n = 275) body composition and physical fitness assessment	171
9.2	Percentile scale of physical development and physical fitness indicators for 12-year-old basketball players (n = 12)	172
9.3	Assessment scale of Lithuanian cadet basketball team players' (U16) physical development and physical fitness indicators	174
9.4	Assessment scale of Lithuanian junior basketball team players' (U18) physical development and physical fitness indicators	174
9.5	Physical development, physical fitness and functional capacity assessment scale for elite women's basketball players	177
9.6	Physical development, physical fitness and functional capacity assessment scale for elite men's basketball players	177

ABOUT THE AUTHORS

Juan Mielgo Ayuso is currently working as a Lecturer of physiology at the University of Valladolid (Spain). He also works as a visiting lecturer in other universities, delivering lectures related to sports nutrition and sports physiology. Juan completed his bachelor's degree in human nutrition and dietetics at the University of Navarra in 1995. Juan continued his education doing his PhD in Biomedical Research at the University of Basque Country in 2013, where his PhD supervisors were Prof. Jesús Seco and Prof. Alfredo Córdova, two of the best sports medical doctors of Spain.

As a sport and health nutritionist, Juan has a great interest in sport nutrition, use of energy, ergogenic aids and its effects on the human body. His PhD thesis observed all aspects related to nutrition, psycho-physical profiles and muscle damage of professional women volleyball players over a competitive season. Taking detailed blood tests, anthropometric and psychometric data, and nutritional information at different points during the season, he observed and analysed the way the women's hormone levels, muscle strength, stress levels, and nutrition were altered over the competitive season, as well as the potential impact and connections between these variables. This study made a great connection between nutrition and sport and exercise physiology in high-level sport, providing a better understanding on the importance of good sports dietary advice, and on the way players' bodies develop, adapt and show damage over a sport competitive season.

During and after completing his PhD, Juan has been working as Performance Nutritionist in different elite teams, where he has managed to transfer his scientific knowledge into practice in the professional world of sport. Thanks to these experiences, he has won numerous awards with the different teams in which he has worked. Apart from this, he has participated in different research projects in nutrition and sport and exercise physiology, especially with elite athletes, and authored a large number of publications.

About the authors xv

Haj Bania possesses a Grade 3 Wheelchair Basketball Coach award, and he is also a British Wheelchair Basketball (BWB) Grade 2/3 Tutor CTS (Level 2/3). He has assisted with writing of various documents, including British Wheelchair Basketball Grade 2 and 3 Coach Courses Award Manuals. Haj is currently Head Coach of the GB Men Wheelchair Basketball Team and led this team to a bronze medal at the Paralympic Games in Rio 2016 and to a gold medal in European Wheelchair Basketball Championship in Worcester 2015.

Darren Cooper began his career as a Graduate Sports Therapist in 2003, and since then has worked with a large variety of sporting athletes, across a vast spectrum of sports, at every level from amateur to Olympic. In 2013 he joined the University of Worcester and is currently a Principal Lecturer in sports therapy. At the same time he began working with the Worcester Wolves British Basketball League (BBL) team and has experienced an array of incidents while courtside and off the court with the team and visiting clubs.

Christopher Holland MSc, PGDip, PGCE, BA (hons), MSST, CSCS, FHEA is the Programme Leader for Sports Therapy and Senior Lecturer in the Institute of Sports and Exercise Science at the University of Worcester, England. He has been teaching on higher education programmes across all areas of sports science since 2005 at both degree and master's levels. His published work focusses on the treatment of ankle sprains, and he has presented this research at international conferences. He is currently a doctoral candidate with a focus on the use of mobilisation techniques to improve outcome measures associated with chronic ankle instability. He has a background as a professional soccer player and has worked as the lead Sports Therapist and Strength and Conditioning Coach for a number of semi-professional teams. He currently works with professional and International age group basketball players providing injury prevention, treatment and rehabilitation as a sports therapist. He also runs a private sports injury clinic, working with athletes from a variety of sports, including distance running, mixed martial arts, fitness competitors and cyclists.

Alexandru V. Stewart Mardan received a master's degree in applied sport and exercise psychology from Ulster University (in 2014) and a master's degree in international sport management from Northumbria University (in 2010). He is an accredited professional member (psychology) with the Irish Institute of Sport and a fully paid up member of the British Association of Sport and Exercise Sciences. He is currently working as an applied sports scientist providing support for NGBs, teams, athletes and coaches in a diverse range of sports, including athletics, basketball, tennis, football and roller derby. His applied work and research interest is focused around coping and managing performance demands. His experiences as a former international 400 m sprinter and as a coaching tutor for England Athletics are unique assets. Alexandru also worked as a Lecturer in sports studies, and he is currently a part-time Progression Coach (Sport and Uniformed Public Services courses) at Newcastle College (in Newcastle upon Tyne, UK).

Florin Nini is a Lecturer in basketball at "Dunarea de Jos" University in Galati (Romania). He is a very experienced coach who is currently coaching the Phoenix Galati professional team in the Romanian First National League. Previously, he was coaching at both club level (including teams such as: BC Steaua Turabo Bucuresti, CS Energia Rovinari and CSM Tirgoviste) and also at national team level – he was the Head Coach of the Romanian Senior Women National Team; Romanian University National Team (men); and Romania U16 and U18 National teams (men).

Since 2017 to present he has been the President of the Committee for the Development of Coaches within the Romanian Basketball Federation.

Rutenis Paulauskas is a doctor of biomedical sciences and Professor at Lithuanian University of Educational Sciences (Vilnius, Lithuania). His central areas of teaching and research pertain to coaching high performance basketball players, teaching sport concepts and skills, and the physical fitness of youth and adolescents. As a Head Coach, he has coached several teams, including: Sakalai (Vilnius), "Nevėžis" (Kėdainiai), "GHASIR" (Beirut), Dinamo Moscow region, "TEO" (Vilnius). He was also assistant coach for Lokomotiv Rostov, CSKA Moscow and Lietuvos Rytas (Vilnius). He trained teams that became champions and prize winners of Lithuanian and Baltic basketball leagues, Russian National Cup winners. Together with the team Lietuvos Rytas, he won the European ULEB Cup. He was a coach of the Lithuanian Junior Men National Team, who became runners up in the European championship. He coached the Lithuanian Senior Women National Team.

He lectures at the University of Educational Sciences (Vilnius) and Lithuanian Sports University (Kaunas); he also delivered lectures at Worcester University (England), Kiel University (Germany) and the University of Granada (Spain). He was a trainer in the "FIBA European Coaching Certificate" program. He is board member of the Lithuanian Basketball Coaches' Association.

Ainhoa Prieto is a qualified Nutritionist and Dietitian (BSc) from the University of Navarra, a Registered Dietitian (RD) within the HCPC and specialized as a Sport Nutritionist (MSc) from the Liverpool John Moores University (LJMU) in the UK. Her great interest in the world of sport made her move to the UK to gain more experience in this field. Her first experience started at the High-Performance Centre at the University of Birmingham Sport, when she received the Leonardo da Vinci scholarship and won the second prize in the Best Placements Awards for her great results. Her following experiences as a practitioner combined both clinical and sport pathways in which she has gained excellent understanding of the disciplines in elite sporting environment, working with Liverpool Ladies FC, both individual athletes and teams competing in BUCS and also under the TASS scheme, and Doncaster Rovers Belles FC, until she reached the highest level in sport working as Head of Sport Nutrition for two professional teams: Deportivo Alavés FC and Baskonia Basketball Club in the city of Vitoria-Gasteiz in Spain. Her job is focused mainly on the first teams but also in the development of all the players from the academies, reaching up to 200 players. Apart from this job, Ainhoa is enrolled as a PhD student in the Faculty of Physical Activity and Sport at the University of the Basque Country, and she is currently on her second year of her doctoral thesis. Her advanced methodological research skills allowed her to identify, evaluate and disseminate the findings of her work as part of scientific publications from the university.

Alexandru Radu is a Senior Lecturer in Sports Coaching Basketball within the Institute of Sport and Exercise Science at the University of Worcester (United Kingdom). He is the Course Leader for the MSc in European Basketball Coaching Science, a post-graduate programme of study delivered by University of Worcester in partnership with Lithuanian Sports University from Kaunas (Lithuania). Other teaching areas he is involved in are: sports coaching, sport management and sports development. His main research areas include sports event management, Olympism and the Olympic movement, sport and mass media and basketball coaching. Two of his key publications are *Basketball: A Guide to Skills, Techniques and Tactics* and *Basketball Coaching: Putting Theory into Practice*. Previously, he lectured at Northumbria University in Newcastle upon Tyne (UK) and at "Al. I. Cuza" University of Iasi (Romania).

In addition to teaching undergraduate and post-graduate students in an academic environment, Alexandru is actively involved in practical coaching; he is Assistant Coach of the Worcester Wolves, a professional basketball team that plays in the British Basketball League (BBL). He is also the Head Coach of the Wales Futures Men National Team. His international coaching experience includes: Assistant Coach of the Romania Women National Team (and participation at Women Eurobasket 2015); Assistant Coach of the Wales Men National Team (and participation at European Championship for Small Countries in 2016); Head Coach of the Wales Under 18 Men National Team (during the 2016–2017 season); Associate Head Coach of the University of Worcester Men First Team (since 2017 to present). He was engaged in developing young players by coaching at various basketball camps in three countries: England, Lithuania and Romania. Furthermore, he is a Basketball England Tutor, and he delivers Level 1 and Level 2 Basketball Coach Award courses.

Miles Thompson is a native of coastal Southern California, and has significant wheelchair basketball coaching experience, since 1996 when he became a high school wheelchair basketball coach. In 1999 he led Team USA Under 19 to a gold medal. His other coaching roles include Head Coach of the University of Alabama (between 2006 and 2014); USA Women National Team defensive coordinator (in 2010; world champions); Head Coach of the Great Britain Women Paralympic Team (since 2014 to present) and participation at Paralympic Games in Rio 2016. He contributed to the following publications: *Skills and Drills of Wheelchair Basketball*; and *Tennis Drills for Youth*. Before competing and coaching wheelchair basketball, Miles was a keen wheelchair tennis player who competed across the world and who took part in two US open doubles finals.

Alejandro Vaquera has a bachelor's in physical education (University of Leon, 1999) and PhD in sports sciences (University of Leon, 2010). For more than 15 years he has taught basketball, sports science and sports physiology at the Faculty of Physical Activity and Sports Sciences at the University of León (Spain). Currently he is a Visiting Professor at the University of Worcester (United Kingdom). Between 2008 to 2016, he was the Director of Sports at University of Leon. Since 2008 to present he has been responsible for University Basketball in the Spanish Sports Government. Holding the Basketball Coach Level 3 award, he has worked as a coach of the University of Leon in the EBA League, and he was Spanish University Champion in 2003. His other roles include: Strength and Conditioning Coach of ACB, LEB Gold teams for more than 10 seasons. He was also Strength and Conditioning Coach of the Spanish National Teams Program (U18 and U20) during the period of 2004–2009, with which he has achieved, among other successes, the bronze medal at the European Championship in Greece 2006, or the classification for the 2007 and 2009 World Cups. With extensive international experience, he has worked as Coordinator of the Physical Preparation of the Referee Department for FIBA Europe from 2007 to 2014, and currently holds this position in FIBA as Global Fitness Coordinator in the Referee Department. His main research areas are basketball training, basketball physiology, integrated training and performance analysis, and he has published more than 100 publications (book chapters, journal papers) and presented at more than 200 conferences worldwide.

1
STRENGTH AND CONDITIONING FOR BASKETBALL PLAYERS AND TEAMS

Alejandro Vaquera and Alexandru Radu

1.1 Introduction

Described by some as an intermittent team sport (Aoki et al., 2016), basketball is a complex, dynamic and spectacular sport that combines cyclic and acyclic movements with and without the ball (Erculj et al., 2007; Trninic, 2003). Several authors have attempted to discuss the wide range of physical abilities and requirements that are part of the game. For example, Nikolaos (2015) stated that basketball involves abrupt and intense direction changes and mentions about the high frequencies of starting, stopping that are part of "a physical contact game" (p. 82). Siegler et al. (2003) argued basketball requires tremendous endurance, speed, agility and power while Erculj et al. (2007) mentioning the short sprints, abrupt stops, fast changes in direction, acceleration and different jumps, shots and passes of the ball. Ben Abdelkrim et al. (2007) together with Delextrat et al. (2015) are amongst the researchers who identified repeated sprint ability, changes in running direction and speed, alongside jumps and high-intensity running amongst the requirements of the game.

Recent studies investigated the distance covered by basketball players. Narazaki et al. (2008) cited Crisafulli et al. (2002), who reported distances between 4.5 km to 5 km during match game time (40 minutes). Similar distances are presented by Fox (2016) and Harney (2016), who indicated that Jimmy Butler, forward at Chicago Bulls, ran the most during the 2016 NBA season, covering 4.40 km (2.74 miles). Earlier, Stein (2012) presented a distance of 9.8 km (6.10 miles) for one of the players involved in his study.

Court time is spent at various intensities, and it alternates with moments of break (recovery) during time-outs or while being substituted (and sitting on the bench). For example, analysing elite basketball level, Janeira and Maia (1998) and McInnes et al. (1995) reported that adult players performed 105 high-intensity bouts while covering a distance of 991 meters (in high intensity) executing 50–60 changes in speed and direction and 40–60 maximal jumps. A similar idea is presented by Ben Abdelkrim et al. (2007), who argued that players may perform a maximum of 1100 discrete movements, with up to 217 high-intensity movements including jumping, shuffling and sprinting during a basketball game. Table 1.1 presents an overview of the most frequent actions that basketball players perform during a game as identified by various authors.

TABLE 1.1 Most frequent actions performed by basketball players during game time

Study/authors	Type of physical activity/movement performed	Data collection method/participants
Narazaki et al. (2008)	Standing: 1.6 ± 0.9 minutes on average Walking: 10.6 ± 0.3 minutes on average Running: 6.2 ± 0.7 minutes on average Jumping: 0.3 ± 0.1 minutes on average (34.1% of play time was spent running and jumping; 56.8% walking; and 9.0% standing).	12 players (6 male and 6 female) from NCAA Division II. 20 minutes practice game – subjects were videotaped for motion analysis.
Scanlan et al. (2012)	Reported 1752 ± 186 movements performed in matches. Standing/walk: 436 ± 44 (duration: 869 ± 48 sec.) Jogging: 551 ± 67 (duration: 865 ± 40 sec.) Running: 295 ± 41 (duration: 407 ± 5 sec.) Sprinting: 108 ± 20 (duration: 99 ± 16 sec.) Low shuffling: 41 ± 5 (duration: 76 ± 14 sec.) High shuffling: 22 ± 5 (duration: 17 ± 4 sec.) Dribbling: 34 ± 2 (duration: 100 ± 14 sec.) Jumping: 43 ± 6 Upper-body movements: 220 ± 18 (Total live time was spent: 39 ± 3% low-intensity; 52 ± 2% moderate-intensity; 5 ± 1% high intensity; 4 ± 1% dribbling).	12 Australian state-level female basketball players. 3 in-season matches (4 × 10 min. quarters). Time-motion analysis.
Matthew and Delextrat (2009)	Reported 652 ± 128 movements across matches Jump: 35 ± 11 movements (1.00 = number of movements per minute played) Sprint: 49 ± 17 (1.67 movements per minute) Run: 52 ± 19 (1.73 movements per minute) Jog: 67 ± 17 (2.23 movements per minute) Stand /walk: 151 ± 26 (5.0 movements per minute) Low-intensity shuffle: 117 ± 14 (3.77 movements per minute) Medium-intensity shuffle: 123 ± 45 (3.97 movements per minute) High-intensity shuffle: 58 ± 19 (1.87 movements per minute)	9 varsity female players (BUCS Premier League – UK) during 9 official games. Games were videotaped for movement analysis.

(Continued)

TABLE 1.1 (Continued)

Study/authors	Type of physical activity/movement performed	Data collection method/participants
Ben Abdelkrim et al. (2007)	Reported 1050 ± 51 movements. Sprint: 55 ± 11 (2.1 seconds average time) High-specific movement: 94 ± 16 (2.0 seconds average time) Jump: 44 ± 7 (1.0 seconds average time) Run: 97 ± 14 (2.3 seconds average time) Medium-specific movement: 197 ± 33 (1.9 seconds average time) Jog: 11 ± 8 (2.2 seconds average time) Low-specific movement: 175 ± 10 (1.7 seconds average time) Walk: 129 ± 10 (2.4 seconds average time) Stand: 147 ± 11 (2.3 seconds average time) (Specific movement refers to shuffling as well as to roll, reverse and cross-over run)	38 elite Tunisian U19 players (belonging to 6 teams) during playoffs. Computerised time-motion analyses were performed.
Ribeiro et al. (2015)	Reported 3873 movements (included in three categories: horizontal displacements; vertical displacements/jumps; contact force). Forward: 1453 frequencies during the entire game. Backward: 713 Side: 235 Dribble: 146 Defence stance: 146 Stand: 801. Rebound: 37 Layup: 20 Jump shot: 40 Block: 40 Dunk: 3 Jump pass: 18 Screen or fault: 95 Box out or 1 vs. 1: 205	12 elite players from 1st division of the Brazilian National Basketball League. Video recording
McInnes et al. (1995)	997 ± 183 movements (a change in movement every 2 sec.). 105 ± 52 high-intensity runs (with one high-intensity run every 21 sec during live time). 60% of live time spent in low-intensity activity. 15% of live time spent high-intensity activity.	8 elite Australian men basketball players

Differences in movement demands have also been identified depending on the position on the court; for example, guards tend to run more than centers (as identified by Oba and Okuda, 2008) – further details can be found in Table 1.2.

Considering all the above, coaches need to possess an understanding and be aware of the importance of physical abilities (such as speed, power, coordination, etc.)

TABLE 1.2 Distance covered during game time by players playing different positions

Study / investigation	Playing position and distance covered	Participants and data collection method
Oba and Okuda (2008)	• 5587 ± 171 meters for **high school players**: Point guard: 5656 meters; Shooting guard: 5749 meters; Forward: 5681 meters. Power forward: 5897 meters; Center: 5433 meters. • 5576 ± 202 meters for **college players**: Point guard: 5635 meters; Shooting guard: 5658 meters; Forward: 5671 meters. Power forward: 5921 meters; Center: 5552 meters. • 6177 ± 264 meters for **WJBL players**: Point guard: 6626 meters; Shooting guard: 6182 meters; Forward: 6541 meters. Power forward: 6146 meters; Center: 6182 meters.	3 basketball games were analysed: one High School Championship game (Women Semifinal); one Collegiate Championship game (3rd place final); and one game in the Women's Japan Basketball League (playoff final). Games were video-recorded and 3-dimensional photography analysis with direct linear transformation (DLT) method was used.
Stein (2012)	Guard: 4.8 miles (6.10 miles including warming up). Forward 1: 3.93 miles (4.53 miles including warming up). Forward 2: 4.02 miles (4.94 miles including warming up). Center: Data not available	American High School players monitored in one game with Nike+Sportswatch GPS device.
NBA Miner (2017)	Point guard: 2.72 miles (average distance per game; played 11 games) Shooting guard: 3.04 miles (played 11 games) Forward: 2.53 miles (played 17 games) Power forward: 2.57 (played 4 games) Center: 2.21 miles (played 17 games)	Data provided for NBA players during the 2015–2016 season (playoff games).
Mercadante et al. (2014)	Point guard: 4713.2 meters (1053.2 in attack; 608.9 in defence; 1612.7 in transition to attack; 1438.4 in transition to defence) Shooting guard: 4454.6 meters (869.0 in attack; 551.4 in defence; 1558.4 in transition to attack; 1475.8 in transition to defence) Forward: 3919.0 meters (757.5 in attack; 498.9 in defence; 1317.1 in transition to attack; 1345.5 in transition to defence) Power forward: 4174.9 meters (788.7 in attack; 508.9 in defence; 1489.9 in transition to attack; 1387.4 in transition to defence) Center: 4114.2 meters (761.6 in attack; 533.5 in defence; 1476.6 in transition to attack; 1342.2 in transition to defence)	One game of the 2011–2012 season New Brazil Basketball league (senior men). Data captured with a video-based manual tracking method (Dvideo System).

Source: Adapted from Oba and Okuda, 2008; Stein, 2012; NBAMiner.com, 2017; Mercadante et al., 2014.

to game performance outcomes and, equally important, how to design and implement activities that are intended to develop and enhance these qualities and abilities. A sound understanding of the game demands will enable basketball coaches in general and strength and conditioning (S&C) coaches in particular to develop specific training programmes which will meet the demands of individual players and of the team as a whole.

Before proceeding with a discussion about physical qualities, the authors considered useful a preliminary overview of concepts such as "strength and conditioning," "physical preparation," "fitness," and so on in the context of basketball. For example, *physical training* is defined by Bompa (1999) as "one of the most, and in some cases the most, important ingredient in training to achieve high performance" (p. 54). Speaking about professional basketball, Laios and Theodorakis (2002) point out the fact that *conditioning* is important for success. Similarly, Manzi et al. (2010) are in agreement with Ben Abdelkrim et al. (2007) when considering *physical conditioning* as a prerequisite to compete at elite level in modern basketball.

Taking into account these views, it could be argued that having a better preparation for all strength and conditioning aspects will improve players' physical abilities, which in turn will lead to increased minutes on court and to better performance outcomes. This is what this chapter will try to explore. Apart from this, the notion of "integrated training" will be proposed by the authors and will be explored at large in the section "Overview of physical abilities relevant to basketball training and coaching: integrated training".

1.2 Training principles and training methods

Training principles are a group of components that have been scientifically proven to increase performance. They can guide coaches in ensuring that their basketball players get the maximum benefits from their training regime (Coleman, 2002). These training principles focus on certain aspects, but some of them are closely related to each other. We cannot apply the training principles as individual ones (entirely on their own) because some of them need to be linked to and performed alongside the other ones to have a full effect during training. All of them can have a great impact on basketball training, and coaches need to integrate them carefully in order to get the full benefit from them.

Individuality

Everyone is different and responds differently to training. Some people are able to handle higher volumes of training, while others may respond better to higher intensities. This is based on a combination of factors like genetic ability, predominance of muscle fibre types, other factors that affect everyday life, chronological or athletic age, and mental state (Morgans et al., 2014).

In basketball we need to train every player paying attention to his/her individuality. In a training session or during the season coaches have to set team goals but also individual goals. Making every player in the team better (at individual level) will consequently impact on the quality of the team (more likely in a positive manner).

Specificity

Training must be matched to the needs of the sporting activity to improve the fitness of the players. This principle confers that one should aim to keep all training as sport-specific as possible, regardless of the type of fitness being trained (Hodge et al., 1996; Young et al., 2001).

There are differences between, let's say, training a basketball player compared to training a football player. Drills have to be specific to the sport and also have to be performed in the specific sports court (or field). There are some similarities between training in most team sports during the pre-season period (especially during the general preparation phase), but once the season starts the majority of the drills have to be done on the court (in basketball's case) and, as it was explained before, with drills specific to the sport that is practiced.

The best way to train the basketball players should include the ball in the drills, and a trend that is more and more popular in the last few years for all the team sports is to integrate small-sided games (SSG) into training. According to Sampaio et al. (2009) and Vaquera et al. (2017), small-sided games are a really good way to train the specificity in basketball because they reproduce perfectly the demands of the basketball game and allow the players to rehearse the fundamental elements of the game (passing, dribbling, shooting, defending, etc.) with a high number of repetitions of these elements in game-related conditions.

Examples of small-sided games include: 2-on-2 and 3-on-3, played in different spaces for example using the full court of half court and with minor modification of rules (one dribble or no dribble, shoot only after three passes between the players in the attacking team, a pick and roll action should be incorporated before the shot, etc.).

Progression

Reaburn and Jenkins (1996) argue that the best way to have a good impact in training and avoid over-training is to start slowly and gradually increase the amount of exercise. On the same topic, Radu (2010) suggests an approach that involves teaching drills and techniques from the simple to the more difficult ones (from simple to complex), and also from the less demanding drills to the most demanding ones (from easy to hard). Additionally, he mentions that progression from known situations to unknown is beneficial too.

As mentioned, for the progression to take place, coaches have to control both the learning process and also the fitness process. A really demanding drill from the learning point of view cannot be applied without training the easy ones before. The same principle applies to the work done with regards to the fitness level: we cannot ask our basketball players to engage in a high intensity drill without a progression from the low intensity drills before.

Overload

Fitness can only be improved by training more than you normally do. To obtain optimal improvement and prevent injury, overload must be individualized and must be progressive (Hodge et al., 1996). So, as it was mentioned at the beginning, some of the training principles are linked to the others in order to ensure that a smooth progression is followed in the load of the training drills and also controlling the individualization of these training loads. By continually and gradually increasing the amount of overload, the body will continue to adapt, allowing further gains to be made.

There are a number of ways to ensure that the overload is achieved – for example, the F.I.T.T. principle summarizes these ways very well (Hodge et al., 1996). There are four key factors which can be manipulated to achieve overload:

- Frequency: The number of training sessions per week.
- Intensity: How hard the work is. Intensity can be controlled using an objective measure as heart rate (heart rate monitors have been used successfully to control the intensity), GPS or just using the subjective assessment of the coach. Monitoring the Rating of Perceived Exertion (RPE; Borg, 1998) can be a good way to match the perception of the players with the one of the coach to have a clear idea about the intensity of the training sessions.
- Time: How long we train for (and how often). This factor is simple and can be controlled just with a watch (or a stop watch).
- Type: The type of exercises that are being performed. Some exercises and drills are really demanding while others are less demanding. The focus of the drill will determine the type of exercise (for example technical or tactical drills).

Adaptation

Over time the body becomes accustomed to exercising at a specific level. This adaptation results in improved efficiency, less effort and less fatigue perception at certain levels of training. For improvements to continue, coaches need to change the stimulus via higher intensity or longer duration of the effort/session.

The adaptation principle is important here because the body adjusts to this training by eliciting a number of responses to meet the requirement of the increased workload it has to deal with. These adaptations vary according to the type of training performed. For example, endurance training can increase blood volume, oxygen transport in the blood and capillary density in the trained muscles (Reaburn and Jenkins, 1996). Resistance training may lead to adaptations including increases in muscle fibre size, lean body mass, ligament and tendon strength and enzyme activity of creatine phosphokinase and myokinase (McArdle et al., 2001).

Recovery

Rest is one of the most important training principles. Rest is required in order for the body to recover from the training and to allow adaptation to take place. An inadequate amount of rest may lead to over training. The body cannot regenerate itself without rest and time to recover.

This principle can be summarized with a simple sentence: the more a player trains, the more sleep player's body needs. It is really important to rest but always after a training load; without an appropriate training load is impossible to link this principle with some other training principles such as adaptation. Rest is also one of the key aspects in injury prevention, especially nowadays with the increased amount of games per season which players experience (Belk et al., 2017).

Detraining

When training ceases, the training effect will also stop. It gradually reduces at approximately one-third of the rate of acquisition (Fisher and Jensen, 1990). The effects of a long period of inactivity on physical fitness showed that an elite athlete could take several weeks to fully recover his fitness after more than 2 weeks off (Godfrey et al., 2005). Detraining allows an athlete to physically and psychologically recover from extended periods of training, allowing them to return to training with renewed enthusiasm but always keeping in mind the need for periods of maintenance training during the year. Once the season is over, the number of training sessions is significantly reduced in a controlled manner (in both volume and intensity). Additionally, a level of physical activity intensity is maintained by practicing other sports such as swimming, tennis, cycling and so on.

1.3 Overview of physical abilities relevant to basketball training and coaching: integrated training

In the last 10 years basketball had changed completely in terms of the physical abilities required and also in the way players use their physical abilities in the game (Cormery et al., 2008). One of the main changes in training in the last decade is how the physical abilities are trained; in modern basketball it is not possible anymore to work them separately. Basketball players have to train their key physical abilities in an integrated way because what happens on the court during match play has to be replicated in training; the better players are able to use two or more abilities as one during the different actions they perform in the game.

As with regards to the young players, it is really important to pay attention to the key development stages and how to train the youngsters in order to make sure that their physical abilities are developed in a rational way (Maldonado and Calleja-González, 2007).

One of the key terms used in basketball fitness all around the world in the last few years is *integrated training*. Integrated training means the way coaches apply the different physical abilities into basketball drills in order to work these physical abilities and at the same time to work the technical /tactical fundamental aspects of the game.

Integrated training refers to a training program that incorporates or integrates multiple types of exercises together into a single programme or physical abilities with technical and tactical skills. It can be also defined as the basketball-specific drills with multifactorial training benefit (technical, tactical and physical benefits; Sampaio et al., 2009).

In any case, integrated training is a specific and efficient way to train basketball players – this is actually one of the most studied and more efficient systems (Sampaio et al., 2009; Vaquera et al., 2017). As part of this section, some of the most relevant physical abilities in basketball will be covered and some examples of integrated training drills will be included for every single ability that is discussed.

Strength

Strength in basketball can be defined as the ability of the neuromuscular system to overcome resistance through muscular activity (concentric work), to act against it (eccentric work) or to maintain it (isometric; Lorenzo and Calleja, 2010). Some of the objectives of the strength workout are to increase muscle mass, to strengthen the connective and support tissues thus contributing to a reduction in the risk of injury, to improve the general body constitution and to enhance capacity in training and competition.

In basketball, strength can be divided in different types:

1 **Sub-maximum strength**: This is the greatest force that the nervous and muscular system is able to develop by means of a maximum contraction but in more than one repetition. This force manifests itself dynamically and this is the way that has to be trained in basketball. A high maximum force does not necessarily imply the ability to manifest it quickly but will help to develop the specific basketball movements that include strength.
2 **Explosive strength**: Authors like González-Badillo and Gorostiaga (2002) identify the explosive force with rapid force. The same authors also define it as the relation between the applied force and the time used for it in the manifestation of the maximum force against any resistance.
3 **Specific strength**: Type of strength provided by the specific basketball actions. In this type of strength, sometimes it is more important the way the player use the strength than the amount of strength a player has.

Quite clearly, strength is one of the key physical abilities in basketball, and it also acts as the base for some other abilities.

Phases of strength training for basketball

It is generally accepted that strength training for basketball should be periodized. Over the course of a year, strength training for basketball should follow several distinct phases or periods. Each of these phases has a very specific objective that leads into the next phase of training – by following a periodized strength regime results will be maximized. The following phases (and objectives) need to be considered as part of a training season:

Off-season – build functional strength

This is the most important phase in strength training for basketball. The body must be prepared before beginning the more intensive strength training for basketball. During the off-season, and even in the early pre-season, coaches should engage players in performing functional exercises that focus on stabilizing muscles and in particular core stability.

The effort and intensity of basketball places a lot of uneven strains on our body. Some joints and tendons are placed under more stress than others. The same muscles are used over and over and grow strong while others are neglected.

A low-intensity functional strength phase helps restore the balance. Some of the goals of this phase are: prepare joints, ligaments and tendons for more intense work in subsequent training phases; strengthen our neglected stabilizer muscles; balance both parts of the body and correct any imbalance between flexors and extensors.

It is important in this phase to dedicate a good amount of time to strengthening your core and all the muscles that sustain your body. They support every specific basketball movement such as twisting, turning, jumping, lateral moves and so on. They are literally the link through which all movements happen.

Off-season/early pre-season – build maximal strength

This is the period of the season where coaches need to focus on gaining strength and especially maximal strength. Once this happens, the S&C coaches will be able to convert it into muscular power through different types of training such us plyometric training.

Late pre-season – convert to muscular power

This is the time for S&C coaches to put all types of strength together. As mentioned above, plyometric training can be used to convert your strength into basketball-specific power.

In-season – specific strength

Over the course of the competitive season, players will lose some maximal strength and they have to maintain muscular power. How players use and apply the specific strength will be the key and will impact on later team performance – see Table 1.3.

TABLE 1.3 Strength training for basketball

August September October November December	January February March April May June	July
Pre-season Maximal strength and power	Season Specific strength	Off-season Functional strength

Rest is *the* most important part of the training program. Rest time will depend on the period of the season and the individualities of the basketball player.

Strength training for basketball, as explained before, should fall into some distinct phases over the course of a season. If you can build a high level of maximal strength first, you can then convert much of those gains into explosive power. A very effective form of power training is called *plyometrics*, and it is ideally suited to basketball.

Strength can be discussed at length, but the most important thing coaches have to consider is to find the way where the basketball players apply the specific strength into the basketball game. One of the best ways to gain specific power in basketball players and the best way to use the explosive strength from the lower body of the players is plyometrics. Plyometric training refers to the performance of stretch-shortening cycle movements that involve a high intensity eccentric contraction immediately following a rapid and powerful concentric contraction (Malisoux et al., 2006). Plyometrics combines elements of both speed and strength in single movement patterns. Players must have a solid strength base before performing and engaging in these types of sessions. The purpose of plyometrics is to improve the players' capacity to apply more force more rapidly (Anderson, 2001).

Plyometric training should progress gradually from lower intensity to higher intensity drills, especially for individuals who lack a significant strength training background. The following aspects (adapted from Anderson, 2001) must be considered when using plyometrics in training.

Volume

Plyometrics volume relates to the number of repetitions per session. For lower body exercises, a repetition is a ground contact. The number of repetitions recommended for a plyometrics training session is beginners, 80–90 ground contacts; intermediate, 90–100 ground contacts; and advanced, 100–120 ground contacts.

Frequency

Typically two to three sessions of plyometrics can be completed in a week. Alternatively, recovery time between sessions can be used to prescribe frequency and is recommended at 48–72 hours. The phase of the training program will also determine how many plyometrics training sessions are suitable per week depending on the training load of this specific phase.

Rest intervals

The effectiveness of a plyometric training session depends on maximal effort and a high speed of movement for each repetition. Rest intervals between repetitions and sets should be long enough to allow almost complete recovery.

Warming up

As with any type of training, an adequate warm-up is required before completing a plyometrics session. Plyometrics should be completed at the beginning of the session when the basketball player neuromuscular system is fresh (when the player is not tired).

Safety considerations

Limited data exists as to whether there is any increased risk of injury through plyometric training. However, due to the stress that repeated shock-tension exercises can place on joints and connective tissue, several safety guidelines have been proposed:

- Increasing the load by adding additional weight through weighted vests or ankle weights is not recommended. Inappropriate load can reduce the speed and quality of movement, negating the effects of plyometrics.
- Balance is also an important factor in the safe performance of plyometric exercises.
- Plyometric training is contraindicated in prepubescent children, as it may cause damage to the epiphyseal plates that have yet to close.
- Finally, the landing surface must possess adequate shock absorbing qualities. Good choices include grass, a suspended floor and exercise mats.

Some examples of integrated training for each type of strength are provided below, together with a brief description of the drill/exercise and possible variations.

Figure 1.1 contains an example of integrated training for strength. Description: 2 players together into the key (3 seconds space). They have to use their strength to protect their ball while dribbling and steal the ball from their teammate. Three sets of 1. Important to make them look for the contact.

Variations: One player with the ball and one without; increased area/space (e.g. inside the 3 points semicircle).

Figure 1.2 contains a few examples of integrated training for plyometrics.

Exercise 1 – Description: Each player will take 4 steps from around middle of the court, switching from right to the left. There is no dribbling and the player will always finish with a shoot to the basket.

Variations: Starting with right leg first or the other; starting from the right or left side of the court; 3–5 sets on each side.

Strength and conditioning for basketball 13

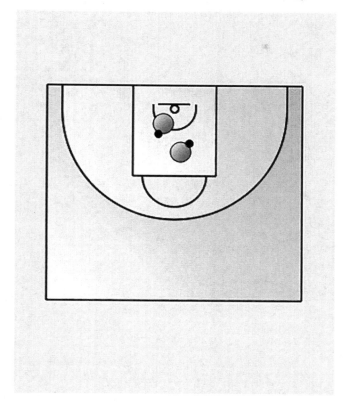

FIGURE 1.1 Example of integrated training (strength)

Exercise 2 – Description: Similar to exercise 1 one but repeating 2 steps in a row with the same leg.

Variations: Same as exercise 1; 5 sets each side of court.

Exercise 3 – Description: Variating from 2 different angles, side to side then into normal jumping direction.

Variations: Same as in previous exercises; different side; starting with different legs; 3–5 sets each side of court.

Endurance

Bompa (1999) defined endurance as "the length of time that an individual can perform work of a given intensity" (p. 344). Endurance is also the body's ability to sustain a certain physical load over longer periods of time without diminishing effectiveness (Bogdanis, 2012). In basketball, endurance can be defined as the ability to repeat efforts at the same intensity from the beginning to the end of the game.

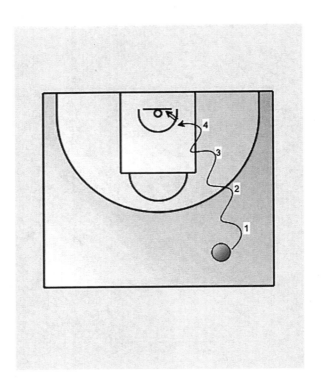
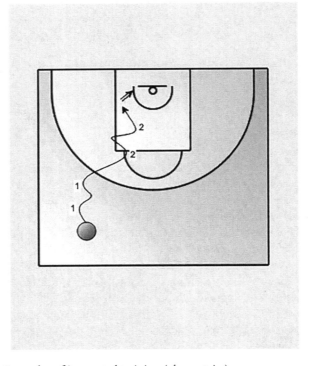

FIGURE 1.2 Examples of integrated training (plyometrics)

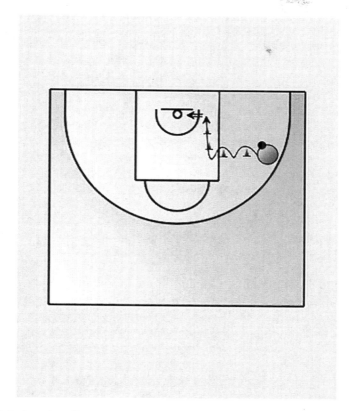

FIGURE 1.2 (continued)

Although endurance training can be performed off the basketball court, nowadays the best way to maintain the specific endurance during the training sessions, games and season is through on-court conditioning drills.

Types

There are two types of metabolism involved in endurance training: aerobic metabolism and anaerobic metabolism (lactic and alactic).

Aerobic literally means "relating to, involving or requiring free oxygen" and refers to the use of oxygen to adequately meet energy demands during exercise via aerobic metabolism. Generally, light-to-moderate intensity activities that are sufficiently supported by aerobic metabolism can be performed for extended periods of time (Plowman and Smith, 2007).

Anaerobic exercise is a physical exercise intense enough to cause lactate to form. Muscle energy systems trained using anaerobic exercise develop differently compared to aerobic exercise, leading to greater performance in short duration, high intensity activities, which last from few seconds to about 2 minutes (McArdle et al., 2006).

This system is subdivided into the anaerobic-alactic (no lactic acid) and anaerobic-lactic (with lactic acid). The anaerobic-alactic system is recognized as the short term system. This system, regarding continuous movement, is responsible for the shortest duration and highest intensity muscular outputs.

The anaerobic-lactic system signifies the process of anaerobic glycolysis. In the context of continuous movement, this system is responsible for medium duration and relatively high intensity muscular output.

The anaerobic-alactic energy system provides massive bursts of energy in very short periods of time. Generally speaking, the anaerobic-alactic energy system can only be dominant for, at most, 20 seconds before the anaerobic-lactic and aerobic energy systems take over.

Another important concept in endurance and also in basketball endurance is the anaerobic threshold. Anaerobic threshold is the exertion level between aerobic and anaerobic training. It is the point during exercise when your body must switch from aerobic to anaerobic metabolism.

Related to basketball training, Lorenzo and Calleja (2010) divided the way to use the different metabolisms (related to endurance into the training exercises) into time periods and intensity: aerobic system – more than 2 minutes, medium intensity; anaerobic-alactic system – between 0 and 30 seconds, sub-maximum intensity; and anaerobic-lactic system – between 30 seconds and 2 minutes, sub-maximum intensity.

As it was mentioned at the beginning of this section, nowadays the best way to train endurance for basketball players is on the basketball court. Some examples for how to train the different types of endurance applying integrated training are provided in Figures 1.3, 1.4 and 1.5.

Figure 1.3 contains an integrated training drill for aerobic endurance. Description: Can be done as an individual player (one at the time) or several players in the same time. The goal is to complete all the cones at both ends of the court (both baskets) by scoring 2 shots in a row from each cone. After every missed shot, the player has to run and go to the other basket. When all the cones at one basket are completed, the player has to go just to the half court in case of a missed shot. Time: 5–7 minutes. Medium intensity (50–60%).

Variations: 3-point shot; 1 made basket at every cone instead of 2; a mix between 2 points and 3 points; etc.

Figure 1.4 contains two exercises exemplifying integrated training drills for aerobic endurance. Exercise 1 description: the aim is to make (to score) 2 shots in a row. A passing player (or the coach) is needed to pass the ball. Five sets of 2 shots each player. Working at sub-maximum intensity.

Variations: Different sides; increasing the numbers of made shots (3 in a row, etc.); different situations on the court: 2-point shots, 3-point shots; etc.

Exercise 2 description: Shooting drill at one basket. After every made basket the player has to go round the closest cone, while after every miss he has to go round the farthest one. 5–7 jump shots in a row.

Strength and conditioning for basketball 17

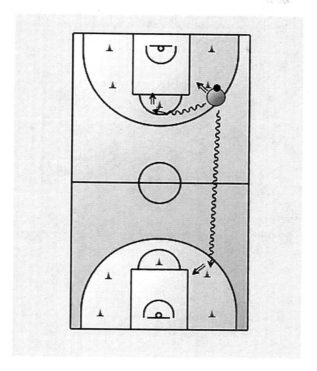

FIGURE 1.3 Example of integrated training (aerobic endurance)

Variations: Different type of shot: catch and shoot, catch-fake-dribble-and-shoot; increase the distance to the cones; etc.

Figure 1.5 contains two exercises that are examples of integrated training for anaerobic-lactic endurance. Exercise 1 description: one player goes from one basket to the other one with dribbling in order to shoot. Four sets of 1. Submaximum intensity.

Variations: Types of shots; length of the drill (45 seconds, 1 minute, 1 minute and 15 seconds, etc.); etc.

Exercise 2 description: Same as first exercise, but this time with one passing player in the half court. Four sets of 1. Submaximum intensity.

Variations: types of shots; length of the drill (45 seconds, 1 minute, 1 minute and 15 seconds, etc.); different type of pass; etc.

Speed

Speed is the ability of a subject to perform different actions in a minimum amount of time and with maximum efficiency (Lorenzo and Calleja, 2010). In basketball, speed can be defined as the physical ability that allows players to make a movement as quickly as possible while on the basketball court.

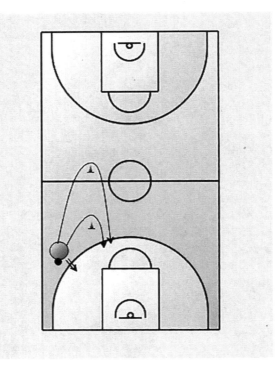

FIGURE 1.4 Example of integrated training (anaerobic–alactic endurance)

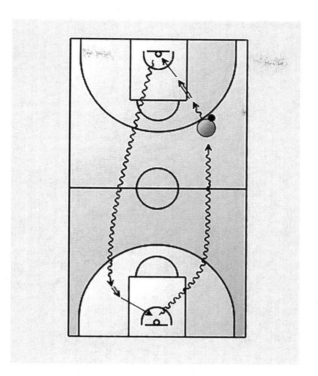

FIGURE 1.5 Example of integrated training (anaerobic-lactic endurance)

Basketball is a dynamic sport that requires movements in multiple planes of motion as well as rapid transitions from walking to sprinting and/or to jumping. The ability to quickly elude defenders, rapidly decelerate to take a jump shot, or explosively jump up to grab a rebound are all skills required to effectively have a good performance in basketball. It is equally important for the players to be able to perform these skills in a variety of directions and in a controlled manner to ensure injuries do not ensue (Balciunas et al., 2006).

There are three different types of speed in basketball, and they are overviewed below.

> *Speed reaction*: The way a basketball player responds as quickly as possible with a movement to a stimulus. In basketball, most of the stimuli are visual (the movement of the ball, of a player, of the defence, etc.).
>
> *Speed*: The speed with which a basketball player performs movement actions while on the basketball court, conditioned by the game action, and in the shortest amount of time as much as possible.
>
> *Drill speed*: The way a basketball player executes a technical gesture/drill as quick as possible.

The best way to train the different types of speed drills is on the court, and they have to be done in the most specific way as much as possible.

In this context, *agility* is another concept related to speed. Agility is the ability to accelerate, decelerate and quickly change direction. Basketball requires many changes in direction, quick movements and explosive jumping (Parsons and Jones, 1998). To ensure the players can perform these skills properly, speed and agility training will be an important training component that needs to be included in the training regimen. These drills can be incorporated into any basketball program to help maximize performance. Once again, the key is to practice them on the basketball court and with specific drills (integrated training). Some examples of speed drills specific to basketball are provided in Figure 1.6, 1.7 and 1.8.

Figure 1.6 contains two exercises that are examples of integrated training for speed reaction. Exercise 1 description: One player facing the basket and his teammate behind. As soon as the teammate behind puts the ball in front (by throwing it gently), the player has to react as soon as possible and shoot to the basket.

Variations: Position on the court; type of shot; type of pass; etc.

Exercise 2 description: One player facing the basket and his teammate playing defence in front of him with a ball. As soon as the defender player passes the ball, he goes to the side that he wants. The offensive player has to react and go to the opposite side, shooting or dribbling to the basket.

Variations: Position on the court; type of shot; situation of the defensive player; etc.

Figure 1.7 contains an example of integrated training for speed. Exercise description: the player has to dribble and to go as soon as possible to score, and afterwards, he has to touch the free throw line, base line and then go to the half court; always at maximum speed.

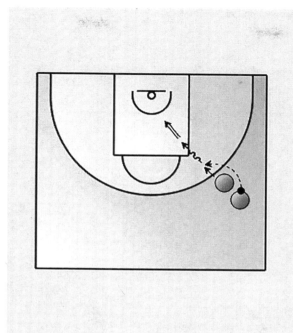

FIGURE 1.6 Example of integrated training (speed reaction)

22 Alejandro Vaquera and Alexandru Radu

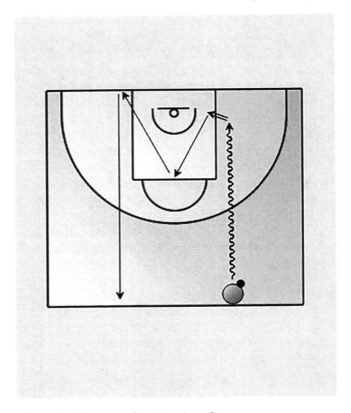

FIGURE 1.7 Example of integrated training (speed)

Variations: Initial starting spot; different type of shots; different moves; include passer/s; etc.

Figure 1.8 contains an example of integrated training for drill speed. Exercise description: using defensive slides, the player has to go from one cone to the other as soon as possible, and afterwards he will get the ball and has to go as soon as possible to shoot to the basket. It is important to always perform the technical drill at maximum speed.

Variations: Different drills; initial starting point; different type of shots; variation of the itinerary; etc.

Flexibility and stretching

Flexibility is commonly described as the range of motion, or movement, around a particular joint or set of joints (Walker, 2013). Flexibility may be defined as the amount of movement that can be achieved in a joint or articulation or the amount of movement that can be achieved through the use of a group of articulations (McCue, 2013).

Strength and conditioning for basketball **23**

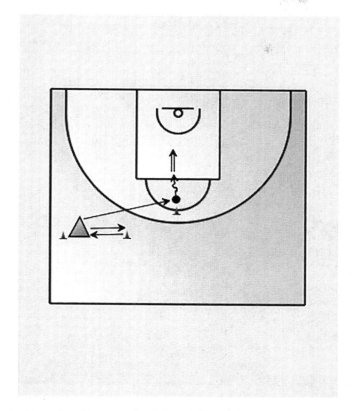

FIGURE 1.8   Example of integrated training (drill speed)

Flexibility in basketball can be divided in two types: static and dynamic. Static flexibility refers to an individual's absolute range of motion that can be achieved without movement. Dynamic flexibility refers to an individual's absolute range of motion that can be achieved with movement. When reference is being made to flexibility in the context of basketball performance, another important term that coaches need to be aware of is *stretching*.

Stretching, as it relates to physical health and fitness, is the process of placing particular parts of the body into a position that will lengthen, or elongate, the muscles and associated soft tissues. Upon undertaking a regular stretching program a number of changes begin to occur within the body and specifically within the muscles themselves. Some of the tissues that begin to adapt to the stretching process include the fascia, tendons, ligaments, skin and scar tissue. Static and dynamic stretching are the two most common types of stretching.

Static stretching

Static stretching means a stretch is held in a challenging but comfortable position for a period of time. Static stretching is the most common form of stretching found and is considered safe and effective for improving overall flexibility. However, many experts consider static stretching much less beneficial than dynamic stretching for improving a range of motion for functional movement, including sports and activities for daily living.

Dynamic stretching

Dynamic stretching means a stretch is performed by moving through a challenging but comfortable range of motion repeatedly. Although dynamic stretching requires more thoughtful coordination than static stretching (because of the movement involved), it is gaining favour because of its apparent benefits in improving functional range of motion and mobility in sports.

One point for consideration is that dynamic stretching should not be confused with old-fashioned ballistic stretching. Dynamic stretching is controlled, whereas ballistic stretching is uncontrolled. Although there are unique benefits to ballistic stretches, they should be done only under the supervision of a professional, because for most people, the risks of ballistic stretching far outweigh the benefits.

Stretching has long been touted as an important part of fitness and exercise because of its alleged effects on injury and performance (Woolstenhulme et al., 2006). Stretching should form a fundamental part of any exercise program and not just as part of the warm-up. In fact, recent research (Shier, 2004; Small et al., 2008) suggests that static stretching may not be beneficial before training or athletic performance. Dynamic stretching seems to be more appropriate as part of the warm-up.

Some guidelines for flexibility and stretching in basketball include: a proper warm-up should be done before performing flexibility and stretching exercises; stretch to the point of discomfort, not any further; breathing is a key part of the stretching session.

Clark and Lucett (2015) indicate the benefits of flexibility training include: decreased chance of injury, prevention or correction of muscle imbalances, improved posture, and enhancement of joint range of motion. Shier (2004) suggested that regular stretching showed an improvement on the following variables: maximal voluntary contraction, contraction velocity, eccentric and concentric contraction force, jump ability and running ability. Woods et al. (2007) indicate stretching should be a long-term part of the fitness routine in order to benefit from the long-term elastic changes within the muscle, which increase range of motion, potentially meaning less muscle-tendon injury. Stretching and especially static stretching can be part of the players' routine but with the purpose to provide the players the benefits mentioned before.

One aspect which was mentioned in previous research is that stretching is not a way to enhance performance or prevent injuries. In this sense, Shier (2004) established that static stretching immediately before activity decreased performance on the following tests: maximum voluntary contraction, power, jump height, jump force and jump velocity. And in relation to injury prevention, Small et al. (2008) indicate there is moderate to strong evidence that static stretching does not reduce injury.

In this context, it is useful to report that 20 NBA S&C coaches who were surveyed by Simenz et al. (2005) stated that the players and the teams they were working with engaged in static flexibility exercises. Same authors (Simenz et al., 2005) reported a mean average duration of 13.5 ± 4.0 minutes for a pre-practice flexibility section. Another interesting finding from their research is that the S&C coaches recommended to their NBA players to hold the static stretch for 14.5 ± 3.9 seconds.

Another interesting concept in flexibility in basketball is the range of motion (ROM). Range of motion (ROM), or range of movement, is so intimately related to flexibility that the terms are often considered having the same meaning. That is, they all describe the extent to which a joint can go in its established spectrum of movements (Walker, 2013). So, from the authors' perspective, it is important to stretch because helps the players to have a better flexibility, a better range of movement and also to train some other physical abilities. Dynamic stretching should be performed before training sessions and games, and static stretching in isolated sessions to gain more range of motion and flexibility.

1.4 Key stages and age groups when to develop the physical abilities in basketball players

Sports scientists have reported that there are critical periods in the life of a young person in which the effects of training can be maximised. This has led to the development of athletic models which identify appropriate training aims at each stage of the player's physical development and they were linked with higher achievements (Leite and Sampaio, 2012).

As it can be observed in Tables 1.4 and 1.5 (adapted from Meinel and Schnabel, 2004 and Maldonado and Calleja-Gonzalez, 2007), there are some ages or stages where basketball players can develop in a faster and better way their physical abilities and their technical and tactical ones. It is important for the coaches to know which physical abilities can be trained in the different ages of the players in order to train them in the "windows" that will make this process much faster (more effective). A similar situation happens with regards to the technical and tactical concepts and consequently; it is important for coaches to be aware of the suitable ages when these concepts need to be taught.

TABLE 1.4 Windows of opportunity to train physical abilities for young players

Physical abilities/age	4	5	6	7	8	9	10	11	12	13	14	15	16	17
Flexibility														
Speed														
Endurance														
Strength														

Adapted from Meinel and Schnabel, 2004.

Once coaches know at what age the different physical abilities and technical/tactical concepts can be trained, it is also important to understand how to control the load of the different situations with youth basketball players (for practices, friendly games, official games, etc.). The information provided in Table 1.6 can help set up the duration and the number of games and practices that are part of the coaching programme in a rational way (NBA and USA Basketball, 2016).

Taking into account all these considerations, an even more important aspect is the rest needed for the young players. Table 1.7 offers the rest guidelines and advice in relation to how many days young players should rest per week, number of months that they should be taking part in organized basketball per year and also the recommended hours of sleep (NBA and USA Basketball, 2016).

One last aspect that needs to be considered is that of the specialization in youth basketball. Although early commitment to a specialized form of training is still recommended in numerous sport programs, coaches should bear in mind that elite sport is composed of early and late maturers. Thus, maturation is a very

TABLE 1.5 Suitable ages to teach technical and tactical concepts to young players

Age	9	10	11	12	13	14	15	16
Technical	★★★★	★★★★	★★★★	★★★★	★★★★	★★★	★★★	★★
Tactical	★	★	★	★	★★	★★★	★★★★	★★★★

Adapted from Maldonado and Calleja-Gonzalez, 2007.

TABLE 1.6 Recommended participation guidelines for basketball at various ages

Age	Game length	Games per week	Practice length	Practices per week
Ages 7–8	20–28 minutes	1	30–60 minutes	1
Ages 9–11	24–32 minutes	1 to 2	45–75 minutes	2
Ages 12–14	28–32 minutes	2	60–90 minutes	2 to 4
Ages 15–17	32–40 minutes	2 to 3	90–120 minutes	3 to 4

Adapted from NBA and USA Basketball, 2016.

TABLE 1.7 Rest guidelines for various age groups

Age	Min rest days per week	Max months per year in organised basketball	Recommended hours of sleep
Ages 7–8	2	4 months	9–12 hours
Ages 9–11	2	5 months	9–12 hours
Ages 12–14	1	7 months	8–10 hours
Ages 15–17	1	9–10 months	8–10 hours

Adapted from NBA and USA Basketball, 2016.

important variable to consider, because the development of an elite basketball player is a long and complex process. These players are often trained the same way and participate in the same age group competitions, which give early maturers, especially males, a huge advantage in performance and in the selection process (Leite and Sampaio, 2012).

1.5 Physical preparation for basketball players – periodisation and training plans for basketball players

Periodisation

As part of the preparation of their teams for the competitions they are engaged with, coaches use a theoretical model (Morgans et al., 2014) called *periodisation*, which is an approach to training that is designed to maximise the abilities of their players (physical abilities alongside the technical and tactical abilities while considering the psychological aspects of being involved in sport). Periodisation provides coaches with a framework which helps with the planning and methodical changes and adaptations that are needed as part of an athlete and a team training programme (Brown and Greenwood, 2005). This is usually done by manipulating the volume and the intensity of training during the weekly training programme, with the aim of optimising athletes' preparation for the coming match (Robertson and Joyce, 2015).

A division of time into smaller, distinctive, more manageable parts is usually referred to as phases of training (Bompa, 1999). These phases (or periods) have very specific aims and goals, and "they are usually designed to bring certain gains related to major components of training" (Radu, 2015, p. 172). In this context, a brief overview of fundamental concepts such as macro-cycle, meso-cycle, micro-cycle, and training session (unit of training) will be provided below.

Macro-cycle

The longest period of time dedicated to training (usually several months) is called the *macro-cycle* (Radu, 2015). Normally the macro-cycle represents the competition year (the whole season), and it can be divided into three component parts (or phases): pre-season, season (official competition) and transition phase (rest and recovery).

An annual training plan should include important information concerning the team and the individual players such as: the months and the weeks; dates for medical control; dates for fitness testing; dates for friendly games and official games; the "what" and "when" in relation to physical training, technical training, tactical training, psychological preparation, theoretical-methodical preparation (volume, intensity, timing in relation to the various phases of training); number of days of rest and recovery.

Meso-cycle

This is a sub-phase of the training programme that is made out of 2–6 weeks of training. Usually, the meso-cycle is made out of 2–6 micro-cycles.

Micro-cycle

A training programme that has duration of one week is usually referred to as micro-cycle (Bompa, 1999). Typically a micro-cycle lasts up to 7 days (1 week of training) and is structured based on several units of training – the actual training sessions.

Weekly training loads differ depending on the number of games played within that week. For example, a reduced training load on the day before a scheduled official game was evident in the study performed by Manzi et al. (2010), with an elite men's professional basketball team in Italian Series A 1 League during a competitive season. When the game took place on Sunday, the training week included the following activities (as reported by the same authors): rest on Monday, strength training and technical training on Tuesday, followed by technical and tactical training on Wednesday, then explosive weights and technical training on Thursday and lastly tactical training on Saturday (the day before the game).

A more recent example for a different situation (two games per week during the season on Thursday and Saturday) is provided by Aoki et al. (2016), who looked at Brazilian professional male basketball players. They engaged in the following activities as part of the weekly programme: physical training, strength and power training on Monday morning followed by technical and tactical training during afternoon session; physical training, speed and agility (and core training) on Tuesday morning and technical and tactical training as part of the afternoon session; only one session on Wednesday afternoon (technical and tactical); game on Thursday evening; technical and tactical session on Friday morning; game during Saturday evening; followed by a full day of rest on Sunday.

Session plan and training sessions

A session plan is a document that contains what the coach intends to do with his/her players in one training session. This is the main tool – and, arguably, the most important tool – a coach is using in order to engage the athletes with the training components.

Balciunas et al. (2006) indicated that coaches who follow the Lithuanian basketball schools programme will usually include as part of a regular 90 minute session basketball specific activities that are grouped into three main parts: an initial warm-up period (up to 20 minutes); followed by exercises designed to improve technical aspects (individual technique for up to 40 minutes) – approximately 10 minutes for dribbling, 20 minutes for shooting and 10 minutes for passing drills; and the last part of the session aimed at tactical training (up to 30 minutes).

1.6 Summary

The physiological demands of basketball are complex. This complexity is partly a consequence of the nature of the exercise pattern; the requirement for frequent changes in both the speed of movement (e.g. walking, jogging, high intensity running and sprinting) and direction makes the activity profile intermittent (Morgans et al., 2014). Strength and conditioning coaches are faced with numerous challenges in their day-to-day activity. The complexity of basketball as a sport and the developments in terms of physical abilities and their application in the modern game (e.g. nowadays basketball players run 5 km per game) determined practitioners to continuously find ways and solutions which are implemented in the annual training programme. Integrated training is an approach that is considering and combining the technical and tactical aspects (technical and tactical training) with physical aspects. A good understanding of the game will enable the S&C coaches to device the most appropriate methods of training and to implement them into the programme; they need to carefully balance the content of the programme by taking into account factors such as strengths and weaknesses of each player; requirements of each position; health status of the player (including presence of an injury); time of the season (pre-season, in-season, recovery/off-season); equipment available; rest and recovery; age; and so on. Physical abilities could be maximised with an appropriate training load and a balance between effort, intensity (in both games and training sessions) and rest. A well-planned and well-thought training session that imitates the conditions which players will face in official competition will have the chance to be effective and to lead to improvements.

References

Anderson, J. (2001) Fit for soccer. *Sport Fitness Advisor* (online). Available at: www.sport-fitness-advisor.com/plyometric.html (accessed on 25th October 2017).

Aoki, M., Ronda, L., Marcelino, P., Drago, G., Carling, C., Bradley, P. and Moreira, A. (2016) Monitoring training loads in professional basketball players engaged in a periodised training programme. *Journal of Strength and Conditioning Research*, Vol. 31, Issue 2, pp. 348–358.

Balčiūnas, M., Stonkus, S., Abrantes, C. and Sampaio, J. (2006) Long term effects of different training modalities on power, speed, skill and anaerobic capacity in young male basketball players. *Journal of Sports Science and Medicine*, Vol. 5, Issue 1, pp. 163–170.

Belk, J.W., Marshall, H.A., McCarty, E.C. and Kraeutler, M.J. (2017) The effect of regular-season rest on playoff performance among players in the National Basketball Association. *Orthopaedic Journal of Sports Medicine*, Vol. 5, Issue 10, pp. 1–5.

Ben Abdelkrim, N., El Fazaa, S. and El Ati, J. (2007) Time-motion analysis and physiological data of elite under-19-year-old basketball players during competition. *British Journal of Sports Medicine*, 41, pp. 69–75.

Bogdanis, G. (2012) Effects of physical activity and inactivity on muscle fatigue. *Frontiers in Physiology*, Vol. 3, Article 142, pp. 1–15. Available at: http://doi.org/10.3389/fphys.2012.00142

Bompa, T. (1999) *Periodization: Theory and methodology of training* (4th edition). Champaign, IL: Human Kinetics.

Borg, G. (1998) *The Borg RPE scale: Borg's perceived exertion and pain scales*. Champaign, IL: Human Kinetics.

Brown, L. and Greenwood, M. (2005) Periodization essentials and innovations in resistance training protocols. *Strength and Conditioning Journal*, Vol. 27, Issue 80–85.

Clark, M.A. and Lucett, S.C. (Eds.). (2015) *NASM essentials of sports performance: Flexibility training for performance enhancement* (pp. 133–166). Burlington, MA: Jones and Bartlett Learning.

Coleman, A.E. (2002) 15 basic training principles for all sports. *Coach and Athletic Director*, Vol. 72, Issue 3, pp. 57–62.

Cormery, B., Marcil, M. and Bouvard, M. (2008) Rule change incidence on physiological characteristics of elite basketball players: A 10-year-period investigation. *British Journal of Sports Medicine*, Vol. 42, Issue 1, pp. 25–30.

Crisafulli, A., Melis, F., Tocco, F., Laconi, P., Lai, C. and Concu, A. (2002) External mechanical work versus oxidative energy consumption ratio during a basketball field test. *Journal of Sports Medicine and Physical Fitness*, Volume 42, Issue 4, pp. 409–417.

Delextrat, A., Badiella, A., Saavedra, V., Matthew, D., Schelling, X. and Torres-Ronda, L. (2015) Match activity demands of elite Spanish female basketball players by playing position. *International Journal of Performance Analysis in Sport*, Vol. 15, pp. 687–703.

Erculj, F., Dezman, B., Vuckovic, G. and Bracic, M. (2007) *Testing and evaluating the motor potential of young basketball players during the 2007 FIBA International Basketball Camp in Postojna*. Available at: http://coaching.fibaeurope.com/default.asp?cid={87FFFFCD-C6BB-4BBD-8975-4B26F438B4BE} (accessed on 5th March 2017).

Fisher, A. and Jensen, C. (1990) *Scientific basis of athletic conditioning*. Philadelphia, PA: Lea & Febiger.

Fox, K. (2016) *The distance run per game in various sports*, in Runner's World (online). Available at: www.runnersworld.com/general-interest/the-distance-run-per-game-in-various-sports/slide/3 (accessed on 12th January 2017).

Godfrey, R., Ingham, S., Pedlar, C. and Whyte, G. (2005) The detraining and retraining of an elite rower: A case study. *Journal of Science and Medicine in Sport*, Vol. 8, Issue 3, pp. 314–320.

Gonzalez-Badillo, J. and Gorostiaga, E. (2002) *Fundamentos del entrenamiento de la fuerza: Aplicación al alto rendimiento deportivo* (Vol. 302). Barcelona, Spain: Inde.

Harney, W. (2016) *How many miles do basketball players run in a game? (compared to other sports)*, at Interbasket.net (online). Available at: www.interbasket.net/news/20397/2016/12/how-many-miles-basketball-player-run-in-game-other-sports/ (accessed on 23rd June 2017).

Hodge, K., Sleivert, G. and McKenzie, A. (Eds.). (1996) *Smart training for peak performance – a complete sport training guide for athletes*. Aukland: Reed, Birkenhead.

Janeira, M. and Maya, J. (1998) Game intensity in basketball: An interactionist view linking time-motion analysis, lactate concentration and heart rate. *Coaching and Sport Science*, Vol. 2, pp. 26–30.

Laios, A. and Theodorakis, N. (2002) The pre-season training of professional basketball teams in Greece. *International Journal of Sports Medicine*, Vol. 6, pp. 146–152.

Leite, N.M. and Sampaio, J.E. (2012) Long-term athletic development across different age groups and gender from Portuguese basketball players. *International Journal of Sports Science & Coaching*, Vol. 7, Issue 2, pp. 285–300.

Lorenzo, A. and Calleja, J. (2010) *Factores condicionantes del desarrollo deportivo*. Bilbao: Diputación Foral de Vizcaya.

Maldonado, S. and Calleja-González, J. (2007) *El entrenamiento de baloncesto en edad escolar*. Donostia/San Sebastian, Spain: Fundamentos del deporte de alto rendimiento.

Malisoux, L., Francaux, M., Nielens, H. and Theisen, D. (2006) Stretch-shortening cycle exercises: An effective training paradigm to enhance power output of human single muscle fibers. *Journal of Applied Physiology*, Vol. 100, Issue 3, pp. 771–779.

Manzi, V., D'Ottavio, S., Impellizzeri, F., Chaouachi, A., Chmari, K. and Castagna, C. (2010) Profile of weekly training load in elite male professional basketball players. *Journal of Strength and Conditioning Research*, Vol. 24, Issue 5, pp. 1399–1406.

Matthew, D. and Delextrat, A. (2009) Heart rate, blood lactate concentration, and time-motion analysis of female basketball players during competition. *Journal of Sports Sciences*, Vol. 27, Issue 8, pp. 813–821, doi:10.1080/02640410902926420

McArdle, W., Katch, F. and Katch, V. (2001) *Exercise physiology: Energy, nutrition and human performance* (5th edition). Chicago: Lippincott Williams and Wilkins.

McArdle, W., Katch, F. and Katch, V. (2006) *Essentials of exercise physiology*. Chicago: Lippincott Williams & Wilkins.

McCue, B.F. (2013) Flexibility measurements of college women. *Research Quarterly: American Association for Health, Physical Education and Recreation*, Vol. 24, Issue 3, pp. 316–324.

McInnes, S., Carlson, J., Jones, C. and McKenna, M. (1995) The physiological loads imposed on basketball players during competition. *Journal of Sports Sciences*, Issue 5, pp. 387–397.

Meinel, K. and Schnabel, G. (2004) *Teoría del movimiento: motricidad deportiva*. Madrid, Spain: Editorial Stadium SRL.

Mercadante, L.A., Panhan, C., Monezi, L., Gaspar, R. and Misuta, M. (2014) *Distance covered in different game situations by high-level basketball players from Brazil*, presented at 32nd International Conference on Biomechanics in Sports, Johnson City. Available at: https://ojs.ub.uni-konstanz.de/cpa/article/view/6054/5534 (accessed on 6th July 2017).

Morgans, R., Orme, P., Anderson, L. and Drust, B. (2014) Principles and practices of training for soccer. *Journal of Sport and Health Science*, Vol. 3, Issue 4, pp. 251–257.

Narazaki, K., Berg, K., Stegiou, N. and Chen, B. (2008) Physiological demands of competitive basketball. *Scandinavian Journal of Medicine and Science in Sports*, Vol. 18, Issue 3, pp. 261–269.

NBA and USA Basketball. (2016) *Youth basketball guidelines*. Available at: https://youthguidelines.nba.com/ (accessed on 25th November 2017).

NBA Miner. (2017) Available at: www.nbaminer.com/player-trackings/ (accessed on 5th July 2017).

Nikolaos, K. (2015) Anthropometric and fitness profiles of young basketball players according to their playing position and time. *Journal of Physical Education and Sport*, Article 14, pp. 82–87.

Oba, W. and Okuda, T. (2008) A cross-sectional comparative study of movement distances and speed of the players and a ball in basketball game. *International Journal of Sport and Health Science*, Vol. 6, pp. 203–212.

Parsons, L. and Jones, M. (1998) Development of speed, quickness and agility for tennis athletes. *Strength & Conditioning Journal*, Vol. 20, Issue 3, pp. 14–19.

Plowman, S. and Smith, D. (2007) *Exercise physiology for health, fitness, and performance*. Philadelphia, PA: Lippincott Williams & Wilkins, p. 61.

Radu, A. (2010) *Basketball – skills, techniques and tactics*. Marlborough: Crowood Press.

Radu, A. (2015) *Basketball coaching: Putting theory into practice*. London: Bloomsbury.

Reaburn, P. and Jenkins, D. (1996) *Training for speed and endurance*. Australia: Southward Press.

Ribeiro, R., Calderani Jr, A., Monezi, L.A., Misuta, M.S. and Mercadante, L.A. (2015) *Physical activity demands in elite basketball games*, presented at 33rd International Conference on Biomechanics in Sports, Poitiers (France). Available at: https://ojs.ub.uni-konstanz.de/cpa/article/view/6622/5981 (accessed on 5th July 2017).

Robertson, S.J. and Joyce, D.G. (2015) Informing in-season tactical periodisation in team sport: Development of a match difficulty index for Super Rugby. *Journal of Sports Sciences*, Vol. 33, Issue 1, pp. 99–107.

Sampaio, J., Abrantes, C. and Leite, N. (2009) Power, heart rate and perceived exertion responses to 3x3 and 4x4 basketball small-sided games. *Revista de Psicología del Deporte*, Vol. 18, Issue 3, pp. 463–467.

Scanlan, A., Dascombe, B., Reaburn, P. and Dalbo, V. (2012) The physiological and activity demands experienced by Australian female basketball players during competition. *Journal of Science and Medicine in Sport*, Vol. 15, pp. 341–347.

Shier, I. (2004) Does stretching improve performance? A systematic and critical review of the literature. *Clinical Journal of Sport Medicine*, Vol. 14, Issue 5, pp. 267–273.

Siegler, J., Gaskill, S. and Ruby, B. (2003) Changes evaluated in soccer-specific power endurance either with or without a 10-week, in-season, intermittent, high-intensity training protocol. *Journal of Strength and Conditioning Research*, Issue 2, pp. 379–387.

Simenz, C., Dugan, C. and Ebben, W. (2005) Strength and conditioning practices of National Basketball Association strength and conditioning coaches. *Journal of Strength and Conditioning Research*, Vol. 19, Issue 3, pp. 495–504.

Small, K., McNaughton, L. and Matthews, M. (2008) A systematic review into the efficacy of static stretching as part of a warm-up for the prevention of exercise-related injury. *Research in Sports Medicine*, Vol. 16, Issue 3, pp. 213–231.

Stein, A. (2012) *How far do you run during a basketball game*, in USA Basketball (online). Available at: www.usab.com/youth/news/2012/08/how-far-do-you-run-during-a-basketball-game.aspx (accessed on 18th March 2017).

Trninic, S. (2003) The integrated in-season training of basketball cadets. *FIBA Assists Magazine*, Issue 5, pp. 14–19.

Vaquera, A., Suarez-Iglesias, D., Guiu, X., Barroso, R., Thomas, G. and Renfree, A. (2017) Physiological responses to, and athlete and coach perception of exertion during small side games. *Journal of Strength Conditioning Research*, July 2017, ahead of print.

Walker, B. (2013) *Ultimate guide to stretching and flexibility* (3rd edition). New York: Lotus.

Woods, K., Bishop, P. and Jones, E. (2007) Warm-up and stretching in the prevention of muscular injury. *Sports Medicine*, Vol. 37, Issue 12, pp. 1089–1099.

Woolstenhulme, M.T., Griffiths, C.M., Woolstenhulme, E.M. and Parcell, A.C. (2006) Ballistic stretching increases flexibility and acute vertical jump height when combined with basketball activity. *Journal of Strength and Conditioning Research*, Vol. 20, Issue 4, pp. 799–803.

Young, W., McDowell, M. and Scarlett, B. (2001) Specificity of sprint and agility training methods. *Journal of Strength and Conditioning Research*, Vol. 15, Issue 3, pp. 315–319.

2
PHYSIOLOGY OF BASKETBALL PLAYERS AND TEAMS

Christopher Holland

2.1 Introduction

Basketball is one of the world's most popular court games, being played in almost every nation. It is a multifaceted team sport requiring the possession of specific physical attributes to be played successfully (Chaouachi et al., 2009; Sallet et al., 2005). In the last few decades there has been a significant accumulation of scientific research devoted to basketball physiology and assessment. Aspects such as height and body composition, aerobic and anaerobic capacity, anaerobic power, strength, as well as speed and agility are of significant importance when considering successful performance, and have important implications in the development of the athlete's training programme (Hoffman, 2003). However, the nature of basketball has changed since the rule changes that were introduced to the game in 2000 and 2010. These rule changes included a reduction in both the time allowed in the back court from 10 to 8 seconds, and attack time from 30 to 24 seconds, whilst the game time has been changed from two 20-minute halves to four 10-minute quarters (FIBA, 2014). These new rules have changed the physical and tactical demands of the game, making the game faster and altering the physiological characteristics of players (Ben Abdelkrim et al., 2007; Delaxtrat and Cohen, 2008).

2.2 Physiological requirements for basketball players

Anthropometry

Unique types of body size and proportion constitute important prerequisites for basketball. An examination of elite level players illustrates a variation in height and mass for positional play, whilst there is a distinct trend towards selecting taller players throughout the team (Ostojic et al., 2006). Height and mass have been shown to increase as a function of the field position from guards to forwards and centres (Hoare, 2000; Sallet, 2005). In a 10-year investigation on basketball players before and after the 2000 rule change, Cormery et al. (2008) reported that the mean height of positional players is now 208 cm (centres), 200 cm (forwards) and 184 cm (guards). This trend was also reported for mass, with centres, forwards and guards showing mean measurements of 110 kg, 96.3 kg, and 79.5 kg, respectively. In a more recent study, guards were again the smallest and lightest players (187 cm ± 4.4; 83.2 kg ± 4.9), followed by forwards (196 cm ± 7.4; 90.4 kg ± 8.2) and then centres (207 cm ± 5.6; 101.7 kg ± 9.6; Pone-Gonzalez et al., 2015). These differences are further evidenced when players are divided into those who are used to playing close to the ring (inside players), and those who play further away (perimeter players). In agreement with the others studies, inside players were taller and heavier (206 cm ± 5.0; 98.6 kg ± 10.9) than perimeter players (189 cm ± 5.6; 86.9 kg ± 7.9). Normative test data for height and mass of players can be found in Table 2.1.

When the five-specific individual playing positions are taken into account, there is further homogeneity between players. In the study by Ben Abdelkrim et al. (2010c) on the physical attributes of elite men's basketball players, significant differences in height between guards (point and shooting), forwards (small and power) and centres were shown. This equated to mean heights of 186 cm (±5.2) for point guards and 194 cm (±3.8) for shooting guards, 196 cm (±3.3) and 202 cm (±3.4) for small and power forwards, whilst centres were again tallest at 204 cm (±4.7). Although the mean body mass of these players followed a similar trend of 78.1 kg (±5.8), 85.6 kg (±5.2), 87.8 kg (±4.4), 95.8 kg (±4.3) and 97.1 kg (±5.4) respectively. When the mean body mass index was calculated (kg/m^{-1}) distinct similarities were observed. Most interestingly the power forwards scored highest at 23.7 compared to the centres 23.2, whilst marginally lower values were seen for point guards (22.4), shooting guards (22.8) and small forwards (22.9). This suggests that the anthropometric characteristics of a player's height and weight may follow a linear trend regardless of playing position.

Although measures of body mass give a clear indication of a player's physical form, a more useful anthropometric measure for the assessment of athletes is that of body composition. With regards to the individual specific positional roles, it is the shooting guards (8.3% ± 1.6) and the small forwards (8.6% ± 0.7) who show lower body fat percentages than the point guards (11.2% ± 0.7), power forwards (11.6% ± 2.5) and centres (14.8% ± 1.9; Ben Abdelkrim et al., 2010c). In terms of standard positional roles, though, Ostojic et al (2006) identify that in general it is guard position that has the lowest body fat percentages (9.9% ± 3.1), followed by the forwards (10.1% ± 3.2) and the centres (14.4% ± 5.6). It is interesting to note that in the study by Cormery et al (2008) that evaluated players from 2000 to 2004, all players showed higher body fat percentages (guards 13.5%, forwards 13.6%, centres 14.9%). In contrast, however, Ponce-Gonzalez et al. (2015) report the percentage of body fat being lower in centres (9.5% ± 0.6) than in guards (10.9% ± 0.7) or forwards (10.3% ± 1.2). This does point to the idea that body fat percentages have been reducing in professional basketball players, as developments in training practices

TABLE 2.1 Normative physiological test data for elite male basketball players (PG – Point Guard, SG – Shooting Guard, SF – Small Forward, PF – Power Forward)

Physiological component		All positions	Guard	Forward	Centre	Source
Height (m)			1.82–1.91	1.89–2.03	2.01–2.13	Pone-Gonzalez et al. (2015)
Mass (kg)			78–88	82–98	92–111	Pone-Gonzalez et al. (2015)
Body fat (%)		8–14	7–13	7–13	9–20	Pone-Gonzalez et al. (2015)
VO$_2$max (ml·kg^{-1}·min^{-1})		45–63	52	45	45	Cormery et al. (2008); Gocentas et al. (2011)
Suicide run (s)		< 30				Delextrat and Cohen (2008)
Wingate test (W·kg^{-1})		10.7 (PP)				Popadic Gacesa et al. (2009)
Peak power (P) mean power (MP)		7.2 (MP)				
Squat strength		1.5 kg·kg^{-1}				Chaouachi et al. (2009)
Bench press strength		0.85 kg·kg^{-1}				Chaouachi et al. (2009)
Isokinetic strength	Quadriceps	297.5 (60°·sec^{-1})	268.7 (60°·sec^{-1})	304.2 (60°·sec^{-1})	321.7 (60°·sec^{-1})	Bradic et al. (2009)
		206.3 (180°·sec^{-1})	187.2 (180°·sec^{-1})	215.6 (180°·sec^{-1})	219.9 (180°·sec^{-1})	
	Hamstrings	172.0 (60°·sec^{-1})	157.1 (60°·sec^{-1})	176.5 (60°·sec^{-1})	183.4 (60°·sec^{-1})	Bradic et al. (2009)
		133.4 (180°·sec^{-1})	122.4 (180°·sec^{-1})	134.3 (180°·sec^{-1})	144.2 (180°·sec^{-1})	
Vertical jump (cm)		55	59	57	54	Delextrat and Cohen (2008); Ostojic et al. (2006)
Agility	T-test	9.2–9.7	9.51 (PG)	10.33 (SF)	10.45	Ben Abdelkrim et al. (2010c); Chaouachi et al. (2009); Delextrat and Cohen (2008)
			10.21 (SG)	10.46 (PF)		
	Lane agility	11.4	11.07 (PG)	11.19 (SF)	12.04	2017 NBA Draft Combine results (draftexpress.com, 2017)
			11.20 (SG)	11.55 (PF)		
Speed	5 m	0.82	0.88 (PG)	1.12 (SF)	11.17	Ben Abdelkrim et al. (2010c); Chaouachi et al. (2009)
			1.10 (SG)	1.15 (PF)		
	10 m	1.7	1.74 (PG)	1.96 (SF)	2.00	Ben Abdelkrim et al. (2010c); Chaouachi et al. (2009)
			1.98 (SG)	1.98 (PF)		
	30 m	4.1	4.28 (PG)	4.04 (SF)	4.32	Ben Abdelkrim et al. (2010c); Chaouachi et al. (2009)
			4.00 (SG)	4.28 (PF)		
	¾ court	3.32	3.25 (PG)	3.32 (SF)	3.41	2017 NBA Draft Combine results (draftexpress.com, 2017)
			3.30 (SG)	3.34 (PF)		

as nutrition are made. While there is some disparity between studies, these results highlight the need for players to display body fat percentages within the range of 8–14% (see Table 2.1 for normative ranges).

Although these anthropometric parameters are not essential factors for success in basketball, they can help determine the most effectual playing positional role. Because the game of basketball involves physical contact, the increased height and mass of centres, and other inside players, could help them dominate in the low-post position, which involves rebounding, box-outs and picks, whilst increased height improves their effectiveness in the aerial zone. In contrast, the smaller guards, and to an extent the other perimeter players, are used to bringing the ball up court, setting up plays and organising the defence, where excessive mass or height may actually hinder successful performance.

An additional anthropometric measure that is often overlooked is that of 'wingspan'. This is the length of a player's arms and hands, from fingertip to fingertip, when fully extended out to the sides. In contradiction to da Vinci's Vitruvian man, research suggests that the average adult male has an arm span 5.3 cm longer than his height (Nwosu and Lee, 2008). This equates to an arm length-to-height ratio of 1.01-to-1. According to historical National Basketball Association (NBA) figures from DraftExpress.com (2017), elite level basketball players have a wingspan that, on average, is 11.8 cm longer than their height. However, figures from the 2017 NBA Draft Combine reveal that although there was a decrease in this average, it was still beyond the normal adult value, with arm lengths being 8.9 cm greater than height. NBA players are therefore reported to have an arm length-to-height ratio of 1.06-to-1 (Epstein, 2013). The importance of excessive reach in relation to height is evident during many basketball specific skills. Longer arms mean that jump shots can be released without the fear of being blocked, whilst also increasing the likelihood of stopping shots during defensive play. Indeed, Epstein (2013) confirms that wingspan is a better predictor of shot-blocking ability than height.

Movement patterns

The movement patterns within basketball are largely unpredictable and result from the spontaneity of the player and the demands of play. During a 40-minute game, players cover between 4,500 to 5,000 m, with a variety of multidirectional movements at varying velocities such as running, dribbling and shuffling as well as jumping (Crisafulli et al., 2002). In a detailed study by Erčulj et al. (2008) on movements during the Slovenian Men's National Championship, it was established that during the active phase of play (playing time), a total distance of 2,476 m (±1,058) was covered at an average velocity of 1.86 m/s (±0.16). As most players do not play the full 40 minutes, this data was extrapolated to calculate the distance covered if playing the entire game, revealing an average total of 4,404 m (±354). Interestingly, when this is added to distance covered during the passive phase of play (game clock not ticking), the total distance was 6,235 m. Additional research suggests that players' work rate in terms of distance covered per minute of play is 114.5

± 8.7 m·min^{-1} (Ben Abdelkrim et al., 2010a). However, many of the movements of basketball play are conducted in a relatively small space (rebounding, blocking, positioning etc.), meaning that the total distances covered may not give a clear indication of the movement demands of the game, leading to potentially erroneous conclusions (McInnes et al., 1995). Indeed, more relevant research uses categories to classify mode and intensity of game movements.

In a study on elite junior players, Ben Abdelkrim et al. (2010a) found that 30% of playing time was spent performing high-intensity activities (sprinting >18.1 km·h^{-1}, sideways running >12 km·h^{-1}, shuffling >9 km·h^{-1} and jumping), with 28% and 42% of time spent in moderate and low intensity activity, respectively. Additional research suggests that older basketball players spend 48% walking, 19% positioning, 17% running, 15% inactive and only 1% jumping (Tessitore et al., 2006). This is in comparison to male and female collegiate players who spend 34.1% of play time running and jumping, 56.8% walking and 9% inactive (Narazaki et al., 2009).

Furthermore, significantly more high-intensity activities are performed in the first half of a game than the second, potentially due to the increase in player fatigue (Ben Abdelkrim et al., 2007, 2010a). The influence of tactical factors towards the end of games needs to be considered, though, as the proportion of fast breaks and straight play decreases as teams are likely to manage further control of ball possession (Ben Adbelkrim et al., 2007). Research has also shown that international level players spend significantly more live time in high-intensity activities compared to their non-international counterparts. This includes sprinting, shuffling and intense static actions (positioning and picking; Ben Abdelkrim et al., 2010b). The findings of these studies reveal that like other team sports, competitive basketball involves important actions during a game that are performed at low-intensity. Nevertheless, it is the ability to perform repeated high-intensity activities, as opposed to the total distance covered, that differentiates elite level play from lower levels.

Aerobic demands

The duration of a basketball game requires a high level of aerobic metabolism to enhance the resynthesis of creatine phosphate, lactate clearance from active muscles and the removal of accumulated intracellular inorganic phosphate (Glaister, 2005). The analysis of the aerobic demands of basketball has focussed on measurements of oxygen consumption (VO_2) and heart rate (HR). In a 20-minute practice game, male National Collegiate Athletics Association (NCAA) players demonstrated mean values for VO_2 and HR of 36.9 ml·kg^{-1}·min^{-1} (±2.6) and 168 b.p.m. (±9) (Narazaki et al., 2009). This corresponds to a value of 64.7% of VO_2 max, and 84% of HR_{max}, which is in accordance with the average values of 69% of VO_2max and 84% of HR_{max} identified during training games by Castagna et al. (2005). These values are noticeably lower than the value of 93% of HR_{max} obtained by Ben Abdelkrim (2009) in a study of under-19 elite Tunisian players during competitive games. Indeed, Montgomery et al. (2010) identified that competitive live games place substantially greater demands on player's physiology than 5-on-5 scrimmage play. Interestingly, Castagna et al. (2005) concluded that the HR and VO_2 responses during court drills were inversely proportional to the number of players participating. This corresponded to mean $\%HR_{max}$ and $\%VO_2max$ values of 88.2% and 73.5% for 3 vs. 3 court drills, and 92.1% and 79% for 2 vs. 2 play. These studies suggest that the intensity of practice games can be comparable with that of actual game play and elicit responses known to be useful for the development of aerobic fitness, but that games involving fewer players are best suited for training at high intensity (Hoff et al., 2004).

An examination of blood metabolite and hormonal responses during basketball games has identified that there is a significant increase in triglycerides and free fatty acids concentration, particularly during the latter parts of the game (Ben Abdelkrim et al., 2009). This shows that there is a greater proportion of fatty acids being used to regenerate adenosine triphosphate and an associated increase in the aerobic energy systems contribution to exercise. This suggests that basketball requires extensive use of aerobic metabolism. Whilst phosphocreatine (PCr) is the likely source of much of the energy needed, the restoration of PCr is dependent on aerobic metabolism (Tomlin and Wenger, 2001). During match play, a fast rate of PCr restoration is needed to sustain high intensity actions, with aerobic metabolism being further employed to sustain low intensity movements.

Although the use of in-game metrics provides a clear indication of the demands of match play, the evaluation of maximal oxygen consumption (VO_2max) affords a more significant insight into the aerobic capacity of players, as this is the best indicator of aerobic fitness. Independent of field position, professional basketball players have been shown to have a mean VO_2max of between 50 and 63 ml·kg^{-1}·min^{-1} (Apostolidis et al., 2003; Laplaud et al., 2004; Sallet et al., 2005; Ziv and Lidor, 2009). The values are commensurate with those obtained by Metaxaz et al. (2009) on Division 1 Greek players (51.3 ml·kg^{-1}·min^{-1}) and Ben Abdelkrim et al. (2009) on elite junior players (52.8 ml·kg^{-1}·min^{-1}), suggesting that aerobic capacity in basketball is independent of age or division. However, these average scores may be somewhat misleading, as position specific differences are not taken into account. This is substantiated by Gocentas et al. (2011), who identified that VO_2max scores were higher for perimeter players (52.2 ml·kg^{-1}·min^{-1}) than post players (46.2 ml·kg^{-1}·min^{-1}). In regards to specific individual playing positions, guards have been shown to have significantly higher aerobic capacity (63.4 ml·kg^{-1}·min^{-1}) than forwards (45.2 ml·kg^{-1}·min^{-1}) or centres (44.8 ml·kg^{-1}·min^{-1}; Cormery et al., 2008). Interestingly, scores of 53.8 ml·kg^{-1}·min^{-1}, 53.4 ml·kg^{-1}·min^{-1} and 51.4 ml·kg^{-1}·min^{-1} for guards, forwards and centres, respectively, were found in elite junior players (Ben Abdelkrim et al., 2009). The comparable results may be due to junior players having not been playing long enough to develop position specific physiology.

The higher aerobic characteristics observed in the guard position are due to these players travelling greater distances, and at higher velocities than the other positions. This give guards a better base for performing on the field with regard to the intensity required by the game (Ostojic et al., 2006). In defence, their activity involves constant movement, primarily guarding opponents in the external position, as well as more assertive versions of man to man defence. In attack, their movements are largely based around the perimeter and out of the line (Erculj et al., 2008). The new regulations introduced in 2000 can also be associated with this disproportionate increase in the aerobic capacity of guards when compared to other positions, primarily due to the greater susceptibility to decreases in backcourt and attacking time (Cormery et al., 2008). This is highlighted in Table 2.1, where normative values for each of the playing positions are identified from the research.

Anaerobic demands

The contribution of anaerobic metabolism in basketball players is important for defensive and offensive transitions, and technical actions such as jumping, shooting, lay-ups, blocking and passing (Castagna et al., 2010; Delextrat et al., 2008). The proportion of in-game activity changes, as well as distances covered in high-intensity actions (running and shuffling), indicate that basketball players undergo a high level of anaerobic stress during several parts of the game (Ben Abdelkrim, 2010a). The nonorthodox directional mode of sideways running and shuffling has also been reported to be more metabolically demanding than standard locomotion (Ziv and Lidor, 2009).

Measurement of blood lactate concentration is often used as an indicator of energy production from the anaerobic glycolytic process, with research indicating that there is a substantial contribution of anaerobic metabolism to energy supply within basketball. During simulated match play over a single 20-minute half, relatively low levels of blood lactate concentrations of 4.2 mmol·L^{-1} (±1.3) (Narazaki et al., 2009) and 3.72 mmol·L^{-1} (±1.39) have been reported (Castagna et al., 2006). This is in comparison to actual match play where elite junior players demonstrate average and mean peak blood lactate of 5.75 (±1.25) and 6.22 (±1.34) mmol·L^{-1}, respectively (Ben Abdelkrim et al., 2010a). In an earlier study, Ben Abdelkrim et al. (2007) reported that guards demonstrated higher blood lactate levels (6.0 ± 1.2 mmol·L^{-1}) than centres (4.9 ± 1.1 mmol·L^{-1}), which is primarily related to the increase in high-intensity activities in which guards are involved in during the latter stages of matches. In line with observations in soccer (Mohr et al., 2003) and field hockey (Ghosh et al., 1991), blood lactate concentrations are seen to be higher in international compared to national level players (Ben Abdelkrim et al., 2010b). This suggests that higher intensity play is a determinant of performance at the elite level. Intensity of play and the associated lactate concentrations have been shown to be affected by the defensive strategy that is employed. This is reflected in an increase in blood lactate values at the end of games when a zone marking system is adopted, and is related to the observed tendency for more vigorous activity during the latter parts of these games (Ben Abdelkrim et al., 2010b). However, blood lactate is only a surrogate indicator of anaerobic metabolism, as concentrations may be on third of the muscle concentrations (Krustrup et al., 2006), and are influenced by the exercise intensity immediately before sample collection. Results from these studies do point to the need for lactic-acid-tolerance training for basketball players in order to improve intramuscular buffering capacity, as the ability to buffer H$^+$ is important for maintaining performance during repeated sprint bouts (Bishop et al., 2004).

It is important for those working within the game to have an understanding of a player's anaerobic capacity and anaerobic power. Indeed, anaerobic capacity is defined as the maximal rate of energy production through the combined phosphagen and glycolytic energy systems (Maud and Foster, 2006) and is required for exercise of between 30 and 90 seconds. In contrast, anaerobic power reflects the ability of the phosphogen energy pathway to support muscle contraction and is required in exercises lasting only a few seconds (Delextrat and Cohen, 2008). Unfortunately, the analysis of player's anaerobic capacity is somewhat limited within the research literature. Delextrat and Cohen (2008) tested players using the "suicide run" test, which is commonly used to assess anaerobic capacity within basketball (McKeag, 2003). Results revealed mean completion times for elite level players of 28.97 s (±0.88), although these were comparable to those obtained in lower level university standard players at 29.03 s (±0.7; Table 2.1).

Although the anaerobic capacity of players is important for sustaining high-intensity actions, results suggest that since the rule changes in 2000, basketball relies more on anaerobic power, which provides a better prediction of athletic success (Bompa, 1993; Delextrat and Cohen, 2008). The Wingate Anaerobic Power Test (WAnT) has been utilised extensively for the purpose of providing information on the anaerobic power of athletes (Zajac et al., 1999). Interestingly, studies conducted before the 2000 rule changes have identified higher levels of relative aerobic power within players than those conducted subsequently, although the majority of such have focussed on elite junior level play. In a study on Youth National team players, peak power was identified as 14.4 $W \cdot kg^{-1}$ (±1.7) and mean power of 9.1 $W \cdot kg^{-1}$ (±1.2; Hoffman et al., 1999). These were commensurate to the levels found in National Youth and Collegiate level players of 14.1 $W \cdot kg^{-1}$ (±1.4) and 9.5 $W \cdot kg^{-1}$ (±1.0; Hoffman et al., 2000). In a later study by Apostolidis et al. (2003), lower values for both peak power (10.7 ± 1.3 $W \cdot kg^{-1}$) and mean power (8.0 ± 0.7 $W \cdot kg^{-1}$) were observed for a similar group of junior players. Interestingly, these lower results are comparable to those found more recently in elite adult players. Popadic Gacesa et al. (2009) established values for peak and mean power of 10.7 ± 1.7 $W \cdot kg^{-1}$ and 7.2 ± 1.0 $W \cdot kg^{-1}$, respectively (Table 2.1). While figures are not reported by Delextrat and Cohen (2008), they conclude that the values obtained within their study concur with these findings. Although the anaerobic power of basketball players actually appears to have dropped following the rule change, they are still higher than those reported in hockey, handball and soccer (Popadic Gacesa et al., 2009). The importance of developing high levels of this component of fitness is therefore key for successful play, allowing players to efficiently shoot and rebound, set screens and box out opponents (Pojskic et al., 2015).

Strength and power

Maximal strength

Research into the strength levels of basketball players has focussed on reporting of 1RM strength (repetition maximum) in both the upper and lower body. The squat and bench press exercises have primarily been utilised as the resistance tests for the assessment of these strength parameters. Early research suggests that 1RM squat strength is a stable performance variable and predictive of seasonal playing time within collegiate players (Hoffman et al., 1991, 1996).

In a study by Chaouachi et al. (2009), 1RM Squat performance of elite players was shown to be 142 kg in absolute terms. When this is expressed relative to body mass, players showed mean lower body strength of 1.5 kg·kg^{-1}. Almost identical values were reported recently in elite Bulgarian players of 142 kg (absolute) and 1.51 kg·kg^{-1} (relative; Jakovljevic et al., 2015). However, higher values of 201.5 kg (2.2 kg·kg^{-1}) have also been reported in senior elite players (Ben Abdelkrim et al., 2010c). A relative 1RM squat in the range of 1.5 × body mass appears to be sufficient to play at the elite level of basketball (Table 2.1). The importance of strength at this level is essential for 'boxing out' and positioning, and has also been shown to be positively correlated to both speed and agility (Chaouachi et al., 2009).

Measurement of upper body strength using 1RM bench press performance has yielded some differing results. In relative terms, the studies by Chaouachi et al. (2009) and Ben Abdelkrim et al. (2010c) on elite players have shown strength levels of 0.84 kg·kg^{-1} and 0.96 kg·kg^{-1}, respectively. In contrast, a study of British university basketball players observed relative bench press performance of 1.12 kg·kg^{-1} (Delextrat and Cohen, 2008). Upper body strength may therefore not be a prerequisite for play at the elite level, and thus sub-elite players may be overtraining their upper bodies. Values above 0.85 kg·kg^{-1} appear adequate for elite level players (Table 2.2). Indeed, the relatively low upper body strength exhibited by elite basketball players in comparison to other team sport players may be related to anthropometry. The importance of 'wingspan' in relation to height for players has been discussed in an earlier section. However, this increase in arm length requires greater bar displacement to occur during the bench press meaning higher levels of force must be generated to complete the lift (Caruso et al., 2012).

Isokinetic strength

Anaerobic leg power and rapid movement performance have been shown to be determinants of successful play in basketball (Sallet et al., 2005). Peak torque values for the lower limb during isokinetic contractions have been investigated in a number of studies. In a pre-season study of players from divisions I to IV of the Greek national league (Metaxas et al., 2009), elite players demonstrated peak torque for quadriceps of 295.4 Nm (60^{0}·sec^{-1}), 209.4 Nm (180^{0}·sec^{-1}), and 150.8 Nm (300^{0}·sec^{-1}). Predictably lower values were demonstrated for hamstrings at of 159.7 Nm (60^{0}·sec^{-1}), 112.6 Nm (180^{0}·sec^{-1}) and 80.4 Nm (300^{0}·sec^{-1}). However, no significant differences in peak torque at any of these angular velocities were found between playing level for either muscle group. Similar mean values of 297.5 Nm (60^{0}·sec^{-1}) and 206.3 Nm (180^{0}·sec^{-1}) for the quadriceps have been observed in elite European players (Bradic et al., 2009). However, although levels of isokinetic hamstring strength at 60^{0}·sec^{-1} were equivalent (172.0 Nm), higher values at 180^{0}·sec^{-1} were evident (133.4 Nm). It must be noted that much of the research into isokinetic strength is conducted prior to starting the training season. Players are therefore returning from a break from strenuous exercise in the off-season, so there may be a noticeable decrease in performance levels. However, following a 5-week preseason resistance training programme, significant improvements in isokinetic knee strength are only evident at slow speeds of $60^{0} \cdot \sec^{-1}$ (Hoffman et al., 1991). Although this is an early study and conducted prior to the 2000 rule change, a number of other studies also suggest that maintaining strength and power during or after a competitive season is problematic for players (Campbell, 1967; Hammer, 1965). As such, notable decreases do occur unless in-season strength maintenance programmes are employed (Rønnestad et al., 2011).

Direct comparisons with some additional research can prove problematic due to the utilisation of different angular velocities. In a study by Harbili (2015), similar values at $60^{0} \cdot \sec^{-1}$ have been found in Turkish division III players of 287 Nm (quadriceps) and 161 Nm (hamstrings). At $240^{0} \cdot \sec^{-1}$ peak torque values of 140 Nm and 88 Nm were observed, which are more comparable to those reported by Metaxas et al. (2009) at $300^{0} \cdot \sec^{-1}$. In a study on isokinetic strength in junior and professional players, similar relative knee strength profiles were found between the groups (Schiltz et al., 2009). Of interest is that when knee-injury history is taken into account, professional players demonstrate isokinetic asymmetries. It is therefore important that when studying the strength capabilities of players, a consideration for previous injuries must be made.

In relation to individual playing position, isokinetic strength at $60^{0} \cdot \sec^{-1}$ and $180^{0} \cdot \sec^{-1}$ for both the quadriceps and hamstrings have been shown to be highest in centres (Bradic et al., 2009). These elite level players showed mean knee extensor peak torques of 321.7 Nm ($60^{0} \cdot \sec^{-1}$) and 219.9 Nm ($180^{0} \cdot \sec^{-1}$), which was significantly different from forwards (304.2 Nm and 215.6 Nm) and guards (268.7 Nm and 187.2 Nm). This was further evident for the knee flexors at the same angular velocities for guards (157.1 Nm and 122.4 Nm), forwards (176.5 Nm and 134.3 Nm) and centres (183.4 Nm and 144.2 Nm). However, centres were the only group to be observed as significantly different from the other positions for the knee flexor muscle group. Table 2.1 provides an overview of the requisite levels of isokinetic strength for quadriceps and hamstrings of players in each position. However, when the different values are normalised for body mass, the significant differences between playing position disappear for both knee flexors and extensors at angular velocities of $60^{0} \cdot \sec^{-1}$ and $180^{0} \cdot \sec^{-1}$.

Dynamic strength

Vertical jump is a prevalent and important movement performed within basketball. Players are not only required to jump high, but to be able to jump higher than their opponents in a given offensive or defensive situation. In studies, mean values of jumping height range from 49.7 cm (Ben Abdelkrim et al., 2010c) to 61.9 cm (Chaouachi et al., 2009). However, research into vertical jump among players of different positions found no significant differences between guards (59.7 cm), forwards (57.8 cm) and centres (54.6 cm; Ostojic et al., 2006; Table 2.1). The importance of vertical jump height is further confirmed in the research of Delextrat and Cohen (2008). Their study identified values for vertical jump height of 56.6 cm for elite players and 51.6 cm for players competing at university level. This equates to jumping performance that is 8.8% greater for players of higher skill level.

Speed and agility

Agility and speed have been considered a physiological prerequisite for successful performance in basketball and a consistent predictor of playing time (Hoffman et al., 1996). This is due to the frequent sudden directional changes associated with match play (Hoffman et al., 2000). The ability to sprint repeatedly and change direction rapidly is a determinant of performance in field and court sports (Reilly et al., 2000; Meir et al., 2001; Keogh et al., 2003), and is influenced by strength, balance, coordination and flexibility (Sheppard and Young, 2006).

Average sprint times of 0.82 seconds (5 m), 1.7 seconds (10 m) and 4.1 seconds (30 m) have been reported in elite players (Chaouachi et al., 2009), with perimeter players exhibiting greater speed than their post playing counterparts (Jakovljevic et al., 2015). Although the study by Ben Abdelkrim et al. (2010c) shows average sprint times that are slightly slower than these, the difference between players with specific positional roles is of note. For sprint times over 5 and 10 meters, point guards are shown to be the fastest at 0.88 and 1.74 seconds, respectively. Over these distances similar sprint times are seen between shooting guards (1.10 s and 1.98 s), small forwards (1.12 s and 1.96 s), power forwards (1.15 s and 1.98 s) and centres (1.17 s and 2.0 s). Interestingly, the speed of point guards over 30 meters is shown to be one of the slowest in the team, and the same as power forwards, at 4.28 seconds. Only centres showed slower times of 4.32 seconds, with both small forwards and shooting guards being noticeable faster over this distance at 4.04 and 4.0 seconds, respectively. Table 2.1 highlights the normative test results over these distances that would be expected for basketball players with specific relation to playing position. Although of interest, the measurement of speed over 30 meters may not be an appropriate measure for basketball players. Under FIBA rules (FIBA, 2014) the court is 28 meter in length and 15 meters in width, meaning that the maximum sprint distance possible is 31.8 meter. However, this would need a player to run diagonally from base line to base line, a feat which is seldom seen within competitive play. Basketball play is interspersed with many short sprints of usually 10 meters or less and usually lasting between 1.7 and 2.1 seconds (Ben Abdelkrim et al., 2007). This means that sprint times over the shorter 5 and 10 meters are more specific to match play situations.

The T-test is now a widely-accepted method of measuring agility in basketball. This drill utilises forward and backward sprinting, as well as side shuffle, all of which are movements performed during match play. A significant and very large relationship has been found between performance in the T-test and the distance covered during a game in high-intensity shuffling (Ben Abdelkrim et al., 2010a). Numerous researchers have utilised this test to evaluate the agility performance of basketball players. The average time achieved has differed within these and shown to be 9.21 seconds (Delextrat and Cohen, 2008), 9.25 seconds (Alemdaroglu, 2012) and 9.7 seconds (Chaouachi et al., 2009). In the Ben Abdelkrim et al. (2010c) study, position specific results again show that point guards demonstrate the best test results at 9.51 seconds, whilst times increase from this for shooting guards (10.21 s), small forwards (10.33 s), power forwards (10.46 s) and centres (10.45 s; Table 2.1).

Within the NBA Draft Combine, both speed and agility are measured differently to those utilised within the research literature. Sprint speed is measured over ¾ of the court (22.86 m) and requires players to sprint from baseline to the opponent's free throw line. Although this distance is seldom used in research literature, it does provide a more basketball specific test of running speed over an increased distance. Agility is measured primarily with the lane agility test, which measures how fast a player can move around the key, which is similar to the T-test, which includes side shuffling as well as forward and backward sprinting. Results from the 2017 Draft Combine (Draftexpress.com, 2017) show an average time over the ¾ court sprint and lane agility test of 3.32 seconds and 11.4 seconds, respectively. For the specific positional roles, point guards are again seen to be the fastest and most agile at 3.25 seconds (¾ court sprint) and 11.07 seconds (lane agility test). In comparison, slower times are identified in shooting guards (3.3 s and 11.20 s), small forwards (3.32 s and 11.19 s), power forwards (3.34 s and 11.55 s) and centres (3.41 s and 12.04 s; Table 2.1).

Such results show the importance of agility and speed for successful match play. In addition, acceleration may be seen as more important than maximal speed for performance in basketball, whilst agility is another important characteristic that must be considered in the physical conditioning of players.

2.3 Principles of physiological testing

A comprehensive set of physiological tests provides coaches with information regarding the current fitness status of players (Drinkwater et al., 2008; Montgomery et al., 2008), and is essential for optimising training programme design, reducing injury risk and maximising performance (Newton et al., 2011). Prior to the implementation of any test or measurement, there are a number of key issues that must be considered.

> *Validity* – To have meaning a test must measure what it is purported to measure and is one of the most important characteristics of performance testing (Morrow, 2011).

Reliability – The consistency or repeatability of a test is important to ensure that difference between athletes and changes in a given athlete can be detected effectively (Newton et al., 2011).

Specificity – The tests selected should be based on their ability to assess key performance components that are particular to performance within the identified sport (Newton et al., 2011).

A test must be reliable to be valid, because tests with results that are highly variable have little meaning or use. However, because a test may not measure what it is supposed to measure, a reliable test may not be valid. To achieve a high level of reliability the procedures for each test must be precisely described and followed consistently. This includes ensuring that extraneous variables that may influence the physiological component being measured are controlled for. If the test does not assess the fundamental performance aspects, injury risk or inform training programme design, then it is not an efficient use of an athlete's valuable time or effort.

The order of tests and the duration of rest periods between tests is fundamental to ensure test reliability and repeatability. An essential principle within performance testing is that no test should affect the performance in a subsequent test. This allows for optimal performance to occur and for valid comparisons to be made to previous testing results. According to the National Strength and Conditioning Association (NSCA; McGuigan, 2016), a battery of physiological tests should occur in the following order:

1. Non-fatiguing tests (e.g. anthropometric tests, flexibility, vertical jump)
2. Agility tests (e.g. T-test, lane agility)
3. Maximum power and strength tests (e.g. 1RM, isokinetic dynamometry)
4. Sprint tests (e.g. 5, 10 and 30 m sprints)
5. Muscular endurance tests (e.g. push-up, sit-up tests)
6. Fatiguing anaerobic capacity tests (e.g. Suicide runs, Wingate test)
7. Aerobic capacity tests (e.g. VO_2max, Yo-Yo intermittent recovery test).

Testing should also be performed when an athlete is not fatigued in order to ensure that their performance capacity is maximised. This usually involves the player abstaining from any high-intensity activity or competition for 48 hours prior to testing. Although this is not always feasible for players competing at the elite level, it is certainly desirable, as it provides some assurance that the results obtained are not affected by extraneous variables related to fatigue and are the best that can be achieved. The planning of a test schedule must therefore be given careful consideration. In many cases this may involve testing programmes being split over a number of days in the confidence that previous test should then not impact on the later ones. An example of a test battery for basketball can be seen in Table 2.2. This provides a clear indication of an appropriate test order for each of the requisite physiological components that could be utilised by coaches and allied professionals.

TABLE 2.2 Example test battery for basketball

Test number	Test	Physiological component
1	Height and mass	Anthropometry
2	Skinfold measurements	Body composition
3	Vertical jump test	Power
4	T-test	Agility
5	1RM squat and bench press	Maximum strength
6	Sprint (5 m, 10 m and ¾ court)	Speed
7	Wingate test	Anaerobic power
8	VO_2max	Aerobic capacity

2.4 Summary

This chapter provides a review of the physiological demands that comprise the game of basketball, along with the physical attributes that players need in order to be successful within the sport. Depending on the position (guard, forward or centre), players possess different body compositions and anthropometric profiles, whilst developing different physical fitness levels that determine their role on the court. Guards are usually the most physiologically developed of all players, demonstrating higher scores for aerobic capacity (Coremry et al., 2008), speed (Ben Abdelkrim et al., 2010c), agility (Ben Abdelkrim et al., 2010c) and dynamic power (Ostojic et al., 2006). In contrast, centres are the largest (height and mass) players (Pone-Gonzalez et al., 2015), and possess higher body fat percentages (Pone-Gonzalez et al., 2015), whilst also exhibiting the greatest levels of lower limb isokinetic strength (Bradic et al., 2009).

The development of training programmes specific to the requirements of basketball participation is an important aspect to adequately prepare players for competition. Information concerning the movement patterns and physiological requirements of the game should form the basis of these programmes (Sallet et al., 2005). During training sessions, coaches can use this information to create more individualised strength and conditioning programs for different positional roles. This will enable them to maximise the players' physiological potential, which is an integral part of successful performance in basketball.

References

Alemdaroglu, U. (2012) The relationship between muscle strength, anaerobic performance, agility, sprint ability and vertical jump performance in professional basketball players. *Journal of Human Kinetics*, 31: 99–106.

Apostolidis, N., Nassis, G.P., Bolatoglou, T., Geladas, N.D. (2003) Physiological and technical characteristics of elite young basketball players. *Journal of Sports Medicine and Physical Fitness*, 44(2): 157–163.

Ben Abdelkrim, N., Castagna, C., El Fazaa, S., Tabka, Z., El Ati, J. (2009) Blood metabolites during basketball competitions. *Journal of Strength and Conditioning Research*, 23(3): 765–773.

Ben Abdelkrim, N., Castagna, C., Fazaa, S.E., Ati, J.E. (2010a) The effect of players' standard and tactical strategy on game demands in men's basketball. *Journal of Strength and Conditioning Research*, 24(10): 2652–2662.

Ben Abdelkrim, N., Castagna, C., Jabri, I., Battikh, T., El Fazaa, S., El Ati, J. (2010b) Activity profile and physiological requirements of junior elite basketball players in relation to aerobic-anaerobic fitness. *Journal of Strength and Conditioning Research*, 24(9): 2330–2342.

Ben Abdelkrim, N., Chaouachi, A., Chamari, K., Chtara, M., Castagna, C. (2010c) Positional role and competitive-level differences in elite-level men's basketball players. *Journal of Strength and Conditioning Research*, 24(5): 1346–1355.

Ben Abdelkrim, N., El Fazaa, S., El Ati, J. (2007) Time-motion analysis and physiological data of elite under-19 basketball players during competition. *British Journal of Sports Medicine*, 41: 69–75.

Bishop, D., Edge, J., Goodman, C. (2004) Muscle buffer capacity and aerobic fitness are associated with repeated-sprint ability in women. *European Journal of Applied Physiology*, 92: 540–547.

Bompa, T.O. (1993) *Periodization of strength*. Toronto, ON: Veritas Publishing Inc.

Bradic, A., Bradic, J., Pasalic, E., Markovic, G. (2009) Isokinetic leg strength profile of elite male basketball players. *Journal of Strength and Conditioning Research*, 23(4): 1332–1337.

Campbell, D.E. (1967) Maintenance of strength during a season of sports participation. *American Corrective Therapy Journal*, 21(6): 193–195.

Caruso, J.F., Taylor, S.T., Lutz, B.M., Olson, N.M., Mason, M.L., Borgsmiller, J.A., Riner, R.D. (2012) Anthropometry as a predictor of bench press performance done at different loads. *Journal of Strength and Conditioning Research*, 26(9): 2460–2467.

Castagna, C., D'Ottavio, S., Manzi, V., Annino, G., Colli, R., Belardinelli, R., Dikic, N., Zinanic, S., Astojic, S., Tornjanski, Z. (2005) *HR and VO2 responses during basketball drills*. In N. Dikic, S. Zivanic, S. Ostojic, eds. Book of abstracts of the 10th annual congress of the European College of Sports Science, Belgrade, Serbia, page 160.

Castagna, C., Manzi, V., Impellizzeri, F., Chaouachi, A., Ben Abdelkrim, N., Ditroilo, M. (2010) Validity of an on-court lactate threshold test in young basketball players. *Journal of Strength and Conditioning Research*, 24: 2434–2439.

Castagna, C., Manzi, V., Marini, M., Annino, G., Padua, E., D'Ottavio, S. (2006) *Effect of playing basketball in young basketball players*. In H. Hoppeler, T. Reilly, E. Tsolakidis, L. Gfeller, S. Klossner, eds. Book of abstracts of the 11th Annual Congress of the European College of Sports Science, 5th–8th July 2006, Lausanne, Switzerland, page 325.

Chaouachi, A., Brughelli, M., Chamari, K., Levin, G.T., Abdelkrim, N.B., Laurencelle, L., Castagna, C. (2009) Lower limb maximal dynamic strength and agility determinants in elite basketball players. *Journal of Strength and Conditioning Research*, 23(5): 1570–1577.

Cormery, B., Marcil, M., Bouvard, M. (2008) Rule change incidence on physiological characteristics of elite basketball players: A 10-year-perior investigation. *British Journal of Sports Medicine*, 42(1): 25–30.

Crisafulli, A., Melis, F., Tocco, F., Laconi, P., Lai, C., Concu, A. (2002) External mechanical work versus oxidative energy consumption ration during a basketball field test. *Journal of Sports Medicine and Physical Fitness*, 42: 409–417.

Delextrat, A., Cohen, D. (2008). Physiological testing of basketball players: Towards a standard evaluation of anaerobic fitness. *Journal of Strength and Conditioning Research*, 22: 1066–1072.

DraftExpress.com. (2017). *Measurements history*. Available at: www.draftexpress.com/nba-pre-draft-measurements/all/all/all/all/1/height/desc

Drinkwater, E.J., Hopkins, W.G., McKenna, M.J. (2008) Design and interpretation of anthropometric and fitness testing of basketball players. *Sports Medicine*, 38(7): 565–578.

Epstein, D. (2013) *The sports gene: Inside the science of extraordinary athletics performance*. New York, NY: Penguin Group.

Erčulj, F., Dežman, B., Vučković, G., Perš, J., Perše, M., Kristan, M. (2008) An analysis of basketball players' movements in the Slovenian basketball league playoffs using the sagit tracking system. *Facta Universitatis*, 6(1): 75–84.

FIBA. (2014) *Official basketball rules 2014.* Available at: www.fiba.com/downloads/Rules/2014/OfficialBasketballRules2014.pdf

Glaister, M. (2005) Multiple sprint work: Physiological responses, mechanisms of fatigue and the influence of aerobic fitness. *Sports Medicine*, 35: 757–757.

Gocentas, A., Jascaniniene, N., Poprzecki, S., Jaszczanin, J., Juozulynas, A. (2011). Position-related differences in cardiorespiratory functional capacity of elite basketball players. *Journal of Human Kinetics*, 30: 145–152.

Gosh, A.K., Goswami, A., Mazumdar, P., Mathur, D.N. (1991) Heart rate and blood lactate responses in field hockey players. *Indian Journal of Medical Research*, 94: 351–356.

Hammer, W.M. (1965) Physiological and performance changes during periods of football training and de-training. *Journal of Sports Medicine*, 5(2): 72–75.

Harbili, S. (2015) Relationship between lower extremity isokinetic strength and anaerobic power in weightlifters, basketball and soccer players. *Isokinetics and Exercise Science*, 23(2): 93–100.

Hoare, D.G. (2000) Predicting success in junior elite basketball players – the contribution of anthropometric and physiological attributes. *Journal of Science and Medicine in Sport*, 3: 391–405.

Hoff, J., Helgerud, J. (2004) Endurance and strength training for soccer players: Physiological considerations. *Sports Medicine*, 34(3): 165–180.

Hoffman, J.R. (2003) *Physiology of basketball.* In D.B. McKeag, ed. Basketball, Oxford, Blackwell Science, pages 12–24.

Hoffman, J.R., Epstein, S., Einbinder, M., Weinstein, Y.A. (1999) The influence of aerobic capacity on anaerobic performance and recovery indices in basketball players. *Journal of Strength and Conditioning Research*, 13(4): 407–411.

Hoffman, J.R., Epstein, S., Einbinder, M., Weinstein, Y.A. (2000) A comparison between the Wingate anaerobic power test to both vertical jump and line drill tests in basketball players. *Journal of Strength and Conditioning Research*, 14: 261–264.

Hoffman, J.R., Fry, A.C., Howard, R., Maresh, C.M., Kraemer, W.J. (1991) Strength, speed and endurance changes during the course of a division I basketball season. *Journal of Strength and Conditioning Research*, 5: 144–149.

Hoffman, J.R., Tenenbaum, G., Maresh, C.M., Kraemer, W.J. (1996) Relationship between athletic performance tests and playing time in elite college basketball players. *Journal of Strength and Conditioning Research*, 10: 67–71.

Jakovljevic, S., Karalejic, M., Pajic, Z., Jankovic, N., Erculj, F. (2015) Relationship between 1RM back squat test results and explosive movements in professional basketball players. *Acta Universitatis Carolinae: Kinanthropologica*, 51(1): 41–50.

Keogh, J., Weber, C.L., Dalton, C.T. (2003) Evaluation of anthropometric, physiological, and skill related tests for talent identification in female field hockey. *Canadian Journal of Applied Physiology*, 28: 397–409.

Krustrup, P., Mohr, M., Steensberg, A., Bencke, J., Kjaer, M., Bangsbo, J. (2006) Muscle and blood metabolites during a soccer game: Implications for sprint performance. *Medicine and Science in Sports and Exercise*, 38(6):1165–1174.

Laplaud, D., Hug, F., Menier, R. (2004) Training-induced changes in aerobic aptitudes of professional basketball players. *International Journal of Sports and Medicine*, 25(2): 103–108.

Maud, P.J., Foster, C. (2006) *Physiological assessment of human fitness* (2nd ed.). Champaign, IL: Human Kinetics.

McGuigan, M. (2016) Principles of test selection and administration. In G.G. Haff, T.N. Triplett, eds. *Essentials of strength training and conditioning* (4th ed.). Champaign, IL, Human Kinetics, pages 249–258.

McInnes, S.E., Carlson, J.S., Jones, C.J., McKenna, M.J. (1995) The physiological load imposed upon basketball players during competition. *Journal of Sports Sciences*, 13: 387–397.

McKeag, D.B. (2003) *Basketball*. Indianapolis, IN: Blackwell Science.

Meir, R., Newton, R., Curtis, E., Fardell, M., Butler, B. (2001) Physical fitness qualities of professional rugby league football players: Determination of positional differences. *Journal of Strength and Conditioning Research*, 15: 450–458.

Metaxas, T., Koutlianos, N., Sendelides, T., Mandroukas, A. (2009) Preseason physiological profile of soccer and basketball players in different divisions. *Journal of Strength and Conditioning Research*, 23(6): 1704–1713.

Mohr, M., Krustrup, P., Bangsbo, J. (2003) Match performance of high-standard soccer players with special reference to development of fatigue. *Journal of Sports and Sciences*, 21: 519–528.

Montgomery, P.G., Pyne, D.B., Hopkins, W.G. (2008) Seasonal progression and variability of repeat-effort line drill performance in elite junior basketball players. *Journal of Sports and Sciences*, 26(5): 543–550.

Montgomery, P.G., Pyne, D.B., Minahan, C.L. (2010) The physical and physiological demands of basketball training and competition. *International Journal of Sports Physiology and Performance*, 5: 75–86.

Morrow, J.R. (2011) *Measurement and evaluation in human performance* (4th ed.). Champaign, IL: Human kinetics.

Narazaki, K., Berg, K., Stergiou, N., Chen, B. (2009) Physiological demands of competitive basketball. *Scandinavian Journal of Medicine & Science in Sports*, 19: 425–432.

Newton, R.U., Cormie, P., Cardinale, M. (2011) Monitoring strength and conditioning progress. In M. Cardinale, R. Newton, K. Nosaka, eds. *Strength and conditioning: Biological principles and practical applications*, Chichester, UK, Wiley-Blackwell, pages 253–270.

Nwosu, B.U., Lee, M.M. (2008) Evaluation of short and tall stature in children. *American Family Physician*, 78(5): 597–604.

Ostojic, S.M., Mazic, S., Dikic, N. (2006) Profiling in basketball: Physical and physiological characteristics of elite players. *Journal of Strength and Conditioning Research*, 20(4): 740–744.

Pojskic, H., Separovic, V., Uzicanin, E., Muratovic, M., Mackovic, S. (2015) Positional role differences in the aerobic and anaerobic power elite basketball players. *Journal of Human Kinetics*, 49: 219–227.

Ponce-Gonzalez, J.G., Olmedillas, H., Calleja-Gonzalez, J., Guerra, B., Sanchis-Moysi, J. (2015) Physical fitness, adiposity and testosterone concentrations are associated to playing position in professional basketballers. *Nutricion Hospitalaria*, 31(6): 2624–2632.

Popadic Gacesa, J.Z., Barak, O.F., Grujic, N.G. (2009) Maximal anaerobic power test in athletes of different sport disciplines. *Journal of Strength and Conditioning Research*, 23(3): 751–755.

Reilly, T., Williams, A.M., Nevill, A., Franks, A. (2000) A multidisciplinary approach to talent identification in soccer. *Journal of Sports Sciences*, 18: 695–702.

Rønnestad, B.R., Nymark, B.S., Raastad, T. (2011) Effects of in-season strength maintenance training frequency in professional soccer players. *Journal of Strength and Conditioning Research*, 25(10): 2653–2660.

Sallet, P., Perrier, D., Ferret, J.M., Vitelli, V., Baverel, G. (2005) Physiological differences in professional basketball players as a function of playing position and level of play. *Journal of Sports Medicine and Physical Fitness*, 45(3): 291–294.

Schiltz, M., Lehance, C., Maquet, D., Bury, T., Crielaard, J.-M., Croisier, J.-L. (2009) Explosive strength imbalances in professional basketball players. *Journal of Athletic Train*, 44(1): 39–47.

Sheppard, J.M., Young, W.B. (2006) Agility literature review: Classifications, training and testing. *Journal of Sports Sciences*, 24: 919–932.

Tessitore, A., Tiberi, M., Cortis, C., Rapisarda, E., Meeusen, R., Capranica, L. (2006) Aerobic-anaerobic profiles, heart rate and match analysis in old basketball players. *Gerontology*, 52(4): 214–222.

Tomlin, D.L., Wenger, H.A. (2001) The relationship between aerobic fitness and recovery from high intensity intermittent exercise. *Sports Medicine*, 31(1): 1–11.

Zajac, A., Jarzabeck, R., Waskiewicz, Z. (1999) The diagnostic value of the 10- and 30-second Wingate test for competitive athletes. *Journal of Strength and Conditioning Research*, 13: 16–19.

Ziv, G., Lidor, R. (2009) Physical attributes, physiological characteristics, on-court performances and nutritional strategies of female and male basketball players. *Sports Medicine*, 39: 547–568.

3

NUTRITION FOR BASKETBALL PLAYERS AND TEAMS

Juan Mielgo Ayuso and Ainhoa Prieto

3.1 Introduction

The game of basketball is characterized by combining repeated bouts of high-intensity activity with interspersed recovery periods. Basketball players usually train and/or play 6 days per week, but sometimes they can also have double training sessions per day and 2–3 games on a week, which leads to greater nutritional demands.

Main goals of nutrition in basketball are focused on maximizing the speed, agility and power of players. In order to reach an optimal performance and recovery, there is a high interest on meeting the nutritional needs before, during and after practices and games.

Due to the busy schedule of training and competition, basketball players can find challenging to follow a healthy diet because they can often feel too tired to cook for themselves. Therefore, it is essential to have a good eating plan in advance to help them establish healthy eating habits. In order to support this eating plan, players need to be educated on the role of nutrients and foods to reach an optimal performance and to improve the recovery process. This education should also be focused on improving their cooking skills to ensure players are able to cook their own meals and snacks to increase their energy stores and avoid fatigue. Likewise, they should be guided about which supplements they can consume in order to improve their performance and/or recovery, making sure they understand that supplements do never replace an optimal diet.

This chapter includes a nutritional guide that a basketball player should follow over a season, including the supplements that a player could use to improve health and performance.

3.2 Nutritional limiting factors

Carbohydrates availability

In intermittent team sports, performance is limited by energy from carbohydrates (Ziv & Lidor, 2009). So, basketball players must store energy in the muscles in the form of glycogen to be able to perform to the maximum. In the same way, players also have a large amount of glycogen stored in the liver if they carry adequate nutrition. When the exercise is intense and prolonged, the player can help maintain the blood glucose level through the consumption of sports drink, which has glucose and other forms of carbohydrate (CHO). The ingested CHO can be used by muscles, heart and brain in a quick way by delaying fatigue. It has also been shown that oral rinsing with CHO improves performance when it is run (Bonci, 2003). In short, given the importance of CHO as fuel for basketball players, it is logical that there are general patterns of CHO consumption in the days and hours prior to training and matches, during and even at the end of the exercise.

Several studies using diet recall techniques with basketball players suggest that athletes do not always reach these goals (Bonci, 2003). The post-exercise recovery phase is also the beginning of preparation for the next workout as elite players usually train or play almost every day and with frequencies several times a day in tournaments.

Hydration

An important nutrient that is often overlooked is water. Maintaining adequate hydration, achieving euhydration is important for aerobic performance, and it is suggested that a water deficit of 2% of body weight may lead to poor performance. Different studies of hydration in basketball players suggest that dehydration is detrimental to performance, showing, among others, deterioration of alertness-related care (Baker, Conroy, & Kenney, 2007), or a progressive decline in basketball practice skills when dehydration levels were 1–4% of body weight (Baker, Dougherty, Chow, & Kenney, 2007). The threshold of water deficit in which the overall deterioration of yield was statistically significant was 2% of body weight (Baker et al., 2007). The consumption of carbohydrate solutions (sports drinks) during intermittent exercise seems to improve sports performance so that athletes with 2% dehydration decreased their shooting skills and on the court, as soon as a euhydration with a solution of 6% of carbohydrates were improved compared to euhydration with a placebo. In this sense, it is important to teach basketball players to maintain adequate hydration. One way of knowing individual proportions of sweat loss and knowing how much fluid intake is required to maintain euhydration can be achieved by weighing each player before and after workouts and/or matches.

Body weight and body composition

An optimum physical performance depends on different factors such as genetic traits, health, diet, environment, training schedule, mood and body composition

(BC). BC is one of the most important pillars of cineanthropometry, and is closely related to the player's ability to achieve maximum performance. The BC plays a crucial role in the athletic performance of indoor sports such as basketball (Ramos-Campo et al., 2014), since an excess of fat mass acts as a dead weight that the basketball player must carry in activities. When the body must be lifted repeatedly as in the various movements on the court and in the continuous jumps that must be made (throwing and rebounding), decreasing performance and increasing energy demands are noticed (Mielgo-Ayuso, Calleja-Gonzalez, Clemente-Suarez, & Zourdos, 2014). However, musculoskeletal mass is an indicator of athletic performance (Ramos-Campo et al., 2014) because it contributes to energy production during high intensity activities and provides absolute strength (such as jump power). In basketball, the body mass of the players was the limiting factor that determined their playing position (Drinkwater, Hopkins, McKenna, Hunt, & Pyne, 2007). Specifically, guards are lighter ($p < 0.05$) and have lower body fat percentages ($p < 0.05$) when compared to forwards and centers (Lamonte, Mckinnex, Quinn, Bainbridge, & Eisenman, 1999). Centers also appear to be heavier ($p < 0.05$) than forwards (Lamonte et al., 1999), but no significant differences were found in the percentage of body fat between those positions. This may reflect that the centers need greater weight in order to perform their game well due to the considerable body contact that exists during the time spent on court when on the blocks and rebounding among other actions (Ramos-Campo et al., 2014).

Training periodization

Basketball players can get up to 28 hours of exercise per week, which includes games and different training sessions, depending on the training phase within the annual plan. The season can last up to 40 weeks in which depending on the particular structure of each team the different periods of the season can vary, both in the number of weeks, sessions and/or competitions (see Table 3.1).

An example of an annual planning of a professional basketball team can be seen in Table 3.2, where in addition to the different periods in which the season is divided, the table shows the work done in each one of them, as well as the division of the different microcycles.

In the same way, in order for players to know what type of training they engage with and thus facilitate nutrition, the coaching team can divide the training according to the intensity of the training – see Table 3.3.

TABLE 3.1 Example of annual distribution of basketball training (own elaboration)

	Weeks	*Sessions*	*Matches*
General preparatory period	6	45	4
Specific preparatory period	4	25	4
Competitive period	22	90	40
Transitory period	8	0	0
Total	**40**	**160**	**48**

TABLE 3.2 General planning of a basketball season (own elaboration)

WEEKS	1	2	3	4	5	6	7	8	9	10	11	12	13	14	15	16	17	18	19	20	21	22	23	24	25	26	27	28	29	30	31	32	33	34	35	36	37	38	39	40
MONTHS	AUGUST				SEPTEMBER				OCTOBER				NOVEMBER				DECEMBER				JANUARY				FEBRUARY				MARCH				APRIL				MAY			
PERIOD	PREPARATORY PERIOD												COMPETITIVE PERIOD																				TRANSITORY PERIOD							
PHASES	GENERAL PREPARATORY PERIOD								SPECIFIC PREPARATORY PERIOD				COMPETITIVE PERIOD																				TRANSITORY 1				TRANSITORY 2			
MICROCYCLE	A	C	C	D	C	C	I	D	C	I	D	C	C	C	D	AC	C	C	D	AC	C	C	D	AC	C	I	D	AC	C	D	AC	D	A	A	A	A	A	A	A	A
TRAINING CONTENT	- General strength - Strength power - Average aerobic power - Compensatory work.				- Active flexibility - General flexibility - Injury prophylaxies				- Hypertrophic power (hp) - Velocity gestual segments. - Injury prophylaxies				- Strength hp - Reaction speed - Sign speed - Development in speed technique - Strengthening soft areas - Coordination				- Strength hp - Reaction speed - Sign speed - Development in speed technique - Strengthening soft areas - Coordination.				- Strength hp - Reaction speed - Sign speed - Development in speed technique - Strengthening soft areas - Coordination.				- Strength hp - Reaction speed - Sign speed - Development in speed technique - Strengthening soft areas - General flexibility				- Strength hp - Reaction speed - Sign speed - Development in speed technique - Strengthening soft areas - Coordination - General flexibility				- Endurance - Other activities - General flexibility - Injury prophylaxies.				- Endurance - Other activities - General flexibility - Injury prophylaxies.			

A: adjustment; D: unload; C: load; I: impact

TABLE 3.3 Zones and characteristics of basketball training (own elaboration)

Zone	Intensity of training/Description
Zone 0	Without load
Zone 1	Recovery
Zone 2	Maintenance
Zone 3	Non stressful load
Zone 4	Intensity load (similar to game)
Zone 5	Game

Dietary nutritional requirements of basketball

Nutritional needs of basketball players

There are few studies that analyse the specific nutritional needs of basketball players. However, in order to implement nutrition in these athletes we must be clear that basketball is a sport of intermittent character, because it combines actions of great intensity and short duration with others of low intensity (McInnes, Carlson, Jones, & McKenna, 1995), and it is this characteristic that will guide us in the development of a nutritional strategy.

In this sense, it has been shown that elite basketball players who received daily nutritional counselling by certified sports dietitians show quality in their diets, especially during game days (Tsoufi, Maraki, Dimitrakopoulos, Famisis, & Grammatikopoulou, 2016).

Energy requirements

The energy needs of a basketball player, as for any other athlete, will be determined by the influence of different factors such as weight and body composition, intensity, duration and frequency of training or competitions, environmental conditions and the state of sportsmanship (Close, Hamilton, Philp, Burke, & Morton, 2016). Although there are several equations that allow estimation of the basal metabolism, such as those of Brody-Klieber or Harris-Benedict, to which various constants are added (according to physical activity to calculate the total energy expenditure), in the field of sports nutrition the validity of these equations is reduced and they are rarely used (Thomas, Erdman, & Burke, 2016).

A simple way to know the energy requirements of the basketball player is by studying their intake along with their body composition. Thus, the evaluation of the results obtained by monitoring of 3 or 7 days, together with a detailed examination of the body composition, provides us with very important information to establish the individualized nutritional goals (increase or decrease of weight, muscle gain, etc.; Mielgo-Ayuso, Maroto-Sanchez, Luzardo-Socorro, 2015). In some high-level basketball teams, these checks are usually performed at least three times during the season: 1) During the pre-season to find out the status of players after the holiday period. 2) Mid-season, between December and January, to plan the second part of the season. 3) Before the last 10 league days, to optimize the state of the players during the most decisive phase of the championship (Martinez et al., 2010).

To provide a specific example, the average caloric intake of a team of 15 players competing in both their national league and the Euroleague was 6209.9 kcal during training days and 4657.4 kcal on matchdays (Tsoufi et al., 2016).

Macronutrient requirements

Carbohydrates Players should be directed to select foods containing CHO to minimize gustatory fatigue and maximize the nutritional quality of the diet (Table 3.4). Two-thirds of the food and snack foods should contain HC. Half of these must be starchy foods (bread, cereal, rice, pasta) and the other half fruit and/or vegetables (Bonci, 2003).

Fibre is very important for normal bowel function; however, high fibre foods such as legumes, bran or cabbage family vegetables can cause gastrointestinal problems if consumed in the food prior to a workout or match. Players should be educated to include all kinds of fruits, vegetables, grains and legumes in their diet, but should eat foods with higher fibre or drink fruit juices after exercise rather than before physical activity.

Many players who get up early to train complain about the lack of time to make a proper breakfast and sometimes do not eat anything before the morning exercise. After nocturnal fasting, the body needs energy to replenish liver glycogen stores, and to provide an energy substrate for exercise. Players who cannot or do not like to eat a full breakfast in the morning can make a small intake of food either solid or liquid – details in Table 3.5.

TABLE 3.4 Food sources rich in CHO

Juices	Fruit juices	Fruit based drinks&	Sport drinks
Fizzy Drinks&	Vegetables	Vegetable juices	
Tomato sauce	Potatoes	Legumes	
Bread	Cereals	Pasta	Rice
Millet	Quinoa		
Bread rolls*	Muffins*	Crackers type biscuits*	Fries and crisps*
Crackers (salted)	Popcorn*	Biscuits*	Pastry*
Sponges*	Cakes*	Ice cream*	Iced yogurt
Sorbets	Fruit ice cream	Sugar&	Honey&
Glucose syrup&	Treacle	Sweets&	CHO rich sport drinks
Sports bars	Fried nuts*	Nut bars	Sport gels
Skimmed milk	Skimmed yogurt		

*Food sources rich in fats
&: Food sources rich in simple sugars
Adapted from Bonci, 2003.

CHO requirements In basketball, carbohydrate intake is one of the fundamental aspects of diet. The recommendations that a basketball player should follow indicate that they should consume diets with a content of 5–7 g/kg on days where the training intensity is moderate-low, and increase these values to 7–10 g/kg/day the high intensity training days, as well as the pre-competition days (Thomas et al., 2016). However, without proper nutritional planning it is complex to perform diets that include amounts greater than 7 g/kg/day of carbohydrates in athletes with a high body mass as is the situation with basketball players and especially centers (Bonci, 2003). Therefore, one of the dietician-nutritionist's priority objectives should be the planning of nutritional strategies that facilitate the intake of carbohydrate-rich diets, which is the main fuel metabolized by basketball players to develop their sport activity (Close et al., 2016) – see Table 3.6.

In this context, Tsoufi and coworkers showed in a team playing Euroleague an intake of 7.6±1.5 g/kg HC on game days by 6.8±0.9 g/kg on training days (Tsoufi et al., 2016). Both figures are in line with the recommendations from other research such as Thomas et al. (2016).

Proteins The main role of proteins is muscle growth and repair, as well as the function of the immune system. Many basketball players believe that protein should be the main ingredient in the diet, especially if they are interested in gaining muscle mass. This may lead to poor carbohydrate feeding, which will lead to poorer performance, slower recovery and an inability to synthesize new muscle tissue (Martínez Sanz, Urdampilleta, & Mielgo-Ayuso, 2013).

The intake of diets rich in proteins for a rapid loss of weight and a suppressive effect of the appetite has become a fashion. But we must remember that this weight loss is due to loss of water, which can impair performance, and loss of appetite that can lead to insufficient caloric intake, which can lead to early fatigue during

TABLE 3.5 Examples of breakfast substitution (own elaboration)

A banana and a handful of cereals
A cereal bar and a yogurt
Biscotti with a little jam
A sports gel or a large spoonful of honey and a glass of water
A glass of juice and a cereal bar
A sports drink high in CHO

TABLE 3.6 Moment of CHO intake in competition (own elaboration)

	24–48 hours before	Pre-competition meal (3–4 hours before)	During competition	Post-competition
CHO (g/kg)	7–10	2	30–60 g/hour	1–1,2

exercise. The basketball player will lose weight, but will end up feeling weak, tired and unable to compete. In addition to dehydration, excess protein in these diets can lead to loss of calcium and electrolytes (Martínez-Sanz & Urdampilleta, 2012).

Likewise, the player who opts for a vegetarian diet should be educated about the importance of protein in the diet, and teach the appropriate sources of vegetable protein – an example could be found in Table 3.7. The only foods that do not provide protein are fruits, beverages (except milk), fats (oils, pasta) and sweets. On the other hand, sources of animal proteins such as meat, poultry, fish, eggs and dairy products supply all the essential amino acids, being the proteins complete (Bonci, 2003). For their part, soy foods are the only source of vegetable protein that provides all the essential amino acids. The rest of plant protein sources do not provide all the essential amino acids, necessitating combinations among several in order to obtain protein requirements (Fuhrman & Ferreri, 2010).

Protein requirements Protein consumption by basketball players is often high. Studies on protein metabolism indicate that an amount of 1.7 g/kg/day is more than sufficient to meet the protein needs of adult players, increasing to 2 g/kg/day in season, in which there is a great muscular destruction or the training is directed to the increase of muscle mass (Martínez-Sanz & Urdampilleta, 2012; Thomas et al., 2016). This amount of protein is easily attainable by foods eaten in diets with an energy intake of more than 3,000 Kcal (Bonci, 2003). Despite this, in the basketball world there is still the "myth" about having to consume protein-rich products to improve performance and muscle mass (Campbell et al., 2007). In this sense, we can find basketball players who consume amounts greater than 3 g/kg/day, although the average during game days is 2.2 ± 0.2 g/kg, while the training days is 2.6 ± 0.6 g/kg (Tsoufi et al., 2016). In fact, an excess of protein can lead to increased deposit of body fat rather than to an increase in lean muscle mass. Therefore, one of the priority actions of the nutritionist should be the reduction of protein consumption, reducing animal origin and boosting the intake of carbohydrates, as well as the consumption of protein sources of vegetable origin (legumes and soybean; Bonci, 2003).

Fats Fat consumption varies widely from one player to another. While some players routinely and effortlessly eat a low-fat diet, others make a real effort to restrict fat intake by minimizing the use of added fats, fried foods and high-fat snacks (Bonci,

TABLE 3.7 Protein-rich food sources

Cow	Beef	Pork	Lamb
Chicken	Duck	Turkey	Eggs
Fish	Crustaceans	Milk	Cheese
Cottage cheese	Yogurt	Soya-based foods*	Nuts*
Nut butter*	Seeds*	Legumes*	Grains*
Vegetables*			

*Vegetarian food sources.
Adapted from Bonci, 2003.

2003). Fat is used as an energy substrate for resistance exercise, and is important for lubrication, thermoregulation and transport of fat-soluble vitamins. Although some players mistakenly believe that eating foods that contain fat will lead to excess body fat, this will only occur if the player eats more calories than their body can use effectively, regardless of whether the food is derived from protein, HC or fat. In fact, high-fat foods promote satiety between meals, which may be advantageous for the player who is trying to lose weight (Close et al., 2016).

Fat is a concentrated source of energy, so you do not have to eat a lot to get a significant number of calories. This can be useful for players who lose weight during the season, but find it difficult to eat large amounts of food. For example, adding olive oil, nuts, seeds or nut butters can provide a good source of fat and protein to add extra calories without having to eat large amounts of food (Bonci, 2003).

Since fat is a source of concentrated calories, it should be used sparingly. In addition, foods containing fat (Table 3.8) take longer to digest than CHO or protein and a high-fat meal before exercise can cause gastrointestinal problems, so the recommendation is that players should minimize the intake of fried foods or creamy sauces before exercise and use these foods as part of the post-exercise refuelling.

Fat recommendations The fats should constitute between 20% and 30% of the total caloric intake (1.0–1.2 g/kg/day), prioritizing the consumption of mono and polyunsaturated fatty acids, as well as omega 3 fatty acids (Martínez Sanz et al., 2013). The anti-inflammatory and vasodilatory properties of docosahexaenoic (DHA) and eicosapentaenoic acid (EPA) have generated great interest in the field of sports nutrition, to improve post-training recovery and competition processes (Simopoulos, 2007).

Micronutrient requirements

There is the misconception of many basketball players that vitamin and mineral supplements will provide energy and can be taken instead of meals (Schroder et al., 2002). However, we must remember that vitamin-mineral supplements are an extra for athletes who have a deficiency either because they eat little continuously or eat an unbalanced diet. Additionally, the moment a basketball player takes a certain supplement with micronutrients he/she should take into account a series of points as those presented in Table 3.9.

TABLE 3.8 Fat rich food sources

Butter*	Cream*	Cured cheeses*	Bacon/sausages*
Oil	Olives	Coconut oil*	Palm oil*
Margarine*	Creamy salad dressings*	Oily salad dressings	Mayonnaise
Linseed	Avocado		

*Saturated fat sources.
Adapted from Bonci, 2003.

TABLE 3.9 Things to consider when a basketball player is keen to consume supplements

Consume a product with 100% of RDA /DRI*.
There is no need of buying an expensive product.
To take a multivitamin-mineral supplement, rather than individual formulations, unless advised by the doctor.
A natural product is not necessarily better, but it can be more expensive.
Supplements need to be consumed daily, within the meals.
* RDA = Recommended Dietary Allowance / DRI = Dietary Reference Intake

While there are no specific recommendations for basketball players, vitamin and mineral needs are higher for a basketball player than for a sedentary individual, but these additional needs can be met comfortably through a varied diet. Also, basketball players regularly consume fortified cereals, sports bars and protein powders that already meet their daily needs and would not benefit from an extra supplement (Schroder et al., 2002).

Minerals Minerals, especially calcium, magnesium and phosphorus are involved in muscle and nervous system function, as well as in bone health. Minerals are needed in much smaller amounts than vitamins, except for calcium. Care should be taken to ensure that players do not over-consume mineral supplements, as mineral requirements can be satisfied through dietary sources of food, without the need for extra supplementation, except in exceptional cases. In fact, with the abundance of supplements available, in addition to fortified foods and beverages, and the belief that more is better, it would be fairly easy for an athlete to exceed their daily mineral needs (Bonci, 2003).

To the player who does not like or cannot tolerate dairy products, a calcium supplement may be necessary to ensure optimum bone health. Again, a supplement is not a substitute for a food, so even if the player takes a daily supplement, a varied and balanced diet is best for the player's health (Bonci, 2003). Sodium and potassium electrolytes are important for maintaining optimal hydration and cardiovascular function, and preventing cramps (Martínez-Sanz, Urdampilleta, & Mielgo-Ayuso, 2013). Basketball players should not overly restrict the use of salt unless advised by the nutritionist or sports doctor. Eating lightly salted foods or using condiments that contain sodium before exercise, as well as using sports drinks during exercise can help prevent sodium loss (Urdampilleta, Martínez-Sanz, Julia-Sanchez, & Álvarez-Herms, 2013). Fruits, juices and sports drinks are excellent sources of potassium, which can be used during and after exercise, as well as the night before matches to ensure optimum levels of potassium. Some post-exercise electrolyte replacement techniques include consuming the types of food presented in Table 3.10.

Basketball players' meal timing

Basketball players should be encouraged to eat before, during and after sports. Basketball requires performing continuous activity throughout the game. The player

TABLE 3.10 Some combinations of electrolyte rich food sources to take post-exercises (own elaboration)

Salted nuts (i.e. walnuts) and orange juice
Banana and salted crackers
Nuts, cereals and walnuts mix
Yogurt with cereals

who is not properly fed will tire before the end of it. Given that both training and matches are frequent and intense, the player needs to have the energy required to perform efforts during the 7 days of the week (Bonci, 2003). Nutrition guidelines are divided into pre-, during and after exercise.

Pre-match nutritional strategies

As they usually play 1 or 2 games per week, the pre-match nutritional measures can be repeated very frequently, so it is very important to introduce modifications during the season to provoke motivation and adherence to the diet.

The first and fundamental point is to ensure HC-rich diet (> 7 g/kg/day) during the 48 hours before the matches (Thomas et al., 2016) – see Appendix 3.1 for additional details. The amount of protein should not exceed 1.8–2 g/kg/day and the lipid intake should not exceed 25–30% of the total caloric intake (1–1.2 g/kg).

The second point that must be rigorously controlled is the level of hydration of the players. A good water balance should be ensured, prioritizing water intake, isotonic drinks and/or fruit juices (preferably natural), avoiding soda and alcoholic beverages (American College of Sports Medicine et al., 2007). There are several ways to control the state of hydration, some as simple as the assessment of urine colour, indicating a good state of hydration when it has a white-transparent coloration (Mielgo-Ayuso, Zourdos, Calleja-Gonzalez, 2015; Urdampilleta et al., 2013). However, this simple method may be affected by the ingestion of certain foods and/or supplements that cause changes in the coloration of urine such as beet juice. Another simple form is based on the determination of specific gravity of the urine by using small refractometers or test strips (Mielgo-Ayuso, Maroto-Sanchez, Luzardo-Socorro, 2015). Values greater than 1,020 indicate symptoms of possible dehydration, with the risk that this can lead to the players not only in the decrease of performance but also in the appearance of injuries especially muscular. However, the simplest method to know dehydration is the pre- and post-exercise weighing, where the difference will indicate the lost liquid. In this case, it will always be tried that this does not exceed 2% (Urdampilleta et al., 2013).

On the other hand, studies have shown that athletes who eat a moderate diet-high in HC, low in fat and low in protein 3 hours before exercise may notice a higher performance during exercise (Thomas et al., 2016). However, some authors indicate that a meal 6 hours before exercise will not confer any advantage during play.

Likewise, it is important to remind the player that dinner late the day before does not replace breakfast. In this sense, as already mentioned, players should be encouraged to eat or drink something to provide energy during matches and/or morning training sessions (Thomas et al., 2016).

Since pre-match meal times vary widely between teams, it may be necessary to encourage players to take a snack before matches, especially if a pre-meal has been ingested ≥3 hours earlier. In the team, there must be some food on hand to ensure that the players can feed optimally facing the competition. Thus, an adequate pre-party meal emphasizes HC, with moderate amounts of protein and a small amount of fat (Thomas et al., 2016) – an example is provided in Table 3.11.

If the pre-game meal is >3 hours before the game, players should be encouraged to eat a snack before the game about 30–60 minutes before the game (Table 3.12).

Nutritional strategies during the match

From a nutritional point of view, the development of a basketball game allows, at certain times, some type of dietary strategy that can be realized taking advantage of the periods in which the game stops. The main objectives of these strategies will be to care for hydration and replenishment of energy to reduce fatigue as much as possible. The recommendation for energy consumption during exercise for a basketball player is 30–60 g of carbohydrate per hour of play (Thomas et al., 2016). However, we must remember that the large number of stops that occur in basketball can mismatch the actual exercise time. Consumption of preferably isotonic beverages, with a carbohydrate concentration of 6% and 8%, should be prioritized, since otherwise there is a risk of gastrointestinal problems due to a slow gastric emptying (Maughan & Shirreffs, 2008). Some semi-solid or solid foods may

TABLE 3.11 Pre-match meal examples

Pasta with tomato-based sauce (with lean minced meat, poultry or seafood)
Turkey sandwich
Rice, vegetables and meat (chicken, lean meat or seafood) stir-fry
Chicken or seafood paella or curry with vegetables
Cereals
Biscuits, pancakes, French toast
Eggs and fruit with bread rolls.

TABLE 3.12 Pre-match and during-match snack examples

Cereal bars
Low fat and low protein sport bars
Fresh fruit (i.e. banana, if the athlete tolerates well)
CHO rich sport drink
Biscuits
Cereals
Yogurt
Salted biscuits

also be introduced, mainly during rest between second and third quarters, which give a high concentration of fast glucose absorption rich in glucose or dextrins (gels, energy bars of rapid assimilation, etc.; Burke, Loucks, & Broad, 2006) – see Table 3.13.

Post-match nutritional strategies

The timing and amount of energy after exercise are critical for optimal and rapid recovery. The so-called "anabolic window" for maximum glycogen resynthesis happens within the first 30 minutes post-exercise. The goal for the players would be for them to have 1–1.5 g CHO/kg with a third/fourth part of protein (for every 4 grams of carbohydrates consume 1 gram of protein) within this time period (Thomas et al., 2016). The intake of this amount of CHO and proteins together with liquids will not only replenish the energy resources, but will also rehydrate the basketball player. The role of dietitians-nutritionists on basketball teams should be to educate players on establishing a habit of bringing a snack to the training session so they can take it after they leave the gym or the locker-room (Bonci, 2003). After the games, there should be foods and liquids facilitated to players so that they can take something appropriate at that time – as per the example provided in Table 3.14. Another option is for players to have powdered preparations with the right proportions of CHO and protein.

At 2 hours post-exercise it is recommended to make a complete meal, which includes foods rich in medium-CHO and slow absorption such as rice, pasta or bread. Because the fibre can slow the assimilation of the ingested CHO, it is advisable to reduce the consumption of fibre during the hours after the physical exercise. Especially the more fibrous vegetables and vegetables, as well as legumes, should be avoided. You should also avoid eating large quantities of food, which will make digestion slow and heavy because it produces a large mass of intestinal contents. For

TABLE 3.13 Examples of foods to take during basketball games

Sport drinks: ~700 ml/hour
Honey: ~2 spoons
Sport gels: 25–30 g of carbohydrates each
Jellybeans: ~4–8 units (depend of size)
Nuts: ~1 handful
Energy bar with rapid assimilation carbohydrates.

TABLE 3.14 Post-match meals

Fruit juice + skimmed milk
Skimmed liquid yogurt + banana
Low fat cheese or boiled ham sandwich
Sport bars with proteins

this, it is preferable to consume small amounts of food frequently. To ensure a complete recovery of glycogen stores, it is important to ingest at least 7 g/kg of CHO before the next training or competition (Thomas et al., 2016).

During this period, hydration is also critical. In addition to taking advantage of incorporating CHO and electrolytes, it should be taken into account that, for each gram of glycogen, 3 ml of water and 20 mg of potassium are required for which an adequate amount of water must be administered. It is recommended for this amount to be a 150% on the losses occurred during the sport practice. No alcohol or gas-rich drinks should be consumed at this time (American College of Sports Medicine et al., 2007).

Nutritional planning of the season on a basketball team

At present, many authors recommend a daily intake of CHO between 5 and 7 g/kg/day to provide sufficient energy for moderate intensity workouts or training aimed at the development of certain physical qualities. If this training is of a high intensity or a duration of between 1–3 hours, the intake of HC up to 6–10 g/kg should be increased, increasing to 8–12 g/kg in very intense or training lasting more than 3 hours (Thomas et al., 2016).

Depending on the time of the season we can find that the basketball players get to do up to three sessions a day (preseason). At this time, CHO availability is high due to the wear and tear of this training volume. However, when the volume is lower or is simply a day of rest, the diet should be oriented to the volume and intensity of the same, which results in a reduction in CHO intake, reaching a mixed diet (Table 3.15).

TABLE 3.15 Possible nutritional strategies to promote an adequate training and match adaptation

Strategy	Strategy description
High CHO availability	High CHO loading to delay fatigue. The final sum of the day will be about 6–10 g/kg.
Average CHO availability	Due to the type of session a mixed diet is indicated, in which CHO is included in 50% with daily maximum of 5–7 g/kg.
CHO-during	Sport drink/meals with CHO during the session to support the load/high volume of training
Recovery	An amount of CHO of 1–1.2 g/kg, together with proteins (0.3–0.4 g/kg) is required for post-exercise recovery and the next training session is scheduled or for the following day
Mixed	Because the previous session is not very stressful, it does not require special attention from the CHO, but without forgetting to add a certain amount.
Caffeine	Add ~3 mg/kg taken 45–60 minutes before or during fatiguing or broken workouts.

On the other hand, during the competitive period and especially in the phases in which players play two matches a day, dietary strategies that incorporate pre-competition that will include the previous 2 days, during and post-competition that will include at least 24 hours after the match (Close et al., 2016) – see Table 3.16.

The training program is based on the principles of periodization. Typically, periodization is a planned variation of the acute training variables (i.e. intensity and volume) that are manipulated to lead an athlete to achieve maximum strength and power for a single competition. However, the basketball player must insist on maximum performance throughout the season and needs to start the season to the maximum of conditions. In addition, the basketball player needs to maintain this level of condition throughout the competitive year. Because the basketball player needs to train different performance components, he simultaneously performs several types of training (e.g. strength, anaerobic, endurance). The training program must be developed so that the simultaneous training can produce the maximum performance gains. Therefore, to maximize the effect of training, appropriate manipulation of the various stimuli must be performed (McKeag, 2008).

Once the nutritionist knows the annual training plan he/she should estimate the nutritional and supplementation needs throughout that time period – see Table 3.17.

Medical basketball health supplements

Vitamin D

The term vitamin D really refers to various forms of this vitamin. There are two forms of vitamin D that are important in humans: ergocalciferol (vitamin D2) and cholecalciferol (vitamin D3) (Larson-Meyer & Willis, 2010). Vitamin D2 synthesis is performed by plants, while vitamin D3 is made by humans on the skin when exposed to the ultraviolet (UVB) rays of the sun. In humans, vitamin D can also be obtained by eating some foods such as blue fish or by fortified foods (milk and dairy products; Larson-Meyer & Willis, 2010). Vitamin D has traditionally been associated with bone metabolism (McDonnell, Hume, & Nolte, 2011), although it is also being examined for its effect on immunity (He et al., 2013; Owens, Fraser, & Close, 2015) and its possible impact on performance (Dahlquist, Dieter, & Koehle, 2015).

In the field of sport, interest in this vitamin has gone unnoticed for many years, although very recent studies have warned about the risk of deficits that may be experienced by some athletes, especially indoor ones (Willis, Peterson, & Larson-Meyer, 2008), like basketball where solar radiation is practically nil.

Although more studies should be developed to allow a better understanding of the mechanisms of vitamin D on sports performance, nutritionists should pay more attention to this vitamin and to carry out a continuous and exhaustive follow-up of serum levels of 25-OH-D in basketball players. In this sense, Dzedzej and colleagues have shown that blood vitamin D levels decrease during the season (as it can be seen in Figure 3.1), with a slight positive correlation with the performance

TABLE 3.16 Example of a weekly plan in a competitive period with two matches during the same week

	Monday	Tuesday	Wednesday	Thursday	Friday	Saturday	Sunday
Morning session	Off	Off	Off	Off	Off	Off	Off
Nutrition Pre/Breakfast	Average CHO Availability	High CHO Availability	Average CHO Availability	Low CHO Availability	High CHO Availability	Average CHO Availability	High CHO Availability
Lunch/ preparation	High CHO Availability	High CHO Availability	High CHO Availability	High CHO Availability	High CHO Availability	High CHO Availability	High CHO Availability
Afternoon session	Court (2 h)	Match (3 h)	Court (2 h)	Court (2 h)	Match (3 h)	Court (2 h)	Court (2 h)
Zone/session goal	3 /Maintenance	5 /Competitive	2 /Recovery	3 /Development	5 /Competitive	2 /Recovery	3–4 / Development
Nutrition during	CHO	CHO + Caffeine	CHO water if difficult to maintain optimal body composition	CHO	CHO + Caffeine	CHO water if difficult to maintain optimal body composition	CHO
Nutrition post	Recovery + Protein	Recovery + Protein	Recovery + Protein	Recovery + Protein	Recovery + Protein	Recovery + Protein	Recovery + Protein
Nutrition post/ dinner	CHO load	Recovery	Mixed	CHO load	Recovery	Mixed	Mixed

TABLE 3.17 Nutritional strategies for each training phase including supplements with potential benefits for basketball players

Nutrition	General Preparatory Period	Specific Preparatory Period	Competitive Period	Transitory Period
Daily intake (CHO, protein and fats)	– CHO: 6 to 12 g/kg/day – Proteins: ~ 1,8 g/kg/day. – Fats: 20–30% (1–1,2 g/kg). – ~40 g of protein before bed – Focus on antioxidant rich food sources	– Higher consumption of CHO between sessions – Focus on antioxidant rich food sources	General preparation with high CHO load 1 or 2 days before competition	To develop or renew adequate nutritional habits for performance – Reduce energy and CHO – Control of body composition
Nutrition during	CHO in most of the sessions with more than 1 h of duration	CHO during important sessions, especially for the long and high intense sessions	CHO during matches	N/A
Nutrition post	In the first 30 min after each session: – Recovery snack + recovery meal if high nutritional requirements – 0.3 g/kg protein after strength session	In the first 30 min after each session: – Recovery snack + recovery meal if high nutritional requirements – 0.3 g/kg protein after strength session – Practice competition recovery strategies	Specific recovery – CHO + protein immediately after the match, as it has been practiced during the especial preparatory period	N/A
Supplements	– Vitamin D – Iron – Creatine – BCAA – Caffeine (for hard sessions) – Antioxidants	– Vitamin D – Iron – Beta-Alanine – Omega 3 – Caffeine (for hard sessions) – Supplementation strategies for competition: caffeine	– Vitamin D – Iron – BCAA – Specific supplements	– Iron – Antioxidants
Notes	Risk of illness in high volume of training weeks	Possible reduction of appetite in hard sessions	It is possible that weekly strategies are similar between them, so variety is required to avoid boredom.	Remind players that this is the best period to optimize iron and antioxidants resources.

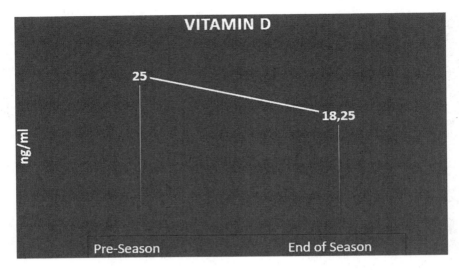

FIGURE 3.1 Variation of vitamin D levels in blood after 8 months of season in the NBA Data obtained from Dzedzej et al., 2016.

of the players (Dzedzej et al., 2016). On the other hand, it has been suggested that all athletes with values <50 nmol/L should be supplemented regularly and at high doses (>1,000 IU) until reaching values ≈75 nmol/L that would reduce the risk of bone lesions and could optimize sports performance (Larson-Meyer & Willis, 2010). In this sense, 90 NBA players had vitamin D deficiency (<20 ng/mL), 131 had insufficiency (20–32 ng/mL), and 58 had adequate vitamin D levels (>32 ng/dL; Fishman, Lombardo, & Kharrazi, 2016).

Iron

Iron (Fe) is one of the nutrients most studied in the scientific literature given its relevance to the health and optimal athletic performance of a basketball player (DellaValle & Haas, 2011). Its deficiency has a direct bearing on sports performance, not only because of its relation to iron deficiency anaemia, but because deficient deposits can negatively affect performance even in situations without established anaemia (Mielgo-Ayuso, Zourdos, Calleja-Gonzalez, 2015). These alterations also affect the recovery of the athlete.

In 2004, iron metabolism (Fe) was studied in international basketball players of different ages (n=103); analysing variables related to EF metabolism such as ferritin and transferrin saturation (IST). The results showed that 22% of the studied players suffered from depletion of Fe deposits (ferritin <22 μg/L), specifically 15% in men and 25% in women. Likewise, 25% showed anaemia (haemoglobin <12 g/dl in women and 14 g/dl in men), being 18% in men and 38% in women. Finally, 7%

also showed iron deficiency anaemia (ferritin <12 μg/L + IST <16%), being 3% in men and 14% in women; Dubnov & Constantini, 2004). Regarding the impact of ferritin and serum iron on the NBA season (8 months), these values fell by 15±40% and 18±33%, respectively as illustrated in Figure 3.2 (Dzedzej et al., 2016).

In this sense, regular blood tests should be performed during the season to control the iron metabolism of players in order to assess iron supplementation (Dubnov & Constantini, 2004; Dzedzej et al., 2016). In the same way, it is advisable to teach the players that foods contain iron, in addition to which they favour their absorption or not, although it has been shown in women and men of team sports that does not influence much (Mielgo-Ayuso et al., 2012).

Antioxidants

Free radicals occur naturally in the body and can have negative effects on the oxidation of DNA, lipids and proteins. While the endogenous antioxidant system placates these negative effects, when there is an imbalance between the production of free radicals and antioxidant defence, oxidative stress occurs. Oxidative stress may be involved in the aging process, cell damage, some pathology, muscle fatigue and overtraining (Ji, 1995). Physical training increases the production of free radicals and the use of antioxidants. Therefore, adequate nutrition is important in the maintenance of antioxidants (Ji, 1995).

Since basketball players engage in intense physical activity, their production of free radicals is likely to increase. Therefore, it is important to provide the necessary

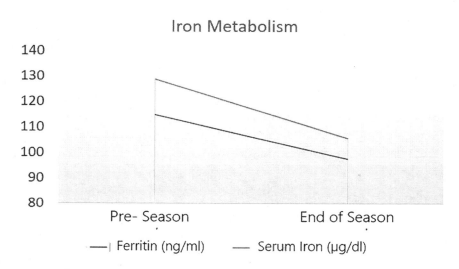

FIGURE 3.2 Modification of iron metabolism (ferritin and serum iron) throughout a basketball season

Data obtained from Dzedzej et al., 2016.

micronutrients that serve as antioxidants to quench the possible negative effects of free radicals. So, when basketball players do not eat a balanced diet, you might consider supplementing with antioxidants.

In this sense, 32 days of treatment with a supplement in professional basketball players containing antioxidants – α-tocopherol (vitamin E), β-carotene and ascorbic acid (vitamin C) – led to higher plasma levels of α-tocopherol and β-carotene in the study group compared to placebo (Schröder, Navarro, Mora, Galiano, & Tramullas, 2001). However, plasma ascorbic acid levels did not rise in the study group, whereas there was a significant decrease in the placebo group (Figure 3.3). It is believed that the levels were maintained by their use to eliminate free radicals and regenerate vitamin E. It is important to note that lipid peroxide (lipid peroxidation is degradation of lipids and may cause damage to the cell membrane) decreased in the study group by 27%, although the difference was not statistically significant with respect to the control group ($p < 0.09$). The authors suggested that this may be related to a reduction of muscle damage during training (Schröder et al., 2001). Similar results were observed in another study (Schröder, Navarro, Tramullas, Mora, & Galiano, 2000), who found an improvement in oxidative stress in elite male basketball players during a competitive season when antioxidant supplements were taken. A third study found that α-tocopherol supplementation may reduce DNA oxidation induced by training (Tsakiris, Parthimos, Tsakiris, Parthimos, &

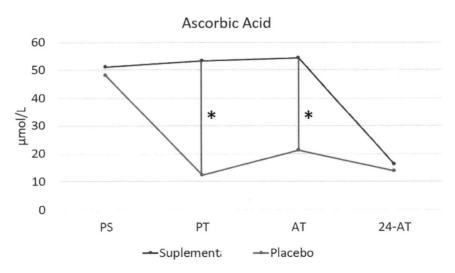

FIGURE 3.3 Ascorbic acid levels in the supplemented and placebo groups in pre-supplementation (PS), pre-training (PT), after training (AT) and 24 hours after training (24h-AT).

* Differences between groups

Data obtained from Schröder et al., 2001.

Schulpis, 2006). In this study, total antioxidant status was highest after 1 month of supplementation.

These studies suggest that basketball players can benefit from supplementing their diet with antioxidants. Interestingly, vegetarian athletes have a higher level of antioxidants such as vitamin C, vitamin E and β-carotene compared to omnivores (Venderley & Campbell, 2006). While the negative effects of free radicals do not usually affect performance, they may possibly lead to overtraining. This may be due to the muscle damage that can be caused by free radicals, can reduce the metabolic capacities of muscle cells (Finaud, Lac, & Filaire, 2006). This speculation should be considered with caution, since there is no direct evidence to support it (Finaud et al., 2006).

Based on what was discussed above, an intake of antioxidant supplements may be recommended in the first weeks of the preseason, as well as in the discharge microcycles and in the transient period, always after analysing the player's diet and see if there may be any deficiency of these antioxidant micronutrients.

Ergonutritional aids to improve training performance and competitions

As already mentioned, basketball requires a continuous work of the whole body, which uses to the maximum all the systems to obtain energy. In this sense, although there are some studies that show the effectiveness of a certain supplementation in basketball performance, there are other supplements that by their characteristics could be suitable for the practice of this sport in order to increase the adaptations to training so that it contributes directly to the competitive success.

Creatine

Creatine monohydrate is one of the best-selling sports supplements among basketball players because it benefits their performance as it increases energy production during high-intensity exercise actions, as well as because it contributes to the increase in muscle mass of basketball players. In addition, Shi (2005) concluded that CHO and creatine supplementation could promote post-exercise recovery in basketball players (Figure 3.4), demonstrating their efficacy in a sport such as basketball characterized by high-intensity efforts (Shi, 2005).

Basketball players as discussed above perform a variety of high intensity actions during a game. For example, it may be necessary to make different sprints throughout the course of the game. Players must also be able to dribble and throw as well as pass the ball to other players for which strength and power is required. Finally, jumping is one of the important skills that players must master if they want to reach the elite. Jumping is an explosive movement that is used while blocking a throw, throwing or looking for a rebound. Throughout the game, players need to be able to have enough energy to perform these high intensity actions. Because of these energy requirements, basketball players can improve their playing skills also through the use of creatine supplements.

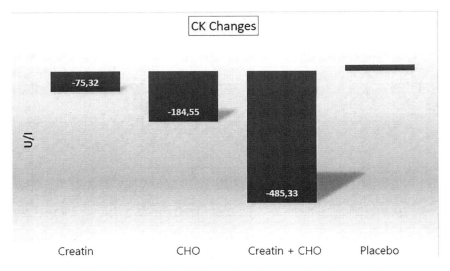

FIGURE 3.4 Changes in CK after 10 days of supplementation after exercise
Data obtained from Shi, 2005.

Also, creatine helps increase muscle mass, not because it stimulates the growth of muscle tissue, but because it increases muscle contractions and reduces fatigue, which helps basketball players train for increased muscle mass.

Because only a certain amount of creatine monohydrate can be stored in the body, taking excessive amounts does not have any extra benefit because too much creatine will be excreted in the urine. There are two classic protocols of supplementation such as fast loading (20 g/d for 5 days) or slow loading (0.03 g/d for 28 days), which seem to be equally effective in obtaining supramaximum stores of muscle creatine. In addition, if we load more slowly (taking about 0.05 g/day, for 6 weeks), less liquid is retained (Boegman & Dziedzic, 2016). The body most effectively absorbs creatine when taken alongside carbohydrate-rich foods like fruits, fruit juices and starches.

During the basketball season, it would be advisable to do 2 or 3 periods of 30–40 days of supplementation that coincide with the most important moments of the season (e.g. Copa del Rey, Playoff, league final, etc.).

Branched amino acids

Branched-chain amino acids (BCAA) are leucine, isoleucine, and valine that make up 40% of the daily requirements of essential amino acids (Campbell et al., 2007). Although a balanced diet will provide adequate branched amino acids (0.64 g/kg/day), the timing of its administration is very important for the acceleration of muscle recovery processes after a high physical exercise intensity. There is strong evidence that high amounts of branched amino acids (≈ 200 mg/kg/day with a 2:1:1 ratio of leucine: isoleucine: valine) at the end of exercise reduce the concentration of the enzymes creatin kinasa (CK) and lactate dehydrogenase (LDH), which are used to determine muscle-induced physical stress (Negro, Giardina, Marzani, & Marzatico, 2008).

In basketball, branched amino acids are added to preparations used at the end of training and competitions. These preparations include products rich in carbohydrates (fruit shakes, biscuits, etc., with water or skim milk) where the appropriate dose of branched amino acids is added.

There is a wide variety of protocols, although it is generally taken half an hour before and after EF with a leucine/isoleucine/valine ratio of 2:1:1 or 4:1:1 (100–200 mg/kg/d during 2 months; De Palo et al., 2001).

Caffeine

Caffeine is an alkaloid that is present in multiple foods and beverages commonly used (coffee, tea, cocoa, chocolate, cola, etc.). Its use as an ergogenic substance is based both on the stimulating effect, with greater resistance to fatigue and decreased recovery time, as well as on metabolic actions, improving aerobic capacity and endurance. Some studies have observed that low doses (1.5–3.5 g/kg) at 40 and 60 minutes before physical exercise can improve performance in short and high muscle power efforts, like those occurring in basketball (Mielgo-Ayuso & Urdampilleta, 2016). However, Tucker and coworkers showed no effect of 3 mg/kg caffeine intake taken 60 minutes earlier on jump power and VO2 max in five elite basketball players (Tucker, Hargreaves, Clarke, Dale, & Blackwell, 2013), while Cheng and colleagues did note that 6 mg/kg intake taken 60 minutes earlier improves the decrease in exercise power of 3 minutes in college players (Cheng, Hsu, Kuo, Shih, & Lee, 2016). Similar results were observed in adolescent basketball players who took 3 mg/kg (Abian-Vicen et al., 2014).

In this sense, an intake of 3 mg/kg 60 minutes before a match could be recommended, and a similar or smaller dose could be taken at the end of the second quarter until a final dose of 6 mg/kg was obtained. Also, a dose of 3 mg/kg can be taken on the days of maximum intensity training. In basketball, it is usually used in the form of a beverage (coffee) or supplementation (caffeine pills) about 2 hours before the game in low doses (1–.5 mg/kg).

Omega-3 fatty acids

In sports, the interest in omega-3 acids is mainly motivated by its anti-inflammatory action (Simopoulos, 2007). High-performance athletes perform very demanding workouts and competitions that help the appearance of muscle injuries and inflammatory processes that must be adequately treated by both diet and other post-exercise recovery mechanisms. In this sense, some studies have suggested the anti-inflammatory benefits of an omega-3 supplementation in athletes.

In basketball, Ghiasvand and colleagues found that supplementation with 2 g of omega-3 (eicosapentaenoic acid [EPA]), together with 400 IU of vitamin E for 6 weeks improved plasma levels of IL-2 and erythrocytes glutathione reductase, in addition to reducing TNF-α, and that the EPA improves the serum level of MDA, reactive species occurs naturally and is a marker for oxidative stress (Figure 3.5; Ghiasvand et al., 2010).

Thus, in basketball the use of omega 3 acids can be of great interest because: 1) Basketball is a muscular sport very aggressive due to the large number of jumps that are made during a training or competition on a hard surface. 2) In addition to this is added that basketball players have a high body mass, which leads to an overload in their joints and muscles of the lower extremities. All this generates a high risk of the appearance of muscular injuries and inflammatory processes. 3) If we add that the diet of many players is generally deficient in foods rich in omega-3, it is evident that the supplementation with these fatty acids is necessary for a large part of the season to supply the deficiencies of the diet and optimize the recovery processes.

The effective doses are 1–3 g/day at a ratio of 2–3 EPA/1 DHA (600–1200 mg EPA and 400–800 mg DHA) and that 66% is provided through a high diet in this type of fatty sardines, anchovies, tuna, horse mackerel, and so on, although some products like dairy products, cookies or eggs are enriched with these fats.

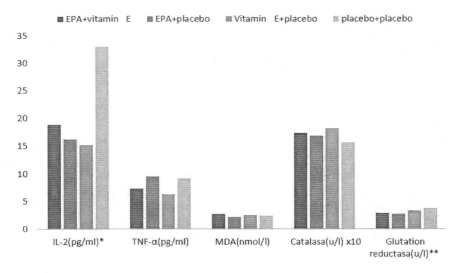

FIGURE 3.5 Plasma levels of IL-2, TNF-A, MDA, and catalase after 6 weeks of supplementation.

* Differences between the group of EPA + vitamin E and the others.

** Differences between the EPA + placebo and vitamin E + placebo groups.

Data obtained from Ghiasvand et al., 2010.

Supplements that require further research

β-alanine

β-alanine is a non-essential amino acid found in different foods of animal origin (meat, fish, eggs and milk; Hill et al., 2007), one of its main actions being the synthesis of carnosine, along with histidine. Carnosine is present in muscle and brain tissues, and its main action for sports is its capacity as a buffering agent for the pH (Derave, Everaert, Beeckman, & Baguet, 2010), which leads to an increase in muscular damping ability, delayed onset of muscle fatigue, and facilitating recovery actions from repeated high-intensity exercises.

Supplementation of β-alanine has been shown to improve the performance of high-intensity exercise. Although some authors have indicated that β-alanine supplementation in highly trained athletes may be important (Hoffman et al., 2008), there is no scientific evidence on the ergogenic effect of β-alanine in basketball today. Recent research has focused on the effect of supplementation with β-alanine and sodium bicarbonate on high-intensity efforts, but performed on resistance exercise. Therefore, analysing the effects of these supplements might be interesting in basketball as it is an intermittent sport with a 40-minute game with a variety of multidirectional moves such as running and dribbling at different speeds and jumping (Crisafulli et al., 2002).

It has been observed that prolonged (>4 weeks) supplementation of β-Alanine (doses between 4–5 g/day) significantly increases muscle deposit of carnosine and reduces metabolic acidosis induced by high-intensity physical exercises (Hill et al., 2007). These studies have aroused great interest in their potential application in sports modalities where lactic anaerobic metabolism plays a determining role, as in the case of basketball. However, despite the potential ergogenic effects of β-Alanine, the adverse effects of prolonged administration of this amino acid are still unknown. More studies are needed to analyse in detail both its ergogenic effects, as well as their adverse effects.

3.3 Summary

Basketball is an intermittent sport in which high intensity actions are combined with moments of recovery which require great physical demands. While basketball is not a sport of endurance, basketball players require a high aerobic capacity which is of vital importance in the recovery processes. The usual actions of basketball require a high anaerobic power such as a rapid change of direction, release from an opponent, jump quickly and repeatedly, and the speed necessary to reach loose balls. Players require high strength in both arms and legs that allow them to jump, block or shoot. Speed and agility are integral aspects of almost all the manoeuvres that basketball players do, both defensive and offensive in training and matches. Adequate flexibility tends to reduce the risk of injury to the player.

Basketball players must store energy in the muscles in the form of glycogen in order to be able to perform to the maximum so that a diet rich in HC is of utmost importance. The basketball player should not forget to be properly hydrated as well as maintaining a correct body weight and composition in order to optimize his performance. The recommendations of HC for a basketball player are 5–7 g/kg on days of moderate-low intensity and 7–10 g/kg/day on days of high intensity, as well as those prior to competition.

The protein requirements are 1.7 g/kg/day, increasing to 2 g/kg/day in periods of the season when there is a great muscular destruction. Fat recommendations are 20–30% of the total caloric intake (1.0–1.2 g/kg/day), prioritizing monounsaturated and polyunsaturated fatty acids, as well as omega-3 fatty acids.

Supplementation with vitamin D and iron during the season may favour the low levels of these micronutrients that are given in basketball players, which will improve their physical performance. Intake of creatine, in addition to providing phospho-creatine for the execution of explosive actions, favours muscle recovery at a dose of 0.03 g/d for 28 days. A dose of ≈200 mg/kg/day of branched amino acids ingested after basketball practice favour muscle recovery.

The intake of 3 mg/kg of caffeine 40–60 minutes before a match or very intense training will delay the onset of fatigue. Supplementation with 2 g of omega 3 (EPA) together with 400 IU of vitamin E for 6 weeks improves the plasma levels of parameters related to inflammation and oxidative stress.

APPENDIX 3.1

Match-oriented diet of a 90 kg basketball player competing on Sunday at 18:00

The two previous days have two training sessions on Friday (morning and afternoon), another training session on Saturday afternoon and the day of the competition will also have a small session in the morning. The player averages 30 minutes of play per game this season.

Intake on Friday	Food sources	g CHO/Kg body weight	% approximated calories intake
Breakfast 08:00	2 toasts with 2 tbsp of jam (40 g CHO)	1 g/Kg body weight	5%
	1 glass of rice milk with coffee 150 ml (15 g CHO)	90 g CHO	
	1 banana (20 g CHO)		
	1 glass of fruit juice 150 ml (15 g CHO)		
Training 9:30	Isotonic drink 8%: 500 ml (40 g CHO)	0.5 g/Kg body weight	5%
		45 g CHO	
Mid-morning 11:00	1 glass skimmed milk 200 ml (12 g CHO) (10 g prot)	1,5 g/Kg de peso	15%
	6 Maria-type biscuits (60 g CHO)	135 g CHO	
	3 bread rolls with 100 g cottage cheese (30 g CHO) (12 g prot)	35 g prot	
	2 slices of cured ham (60 g) con 2 bread slices (20 g CHO) (10 g prot)		
Lunch 14:00	Vegetable salad (300 g) (10 g HC).	2 g/Kg body weight	25%
	150 g de raw pasta with tomato sauce and tinned tuna (85 g CHO) (28 g prot)	180 g CHO	
	2 chicken fillets (200 g) with boiled potato (150 g) (30 g CHO) (20 g prot)	30 g prot	
	2 bread slices (20 g CHO)		
	1 pear (10 g CHO)		
	6 chocolate ounces (30 g HC)		
Training 17:00	Isotonic drink 8% (80 g CHO)	1 g/Kg body weight	10%
		90 g HC	
Mid-afternoon 19:00	1 glass skimmed milk 200 ml with a croissant (52 g CHO) (10 g prot)	1.5 g/Kg body weight	10%
	2 bread slices with 6 turkey slices 180 g (20 g CHO) (15 g prot)	135 g CHO	
	2 bananas (40 g CHO)	25 prot	
	Quince 100 g (30 g CHO)		
Dinner 21:00	Hypertonic recovery drink 3:1 15% CHO 5% prot 500 ml (80 g CHO) (26 g prot)	2 g/Kg body weight	20%
	200 g spinach with 100 g mushrooms (10 g CHO)	180 g CHO	
	Rice (60 g raw) with 2 pan fried eggs, 1 beef fillet 100 g, and tomato sauce (40 g CHO) (30 g prot)	55 g prot	
	1 glass fruit juice (200 ml) (20 g CHO)		
	2 bread slices (20 g CHO)		
	1 peach (10 g CHO)		
Supper 22:30	1 apple (10 g CHO)	0.5 g/Kg body weight	10%
	1 muffin (20 g CHO)	45 g CHO	
	2 chocolate ounces (10 g CHO)		

Breakfast 9:00	2 toasts with 2 tbsp of jam (40 g CHO) 1 glass of rice milk with coffee 150 ml (15 g CHO) 1 glass of skimmed milk (12 g CHO) (10 g prot) 3 tbsp of cereals (22 g CHO).	1 g/Kg body weight 90 g CHO 10 g prot	10%
Mid-morning 11:00	1 orange (10 g CHO) 2 bread slices with 2 turkey slices (60 g) (20 g CHO) (10 g prot) 3 chocolate ounces (15 g CHO)	0,5 g/Kg body weight 45 g CHO 10 g prot	5%
Lunch 14:00	90 g raw lentils (30 g CHO) (20 g prot). 2 pork slices (200 g) with mashed potato (150 g) y guisantes (60 g). (40 g CHO) (20 g prot). 2 bread slices (20 g CHO). Quince 100 g with 4 Maria-type biscuits (60 g CHO).	1,5 g/Kg body weight 150 g CHO 40 g prot	20%
Mid-afternoon snack 1 17:00	1 Banana (20 g CHO). 4 Maria-type biscuits (30 g CHO).	0,5 g/Kg body weight 45 g CHO	5%
Training 18:00	Isotonic drink 8%: 500 ml (40 g CHO).	0,5 g/Kg body weight 45 g CHO	5%
Mid-afternoon snack 2 20:00	2 natural yogurts with honey (20 g CHO) (10 g prot). Hypertonic recovery drink 3:1 15% CHO 5% prot 500 ml (80 g CHO) (26 g prot)	1,5 g/Kg body weight 135 g CHO 36 g prot	15%
Dinner 21:00	Lettuce salad (100 g) tomato (100 g) y corn (100 g) (25 g CHO) 150 g raw pasta with two garlic cloves and 2 tbsp olive oil and 2 chicken fillets (75 g CHO) (20 g prot) 2 bread slices (20 g CHO) 1 glass fruit juice (150 ml) (15 CHO) 1 banana (20 g CHO) 2 melon slices (20 g CHO)	2 g/Kg de peso 180 g HC 20 g prot	20%
Supper 22:30	1 glass skimmed milk (12g CHO) (10 g prot) 1 muffin (20 g CHO) 4 chocolate ounces (20 g CHO) 3 bread rolls with 100 g cottage cheese (30 g CHO) (12g prot)	1 g/Kg body weight 90 g CHO 22 g prot	10%

(Continued)

APPENDIX 3.1 (Continued)

Intake on Sunday	Food sources	g CHO/Kg body weight	% approximated calories intake
Breakfast 08:00	1 glass of rice milk with coffee 150 ml (15 g CHO) 1 muffin (20 g CHO) 1 banana (20 g CHO) 1 glass of skimmed milk (12 g CHO) (10 g prot) 3 tbsp of cereals (22 g CHO)	1 g/Kg body weight 90 g CHO 10 g prot	10%
Training 10:00	Isotonic drink 8%: 500 ml (40 g CHO)	0,5 g/Kg body weight 45 g CHO	5%
Mid-morning 11:00	Hypertonic recovery drink 3:1 15% CHO 5% prot 500 ml (80 g CHO) (26 g prot) 1 bread slice with 1 slice (60 g) of cured ham (10 g CHO) (10 g prot)	1 g/Kg body weight 90 g CHO 36 g prot	10%
Lunch 13:30	150 g raw pasta with tomato sauce (75 g CHO) 2 chicken fillets (100 g) with 2 baked potatoes (200 g) (40 g CHO) (20 g prot) 1 glass juice (150 ml) (15 g CHO) 1 portion (170 g) rice pudding (30 g CHO) (5 g prot) 6 María-type biscuits (30 g CHO) 1 apple (10 g CHO)	2 g/Kg body weight 180 g CHO 25 g prot	25%
Mid-afternoon snack 1 16:00	1 banana (20 g CHO) 2 cereal bars with chocolate chips (30 g CHO) 1 cup of coffee 100 g quince with 1 bread roll (40 g CHO)	1 g/Kg body weight 90 g CHO	10%
Match 18:00	Isotonic drink 8% 1 l (80 g CHO)	1 g/Kg body weight 90 g CHO	10%
Mid-afternoon snack 2	Hypertonic recovery drink 3:1 15% CHO 5% prot 250 ml (40 g CHO) (13g prot)	0,5 g/kg body weight 45 g CHO 13g prot	5%
Dinner 21:00	150 g raw rice with 1 pan fried egg and 1 beef fillet (100 g) (75 g CHO) (20 g prot) 2 bread slices (20 g CHO) 6 bread rolls with 100 g cottage cheese (60 g CHO) (12g prot) 1 glass fruit juice (150 ml) (15 g CHO)	2 g/Kg body weight 180 g CHO 32 g prot	20%
Supper 23:00	1 muffin (20 g CHO) 2 bread slices with 8 chocolate ounces (60 g CHO)	1 g/Kg body weight 90 g CHO	5%

References

Abian-Vicen, J., Puente, C., Salinero, J. J., Gonzalez-Millan, C., Areces, F., Munoz, G., Munz-Guerra, J., & Del Coso, J. (2014) A caffeinated energy drink improves jump performance in adolescent basketball players. *Amino Acids, 46*(5), 1333–1341.

American College of Sports Medicine, Sawka, M. N., Burke, L. M., Eichner, E. R., Maughan, R. J., Montain, S. J., & Stachenfeld, N. S. (2007) American college of sports medicine position stand: Exercise and fluid replacement. *Medicine and Science in Sports and Exercise, 39*(2), 377–390.

Baker, L. B., Conroy, D. E., & Kenney, W. L. (2007) Dehydration impairs vigilance-related attention in male basketball players. *Medicine and Science in Sports and Exercise, 39*(6), 976–983.

Baker, L. B., Dougherty, K. A., Chow, M., & Kenney, W. L. (2007) Progressive dehydration causes a progressive decline in basketball skill performance. *Medicine and Science in Sports and Exercise, 39*(7), 1114–1123.

Boegman, S., & Dziedzic, C. E. (2016) Nutrition and supplements for elite open-weight rowing. *Current Sports Medicine Reports, 15*(4), 252–261.

Bonci, L. J. (2003) Nutrition guidelines for basketball. In D. B. McKeag (Ed.), *Handbook of sports medicine and science: Basketball* (1st ed., pp. 25–37). Malden, MA: Blackwell Science Ltd.

Burke, L. M., Loucks, A. B., & Broad, N. (2006) Energy and carbohydrate for training and recovery. *Journal of Sports Sciences, 24*(7), 675–685.

Campbell, B., Kreider, R. B., Ziegenfuss, T., La Bounty, P., Roberts, M., Burke, D., . . . Antonio, J. (2007) International society of sports nutrition position stand: protein and exercise. *Journal of the International Society of Sports Nutrition, 4*(8).

Cheng, C. F., Hsu, W. C., Kuo, Y. H., Shih, M. T., & Lee, C. L. (2016) Caffeine ingestion improves power output decrement during 3-min all-out exercise. *European Journal of Applied Physiology, 116*(9), 1693–1702.

Close, G. L., Hamilton, D. L., Philp, A., Burke, L. M., & Morton, J. P. (2016) New strategies in sport nutrition to increase exercise performance. *Free Radical Biology and Medicine, 98*, 144–158.

Crisafulli, A., Melis, F., Tocco, F., Laconi, P., Lai, C., & Concu, A. (2002) External mechanical work versus oxidative energy consumption ratio during a basketball field test. *The Journal of Sports Medicine and Physical Fitness, 42*(4), 409–417.

Dahlquist, D. T., Dieter, B. P., & Koehle, M. S. (2015) Plausible ergogenic effects of vitamin D on athletic performance and recovery. *Journal of the International Society of Sports Nutrition, 12*, 33. doi:10.1186/s12970-015-0093-8. eCollection 2015.

De Palo, E. F., Gatti, R., Cappellin, E., Schiraldi, C., De Palo, C. B., & Spinella, P. (2001) Plasma lactate, GH and GH-binding protein levels in exercise following BCAA supplementation in athletes. *Amino Acids, 20*(1), 1–11.

DellaValle, D. M., & Haas, J. D. (2011) Impact of iron depletion without anemia on performance in trained endurance athletes at the beginning of a training season: A study of female collegiate rowers. *International Journal of Sport Nutrition and Exercise Metabolism, 21*(6), 501–506.

Derave, W., Everaert, I., Beeckman, S., & Baguet, A. (2010) Muscle carnosine metabolism and beta-alanine supplementation in relation to exercise and training. *Sports Medicine (Auckland, N.Z.), 40*(3), 247–263.

Drinkwater, E. J., Hopkins, W. G., McKenna, M. J., Hunt, P. H., & Pyne, D. B. (2007) Modelling age and secular differences in fitness between basketball players. *Journal of Sports Sciences, 25*(8), 869–878.

Dubnov, G., & Constantini, N. W. (2004) Prevalence of iron depletion and anemia in top-level basketball players. *International Journal of Sport Nutrition and Exercise Metabolism, 14*(1), 30–37.

Dzedzej, A., Ignatiuk, W., Jaworska, J., Grzywacz, T., Lipinska, P., Antosiewicz, J., Korek, A., & Ziemann, E. (2016) The effect of the competitive season in professional basketball on inflammation and iron metabolism. *Biology of Sport, 33*(3), 223–229.

Finaud, J., Lac, G., & Filaire, E. (2006) Oxidative stress: Relationship with exercise and training. *Sports Medicine (Auckland, N.Z.), 36*(4), 327–358.

Fishman, M. P., Lombardo, S. J., & Kharrazi, F. D. (2016) Vitamin D deficiency among professional basketball players. *Orthopaedic Journal of Sports Medicine, 4*(7), doi: 10.1177/2325967116655742.

Fuhrman, J., & Ferreri, D. M. (2010) Fueling the vegetarian (vegan) athlete. *Current Sports Medicine Reports, 9*(4), 233–241.

Ghiasvand, R., Djalali, M., Djazayery, S., Keshavarz, S., Hosseini, M., Askari, G., . . . Fatehi, F. (2010) Effect of eicosapentaenoic acid (EPA) and vitamin e on the blood levels of inflammatory markers, antioxidant enzymes, and lipid peroxidation in iranian basketball players. *Iranian Journal of Public Health, 39*(1), 15–21.

He, C. S., Handzlik, M., Fraser, W. D., Muhamad, A., Preston, H., Richardson, A., & Gleeson, M. (2013) Influence of vitamin D status on respiratory infection incidence and immune function during 4 months of winter training in endurance sport athletes. *Exercise Immunology Review, 19*, 86–101.

Hill, C., Harris, R. C., Kim, H., Harris, B., Sale, C., Boobis, L., Kim, C., & Wise, J. A. (2007) Influence of β-alanine supplementation on skeletal muscle carnosine concentrations and high intensity cycling capacity. *Amino Acids, 32*(2), 225–233.

Hoffman, J. R., Ratamess, N. A., Faigenbaum, A. D., Ross, R., Kang, J., Stout, J. R., & Wise, J. A. (2008) Short-duration beta-alanine supplementation increases training volume and reduces subjective feelings of fatigue in college football players. *Nutrition Research (New York, N.Y.), 28*(1), 31–35.

Ji, L. (1995) Oxidative stress during exercise: Implication of antioxidant nutrients. *Free Radical Biology and Medicine, 18*(6), 1079–1086.

Lamonte, M. J., Mckinnex, J. T., Quinn, S. M., Bainbridge, C. N., & Eisenman, P. A. (1999) Comparison of physical and physiological variables for female college basketball players. *The Journal of Strength & Conditioning Research, 13*(3), 264–270.

Larson-Meyer, D. E., & Willis, K. S. (2010) Vitamin D and athletes. *Current Sports Medicine Reports, 9*(4), 220–226.

Martínez-Sanz, J. M., & Urdampilleta, A. (2012) Necesidades nutricionales y planificación dietética en deportes de fuerza. *Motricidad. European Journal of Human Movement, 29*, 95–114.

Martínez Sanz, J. M., Urdampilleta, A., & Mielgo-Ayuso, J. (2013) Necesidades energéticas, hídricas y nutricionales en el deporte. *Motricidad. European Journal of Human Movement, 30*, 37–52.

Martinez, A. C., Seco Calvo, J., Tur Mari, J. A., Abecia Inchaurregui, L. C., Orella, E. E., & Biescas, A. P. (2010) Testosterone and cortisol changes in professional basketball players through a season competition. *Journal of Strength and Conditioning Research, 24*(4), 1102–1108.

Maughan, R. J., & Shirreffs, S. M. (2008) Development of individual hydration strategies for athletes. *International Journal of Sport Nutrition and Exercise Metabolism, 18*(5), 457–472.

McDonnell, L. K., Hume, P. A., & Nolte, V. (2011) Rib stress fractures among rowers: Definition, epidemiology, mechanisms, risk factors and effectiveness of injury prevention strategies. *Sports Medicine (Auckland, N.Z.), 41*(11), 883–901.

McInnes, S. E., Carlson, J. S., Jones, C. J., & McKenna, M. J. (1995) The physiological load imposed on basketball players during competition. *Journal of Sports Sciences, 13*(5), 387–397.

McKeag, D. B. (2008) *Handbook of sports medicine and science, basketball*. Malden, MA: John Wiley & Sons.

Mielgo-Ayuso, J., Calleja-Gonzalez, J., Clemente-Suarez, V. J., & Zourdos, M. C. (2014) Influence of anthropometric profile on physical performance in elite female volleyballers in relation to playing position. *Nutricion Hospitalaria, 31*(2), 849–857.

Mielgo-Ayuso, J., Maroto-Sanchez, B., Luzardo-Socorro, R., Palacios, G., Palacios Gil-Antunano, N., Gonzalez-Gross, M., & EXERNET Study Group. (2015) Evaluation of nutritional status and energy expenditure in athletes. *Nutricion Hospitalaria, 31*(Suppl 3), 227–236.

Mielgo-Ayuso, J., & Urdampilleta, A. (2016) *CAFEÍNA: Rendiminento deportivo y riesgos médico-nutricionales*. Oiartzun: Elikaesport.

Mielgo-Ayuso, J., Urdampilleta, A., Martinez-Sanz, J., & Seco, J. (2012) Ingesta dietética de hierro y su deficiencia en las jugadoras de voleibol femenino de élite. *Nutricion Hospitalaria, 27*(5), 1592–1597.

Mielgo-Ayuso, J., Zourdos, M. C., Calleja-González, J., Urdampilleta, A., & Ostojic, S. (2015) Iron supplementation prevents a decline in iron stores and enhances strength performance in elite female volleyball players during the competitive season. *Applied Physiology, Nutrition, and Metabolism, 40*(6), 615–622.

Negro, M., Giardina, S., Marzani, B., & Marzatico, F. (2008) Branched-chain amino acid supplementation does not enhance athletic performance but affects muscle recovery and the immune system. *The Journal of Sports Medicine and Physical Fitness, 48*(3), 347–351.

Owens, D. J., Fraser, W. D., & Close, G. L. (2015) Vitamin D and the athlete: Emerging insights. *European Journal of Sport Science, 15*(1), 73–84.

Ramos-Campo, D. J., Martínez Sánchez, F., Esteban García, P., Rubio Arias, J. Á, Bores Cerezal, A., Clemente-Suarez, V. J., & Jiménez Díaz, J. F. (2014) Body composition features in different playing position of professional team indoor players: Basketball, handball and futsal. *International Journal Of Morphology, 32*(4), 1316–1324.

Schröder, H., Navarro, E., Mora, J., Galiano, D., & Tramullas, A. (2001) Effects of α-tocopherol, β-carotene and ascorbic acid on oxidative, hormonal and enzymatic exercise stress markers in habitual training activity of professional basketball players. *European Journal of Nutrition, 40*(4), 178–184.

Schroder, H., Navarro, E., Mora, J., Seco, J., Torregrosa, J. M., & Tramullas, A. (2002) The type, amount, frequency and timing of dietary supplement use by elite players in the first Spanish basketball league. *Journal of Sports Sciences, 20*(4), 353–358.

Schröder, H., Navarro, E., Tramullas, A., Mora, J., & Galiano, D. (2000) Nutrition antioxidant status and oxidative stress in professional basketball players: Effects of a three compound antioxidative supplement. *International Journal of Sports Medicine, 21*(02), 146–150.

Shi, D. (2005) Oligosaccharide and creatine supplementation on glucose and urea nitrogen in blood and serum creatine kinase in basketball athletes. *Journal of Huazhong University of Science and Technology. Medical Sciences, 25*(5), 587–589.

Simopoulos, A. P. (2007) Omega-3 fatty acids and athletics. *Current Sports Medicine Reports, 6*(4), 230–236.

Thomas, D. T., Erdman, K. A., & Burke, L. M. (2016) Position of the academy of nutrition and dietetics, dietitians of Canada, and the American college of sports medicine: Nutrition and athletic performance. *Journal of the Academy of Nutrition and Dietetics, 116*(3), 501–528.

Tsakiris, S., Parthimos, T., Tsakiris, T., Parthimos, N., & Schulpis, K. H. (2006) Alpha-tocopherol supplementation reduces the elevated 8-hydroxy-2-deoxyguanosine blood levels induced by training in basketball players. *Clinical Chemistry and Laboratory Medicine, 44*(8), 1004–1008.

K., & Grammatikopoulou, M. G. (2016) A case study on the effect of professional dietary counseling: Elite basketball players eat healthier during competition days. *The Journal of Sports Medicine and Physical Fitness, 57*(10), 1305–1310.

Tucker, M. A., Hargrforwards, J. M., Clarke, J. C., Dale, D. L., & Blackwell, G. J. (2013) The effect of caffeine on maximal oxygen uptake and vertical jump performance in male basketball players. *Journal of Strength and Conditioning Research*, 27(2), 382–387.

Urdampilleta, A., Martínez-Sanz, J., Julia-Sanchez, S., & Álvarez-Herms, J. (2013) Protocolo de hidratación antes, durante y después de la actividad físico-deportiva. *Motricidad. European Journal of Human Movement*, 31, 57–76.

Venderley, A. M., & Campbell, W. W. (2006) Vegetarian diets: Nutritional considerations for athletes. *Sports Medicine (Auckland, N.Z.)*, 36(4), 293–305.

Willis, K. S., Peterson, N. J., & Larson-Meyer, D. E. (2008) Should we be concerned about the vitamin D status of athletes? *International Journal of Sport Nutrition and Exercise Metabolism*, 18(2), 204–224.

Ziv, G., & Lidor, R. (2009) Physical attributes, physiological characteristics, on-court performances and nutritional strategies of female and male basketball players. *Sports Medicine*, 39(7), 547–568.

4

PSYCHOLOGY FOR BASKETBALL PLAYERS AND TEAMS

Alexandru V. Stewart Mardan

4.1 Introduction

Mental preparation is one of the key determinants of basketball performance (Kendall et al., 1990; Gould et al., 2002). The way that a player thinks and behaves in practice or during competitions can mean the difference between winning or losing. In a similar way, the interaction between those players as a team, impacts on the way they deal with pressure situations which in turn can facilitate or be detrimental to the success of the team. The chapter represents a rationale for using sport psychology in basketball, and explores basic applied techniques that can be used to enhance performance and minimise the factors that can impact negatively upon player and team performance.

This chapter is aimed to benefit a diverse audience. It will appeal to sport and exercise students at undergraduate level who are interested in exploring the theory to practice from a basketball perspective, but also to coaching teams and individual players who wish to discover and potentially apply some of the principles in their practice.

The chapter is divided in four parts in an attempt to keep the chapter structured and easy to follow. The first part, the introduction, offers an overview of the topic and presents briefly the context in which relevant organisations are trying to harness sport psychology as a domain and as a profession.

The second part will look at what does it mean to be mentally prepared in basketball, exploring mental training tools and mental skills, trying to clarify the difference between the two, while introducing terms such as mental toughness and contextual intelligence.

The third part will look at potential psychological factors influencing basketball performance, looking closely at a particular situation from the game context, in order to gain a more practical perspective.

The fourth part will explore three psychological skills and a mental strategy: goal setting, self-talk, imagery and pre-performance routine for free throws shooting. The three skills are approached differently, for goal setting and self-talk looking more at characteristics and skill development, while for imagery exploring briefly the underpinning theories and identifying applied models. Then will look to see why pre-performance routines are considered an effective strategy to facilitate performance from the free throw line. Again, the text will tap into the relevant background theories and use a case study to translate the theory into practice.

Before starting to discuss the topic, there is a necessity to specify that there are numerous ways in which psychology can be applied in sport and exercise settings. According to the American Psychological Association (APA, 2017), sport psychology is seen as a "proficiency" that utilises knowledge and principles from psychology in dealing with sport performance, as well as athlete wellbeing and any other systemic issues related to sport participation and sport settings in general. The definition focuses heavily on the skill needed in order to apply psychology in sport, a perspective concerned more with the skill that one can practice sport psychology. Somehow in contrast, FEPSAC (European Federation of Sport Psychology, 1995) adopted a broad definition, looking more at the scope of the discipline: "Sport psychology is concerned with the psychological foundations, processes and consequences of the psychological regulation of sport related activities of one or several persons acting as subject(s) of the activity" (p. 1). Additionally, the statement points out that a sport psychologist is likely to be involved in all three areas of practice: research, education and application. In the UK, sport psychology as a profession has been regulated by the British Psychology Society (BPS), requiring that candidates firstly obtain a degree in psychology and a master's degree in sport and exercise psychology. An alternative pathway has been provided by the British Association of Sport and Exercise Sciences (BASES), which offers an accreditation programme similar with the BPS. The BASES programme is developed on a sport science degree and continued with a Masters degree in sport and exercise psychology. In order to obtain the accreditation, both routes require a rigorous but lengthy supervised experience programme. In Ireland, the Irish Institute of Sport offers an accreditation process as well, based on applicant's qualifications (master's), training and experience considered together. Whichever the path, today, the profession of sport and exercise scientist specialised in sport psychology has yet to be fully integrated, with the process of accreditation justifying the ethical and professional duty of care, but remaining disproportionate with the lack of employment or consultancy opportunities.

The complex discipline of sport and exercise psychology, including issues and opportunities within the development of applied work, is not the scope of this chapter. The content below will focus on the role that mental training has on basketball and athletic performance.

4.2 Rationale for psychological preparation in basketball

It is notorious, known from press interviews and TV appearances, that current and former great basketball players and coaches attribute their success on the mental preparation and mental attitude (see e.g. Van Gundy, 2017). Not only anecdotal evidence, but multi-sport studies including basketball related ones, have identified a number of mental skills to characterise elite athletes (Gould et al., 2002). Most recently, many teams and coaches are looking to develop "mentally tough" athletes and teams. However, mental toughness is still considered an umbrella term and the concept is still debated within the specialist literature (Jones et al., 2002; Gucciardi et al., 2012; Clough et al., 2012; Crust & Azadi, 2010), lacking conceptual clarity and an effective way to measure it. A number of studies (Connaughton et al., 2010; Driska et al., 2012; Weinberg et al., 2011) suggest that mental toughness can be fostered or hindered by a number of factors, including coach encouragement of mental skill development, a training environment that values skill mastery and enjoyment, as well as a strong social support in and out of sport. Nonetheless, every coach wishes to have a mentally tough player on the court, who can:

- generally, cope better than his/her opponents with the many demands (competition, training, lifestyle) that sport places on them as performers.
- specifically, be more consistent and better than his/her opponents in remaining determined, focused, confident, and in control under pressure.

Similarly, a psychological profile of a successful athlete might include (Jones et al., 2007):

- Healthy commitment;
- High levels of self-confidence;
- Positive interpretation of anxiety;
- Awareness of the impact on performance of their own thoughts and feelings;
- High levels of concentration;
- Ability to rebound from mistakes;
- Ability to cope well with stress;
- Successfully using goal setting strategies;
- Successfully using self-talk and imagery in training and competitions;
- Ability to control emotions inside and outside sporting environment.

A player displaying a mentally tough profile, as above, it is widely accepted as having increased chances to become an elite performer, and consequently successful in competitions. Looking at the association between mentally tough players or displaying a psychological profile of a successful athlete and sporting performance, Williams and Krane (2015) ask to remain critical when interpreting studies that claim direct causation. The skills could be developed as a result of the sporting success or that players displaying certain psychological characteristics are more likely to join elite-level sport. It is worth noticing here the difference between a psychological skill strategy (imagery, goal setting, self-talk, biofeedback, progressive muscle relaxation) and a mental skill characteristic attributed to sporting success (self-confidence, motivation, coping with stress, concentration, awareness, etc.).

A psychological skill training program will aim to educate players and develop strategies in order to foster and strengthen mental skill qualities.

That leads to the question: Are psychological interventions that are aimed to develop mental skills, effective in improving sport performance? Past studies and reviews show positive performance effects (Vealey, 1994; Weinberg & Comar, 1994; Meyers et al., 1996; Fournier et al., 2005) but sport psychology consultants have still to develop the appropriate measuring tools to clearly demonstrate that what they do makes a difference in the performance and wellbeing of their clients.

How are practitioners delivering interventions? There are currently a number of models of delivery (Aoyagi et al., 2012), each of them usually being employed depending on the consultant's philosophy of practice and perceived competence and specialisation, but also depending on the resources available to access the service of an accredited sport psychologist. Considered not to be necessary to be involved previously with the sport, when delivering interventions, it is imperative for practitioners to be aware of the intricacies of playing and coaching basketball. Being "contextual intelligent", as becoming familiar with the language, with the physical and psychological demands of basketball, with the structure and patterns in which the team functions, as well as learning the attitudes and building the trust to be influential, is the foundation for a successful intervention (Brown et al., 2005). "The ultimate goal" of a psychological skills training program is to develop the ability in players to manage effectively their thoughts, feelings and behaviours while pursuing their sporting career goals (Weinberg & Gould, 2015).

4.3 Psychological preparation for competition in basketball

How many times do we consider mental factors accountable for poor performance? Lack of concentration, nerves, lack of confidence, just to name a few, are mentioned so often in basketball settings. Interestingly still today, coaches and players are trying to fix the lack of mental skills with increased practice of physical skills. In a game situation, this can be illustrated as following. Christine is an 18-year-old basketball player. She is a very skilled shooter and has been selected to play basketball for the university team in her freshmen year. In the very first important game of the season, her team is losing by one point 70–71. Christine is fouled and awarded two free throws with 3 seconds left to play. Despite the coach telling her to relax and perform just like in training, she cannot stop thinking how important this game is and how awful would be if she would miss the shot. She also starts thinking about how disappointing would be for the team, her family and friends if she would fail to score and win the game. Those thoughts are making her lose confidence and she starts feeling more and more anxious about it. As a result, she is shaky at the line, and rushes the shot, failing to use the leg power while jerking the movement. She misses both shots and the team loses the game. Next practice session, the coach asks Christine to perform extra shooting from the free throw line in an attempt to improve her technical ability. By putting more practice, the coach truly believes that is addressing the issue which leads to missing the free throws during the game. However, Christine already has a solid technique and high accuracy percentage from the line. The reason why her technique suffered was because of tensing up under pressure. The technical staff could deal with the issue above by helping Christine to learn some of the psychological strategies to cope under pressure, build her confidence and remain focused in a similar situation. For example, she could be helped to develop free throw pre-performance routine. Additionally, free throw shooting sessions could be designed to simulate similar conditions as experienced during the game. The situation above is developed upon an example used by Weinberg and Gould (2015) to highlight the often missed aspect of mental mindset when evaluating sporting behaviour. To offer another example, imagine a novice player who struggles to cope with the stress of defending a key opponent. Struggling to manage her nerves, our player will end up committing three personal fouls in only 5 minutes of playing. This could be seen as lack of physical preparation, or lack of defending skills, when in fact the real reason behind the poor performance was the inability to regulate her physiological and cognitive anxiety prior and during the game.

A number of mental skill training programs have been specifically designed to help players and coaches in basketball (Brown & Burke, 2003; Burke, 2006; Henschen & Cook, 2003; Lidor et al., 2007). Those interventions or consultations are aimed to develop skills for dealing with psychological demands in competitions or training. For example, Burke (2006) proposed psychological techniques such as imagery, self-talk, pre-performance routines, to deal with playing under pressure, lack of confidence or when dealing with injuries and sitting on the bench. The skills and situations above are concerned with individual needs, but this does not mean that sport psychology has nothing to offer to facilitate the entire team. Weinberg and Gould (2015) point out four major areas where mental preparation is key: group and team dynamics, group cohesion, leadership and communication. Each area impacts on the way the team performs and therefore influences performance itself. An example of a both individual and team specific intervention is described by Lidor et al. (2007). Working for the entire season with an European elite basketball team, the consultant implemented a mental skill program depending on the critical phases of the year, preparation or competition, stressing the importance of integrating psychological training with other components of performance such as work on physical, technical and tactical aspects. Unfortunately, despite presenting both subjective and objective measures used to evaluate the effectiveness of the program, those measures lack the specificity and fail to link the various techniques used with the team and individual performance.

4.4 Psychological preparation content for basketball players

With this in mind, this chapter will look more closely to some of the individual skills and techniques aiming to improve individual performance. The mental strategies selected to be further discussed are *goal setting*, *imagery* and *self-talk*. Additionally, it will be looking more closely at *pre-performance routines* as a strategy to facilitate free throw performance.

Goal setting

Goal setting is arguably one of the most frequently used technique in applied sport psychology, being linked with positive changes in motivation (Locke & Latham, 2002), confidence and coping with stress (Greenglass et al., 1999). Instinctively or deliberately, pretty much all basketball players and coaches set goals in practice or competitions:

- I want to win the game;
- I want to score 20 points;
- I want to make the starting line-up for the next game;
- I want to improve my vertical jump;
- I want to be more confident at the 3 point line.

Unfortunately, setting inappropriate goals without an understanding of the goal setting processes and principles will lead to a missed opportunity to get the benefits associated with effective goal setting. According to Locke and Latham (2002), a goal is an objective or aim of action to get a specific standard or proficiency on a task, usually within a specified time limit. Burton (1989), same as Martens (1987), separated outcome goals from performance goals. An outcome goal refers to the result or the outcome of a performance; for example, winning a game or qualifying for the playoffs. It is a very attractive goal, impacting heavily on the motivation fuelled by winning in direct competition with others. A performance goal refers to performance on a specific task – for example, having 85% at free throws during the season, or having an average of six defensive rebounds per game. Usually it directs focus on tasks and behaviours that have direct impact on competitiveness. Hardy et al. (1996) added process goals as a third category. Those goals, sometimes named action goals, refer to focusing attention towards the tasks at hand, especially looking to improve previous performance on that task. For example, focusing on boxing out prior rebounding, or employing a pre-performance routine before shooting a free throw. The literature highlights the importance of employing all three types of goals (Burton & Raedeke, 2008) for both competitions and training (Orlick & Partington, 1988).

Summarising research that looked to examine current uses of goal setting, Weinberg and Gould (2015) stress out that athletes and coaches set long- and short-term goals, but many lack an adequate action plan for achieving their goals. To address this issue, Cruickshank et al. (2015) proposed a nested approach to goal setting. With this strategy, performance/process goals are employed on short term basis to meet performance/process goals on medium term, which furthermore are set to meet the outcome goals on the long term. The system provides the flexibility needed to adjust goals accordingly, while making sure that players are focused on the process having the big picture in mind. For example, the team wants to achieve a top 1–4 position by the end of the season (outcome goal). The process then involves breaking down the season in different phases and setting performance and process goals based on training and competition plans that address key points towards achieving the outcome goal. An example of medium term performance goal is planning and asking the team to attend three strength and conditioning sessions per week, during the pre-season. If conditioning is identified as a performance factor that needs to be improved, the coach/strength and conditioning specialist can further point out what exactly needs improved during the fitness preparation. It could be endurance, maximum strength or lifting technique, and you can then have each player work on individualised programs, working towards their own fitness goals (performance and process goals). Some of them might focus on employing a series of new exercises in the gym, some might focus on lifting correctly a certain weight or some might focus on achieving certain times or distances when completing various fitness tests (standing long jump).

Although goal setting can be an easy psychological skill to be used, coaches and athletes should have some awareness on the common problems in setting goals. Failing to recognize individual differences could lead to athletes becoming disengaged and less motivated, especially if goals that have been established by the coach for the entire team are not seen to be relevant by individual players. Another common problem is failing to identify goals that are not realistic and which have the potential to influence long term commitment and confidence. Weinberg and Gould (2015) identified that, in practice, coaches fail to understand the time commitment needed to implement a goal setting programme and that a lack of planning for when and how to use the strategy will reduce considerably the effective implementation of the programme.

Self-talk

One of the key abilities to cognitive control is self-talk. Within the cognitive behaviour therapies, self-talk has been employed as an effective method to change people's thoughts, interpretations and actions. Meichenbaum (1977) suggested that self-instructions are capable of affecting individuals' attention and appraisal, which leads into influencing behaviour. Hardy (2006) identified quite a broad range of definitions for self-talk, but tried to bring together one to include various dimensions: statements addressed to self, multidimensional in nature, including interpretive elements in relation with the content of the statement used, and having at least two functions for the athletes: functional and motivational. Gould et al. (1992) study with Olympic wrestlers identified that self-talk was used as a technique to promote positive expectations and to direct focus on relevant cues. More recently, a meta-analysis by Hatzigeorgiadis et al. (2011) concluded that self-talk is an effective strategy to facilitate sporting performance and skill acquisition. Looking at the underlying mechanism of self-talk, Theodorakis et al. (2008) identified five different areas through which self-instructions facilitate positive sport performance: enhancing concentration on relevant cues, setting off automatic execution, increasing confidence, coping with stress, regulating effort. An example of the use of self-talk in basketball can be the moment when a player prepares to execute a free throw. Simple words such as "hands up", "bend knees" or "relax" can help the player to cope with the pressure or to facilitate concentration and technical execution.

Studies focused to understand the characteristics of self-talk, have identified two dimensions or two categories: instructional self-talk and motivational self-talk (Hatzigeorgiadis et al., 2011). In basketball instructional, self-talk can relate to situations when players are looking to focus attention on relevant cues ("follow the ball"), improve technique or improve play ("don't jump at shot fake") or follow strategy ("defend the zone"). In contrast, a motivational self-talk can help a basketball player to maximize effort ("push hard"), to stay motivated ("let's win this game") or even enhance positive mood ("I enjoy this"). A review by Tod et al. (2011) identified positive, instructional and motivational self-talk to facilitate performance. Same study argue that negative self-talk is not necessarily detrimental to sporting performance and their finding has implications in the applied world, where thought stopping techniques have been employed to decrease the negative self-talk said by players.

In order to maximize the benefits of using self-talk to facilitate learning and enhance performance, specialists in the area recommend recognizing and addressing issues related with four dimensions: task characteristics, athlete characteristics, the specifics of self-talk and the characteristics of the intervention. However, given the wide applicability of the self-talk strategy, Hardy (2006) argues that there is still a lack of research looking to identify the theoretical background underpinning the construct. For example, self-talk has been integrated in theories related with attention and concentration (Mallett & Hanrahan, 1997), information processing (Landin, 1994), self-efficacy (Bandura, 1977), theory of cognitive development (Hardy, 2006). It is then of most importance that any further research studies or practical interventions are identifying the underpinning theories to support their topic focus.

To illustrate the potential influence that self-talk strategy has on a basketball shooting task, a related study is described below. Theodorakis et al. (2001) employed self-talk as a strategy to enhance a basketball shooting task. Focus of the study was to compare two different types of self-talk, which were sought to affect the speed and accuracy of shooting execution. Sixty participants were split in three groups and asked to shoot for three minutes from 4.5 m distance to the hoop. The only instruction was to execute as many successful shots as possible. After the first trial, the two experimental groups received new instructions, while the control group received the same general initial instruction. One group was instructed to use the cue word "relax" prior to shooting, while the second group was instructed to use the word "fast" prior to every attempt. All three groups performed the task again for two more 3 minute trials. Results showed that the only group to increase performance was the experimental group using the cue word "relax". Theodorakis et al. (2001) concluded that the study confirms the potential impact that self-talk strategies can have on basketball related task. However, the nature and content of the task needs to be matched by the relevant self-talk strategy. A limitation of this particular study was the lack of control over the actual use of self-talk strategies by the participants. The results also cannot be interpreted as absolutely relevant for real game situations, where the context and demand placed on the shooting task is completely different compared with the self-paced trial from the study above.

Imagery

Imagery or visualization or mental rehearsal has been currently one of the most employed interventions by sport psychology consultants when dealing with a variety of sport related issues. Nevertheless has been a popular tool employed to foster skill acquisition and re-learning or simply to enhance performance (MacIntyre & Moran, 2007). However, despite being considered an effective tool and despite a plethora of anecdotal evidence that elite athletes are mentally rehearsing key skills before executing them in competitions, specialists have argued that imagery research still needs to solve a number of issues: lack of studies on elite athletes (Morris et al., 2005), an unbalanced choice between psychometric self-reported questionnaires and qualitative studies that have the ability to reveal how athletes employ imagery (MacIntyre & Moran, 2007).

A number of theories and models have tried to explain mental imagery. Chronologically, the neuromuscular theory was developed first, theory which indicated that imagery practice would elicit muscular activity in the muscles involved in the particular skill rehearsed. However, research shows little or no evidence for that claim (Murphy & Martin, 2002). Secondly, the cognitive theories disconsidered the peripheral musculature, and claimed that mentally rehearsing a skill can potentially strengthen the brain central representation or motor schemata of that skill. Limitations of the cognitive theories are a weak explanation of underlying mechanism alleged to imagery effects, as well as the difficulty to explain why elite performers who already possess a well-established mental representation of the skill still benefit from mental imagery. The bio-informational theory of imagery (Lang, 1979), developed in an attempt to understand people's psychophysiological reactions to feared objects, saw mental images as propositional representations or cognitive codes in language form. Lang (1979) categorised those propositional representations in stimulus, response and meaning propositions. The theory has been less tested in sport related context but influenced imagery interventions in a number of ways; it highlighted the need to individualised imagery scripts, pointed out the need to address both stimulus and response within the imagery script, and emphasized the need to integrate emotional factors when developing imagery scripts. Most recently, a number of new findings have added to the current understanding of imagery. Firstly, Kosslyn et al. (2001) argued that imagery is functional equivalent to perception, as shown in neuroimaging studies that the two share similar neural pathways in the brain. Secondly, Hall (2001) suggested that mental practice is functionally equivalent to physical practice, as imagery and motor movements are guided by the same central mental representations. The most current understanding of mental imagery is pointing towards an activity mediated cognitively that imitates perceptual, motor and to a certain extent also emotional experiences in the brain.

Based on the functional equivalence model, Holmes and Collins (2001) proposed the Physical Environment Task Timing Learning Emotion Perspective (PETLEP) model to mental imagery. In their proposal, in order to be effective, an imagery script intervention should consider seven factors: physical, environmental, task, timing, learning, emotional, perspective. The physical factor suggests that during imagery athletes should try to replicate their actual performance using the same body position, stance, the equipment involved in the task or clothing – for example, having the player at the free throw line, bending their knees and simulating the throw while visualising it. Environment suggests that the exercise should be performed in the similar environment where the competition takes place, recommending the use of videos and photos of the venues – for example, performing the mental skill training on the court rather than in the office. Task refers to having the same task that needs to be executed in competition to be imagined during visualization training. The timing component suggests that the pace of the imagery task to be identical with the pace during the performance, as so often a good timing is what facilitates optimal performance during games. Learning component means that the imagery task should be updated as the skill improves and progress is made or if a player needs to re-learn the skills coming back from injury. The emotion factor requires players to account during the imagery any emotion that would typically be experienced during that skill execution. For example, different game situations and context can trigger a variety of emotions, and when practicing the skill they should be taken in consideration too, for the imagery to reflect the real situation. Finally, the perspective component refers to the option of using an internal (first person) perspective or an external (third person) perspective when performing the skill. For example, first person perspective means visualising the ball trajectory as looking at the rim from the shooting position. The first person perspective it is sought to facilitate feeling the task or skill with all senses and especially having the muscular, kinaesthetic sensation of the performance. In comparison, the third person perspective would be similar to watching yourself performing the task like watching the game on the TV. Both perspectives have been recognised as efficient depending on the imagery ability of the athlete or depending on the characteristics of the tasks. For example, Mahoney and Avener (1977) proposed that an internal perspective is more efficient for learning postural skills in gymnastics given the kinaesthetic feeling. In contrast, White and Hardy (1995) discovered that external perspective was more efficient for developing a gymnastics routine, which arguably can be defined as a combination of individual postural skills linked together. The debate between effectiveness of internal versus external perspectives is still current in the literature. To add more to the puzzle, Mahoney et al. (1987) found that elite athletes make use more of the internal perspective compared with non-elite athletes, suggesting that first person imagery can be related linked to a higher sporting performance. Hall et al. (1990) argued that elite athletes are consistently investing more time in sport related cognitive activities, including imagery, which might explain why imagery is used more by the elite athletes during both in competition and in training compared with non-elite athletes.

An applied model for imagery use in sport has been developed by Martin et al. (1999), based on the cognitive or motivational function of imagery (Paivio, 1985). According to Paivio (1985) cognitive mental imagery breaks down into cognitive general or rehearsing the strategy (visualising an entire offensive set play) and cognitive specific to a task (rehearsing shooting skills necessary for free throws). Furthermore, motivational specific function refers to visualising particular actions it takes to score a double-double next game, while motivational general function can be either arousal imagery (visualisation associated with arousal and stress) or mastery imagery (visualisation associated with being confident, in control). An example of motivational general – arousal imagery is when a player uses relevant images to get psyched up and feel prepared for competition. An example of motivation general – mastery imagery is when a player visualizes successfully overcoming any challenge might face during the game. The applied model states that it is important to match the desired outcome with the specific function of the imagery employed (CS, CG, MS, MG-A, MG-M). For example, if a player wants to learn a particular dribbling skill, he or she should employ a cognitive specific imagery, mentally rehearsing the skill. Alternatively, if the player is lacking confidence, visualising situations where he or she performed the skill well and defeated her opponents, motivational general – mastery imagery approach, will be more efficient. However, the model has its limitations, one of them being the fact that focuses only on preparation in training and competition, and not in other situations such as rehabilitation (Sordoni et al., 2000).

Pre-performance routine – shooting free throws

To provide an example of how mental skills strategy can be used to enhance skill execution, the final part of the chapter will look at free throws pre-performance routines. It is easily noticeable that many players are using preparatory actions such as bouncing the ball several times before performing free throw shots, visualising the throw, using self-talk to trigger the right movement sequence or to focus on the relevant cues. The skills best thought to benefit the pre-performance routines are closed skills, skills that are self-paced, as the player has no interference from other players and the speed of the execution is not influenced by external factors (Moran, 1996). In basketball, free throws shots are considered to be a closed skill (Jackson & Baker, 2001). The support for using pre-performance routines is backed up by the theory concerned with improving concentration (Lavalle et al., 2004) and has been proposed to help prevent choking under pressure (Singer, 2000). Firstly, they help players to create the right focus before executing the skill by helping them to focus on the relevant cues. For example, bouncing the ball gives the player the opportunity to set herself into the right stance, before fixing the rim prior shooting. Secondly, they help players to focus on the here and now, rather than on past events or any potential future outcomes. For example, having a player at the line thinking about the impact of missing the shot could increase anxiety and trigger a hasted execution. Thirdly, the routine prevents players to focus on the mechanics of a well learned skill, already performed best automatically. Attempting to control the skill could lead to an inappropriate conscious control (Beilock & Carr, 2001), often linked with pressure situations and under performance. An interesting finding regarding pre-performance routines in basketball free throws was linked with the temporal and behavioural consistency of the routine. In their naturalistic study, Lonsdale and Tam (2008) observed nearly 300 free throw routines during 14 National Basketball Association playoff games. After identifying each player's routine sequence, the scientists were able to identify shots performed with the routine sequence being followed or not followed. The analysis revealed that players were more successful when routine followed the temporal and behavioural dominant sequence. For example, when a player took too long to execute the shot compared with his dominant sequence, he was more likely to miss that shot. Similarly, if another spin or dribble, or shorter pause to look at the basket, was added to the routine, the accuracy was likely to drop. In the study above, the difference was 83.77% when routine was followed compared with 71.43% when the routine sequence was not followed. The difference is significant, as it accounts for 3.5 points per game, in the context in which four of the fourteen games have been decided on 4 points or less, and therefore would have impacted the outcome of the game and series. Although the study found a clear relation between the temporal and behavioural consistency and accuracy of the throws, the restricted non-experimental design of the study cannot link causation of the routine consistency with the successful performance. However, the study confirms the potential benefit of helping players developing consistent pre-performance routines prior to executing free throws. Additionally, the routine is best used to facilitate appropriate attentional focus, which according to relevant research should be an external focus (e.g. the rim of the hoop) and not an internal focus (e.g. extending the elbow; Wulf & Prinz, 2001; Wulf & Su, 2007).

What is the difference between a superstition and a pre-performance routine? The big difference is that superstitions are attributing control to an external factor, while pre-performance routines are relying and are based on an internal locus of control (Schippers & Van Lange, 2006). Wearing two pair of shorts or bright yellow socks while always stepping on the court with the right foot first is not a way of readying the player for executing a given task or skill. Both players and coaches should be aware of the thin line between creating a routine or allowing a superstitious ritual to develop.

In conclusion, pre-performance routines appear to be a useful tool to reduce the chances of choking under pressure when performing free throws in basketball. However, evidence suggests that they are complex in nature, and it is not clear how players acquire them intuitively. Pre-performance routines present a temporal, behavioural and kinaesthetic component, while summarising several psychological skills when performed: self-talk, imagery, relaxation or centring. Studies recommend that practitioners develop routines in according with relevant research and theories and evaluate the effectiveness of those routines (Singer, 2000; Mesagno & Mullane-Grant, 2010). Some concerns still exist regarding the placebo effect of superstitions in comparison with the benefits of the routines, while the current theories are still limited in regards to what they can explain. As athletes are unique individuals, so the pre-performance routine interventions should account for the particular need of the player. Just as important, players and practitioners need to be aware when a routine needs to be readjusted to avoid becoming an automatic one.

4.5 Summary

As in with any other sport, mental preparation is considered to be a key determinant for performance. Basketball makes no exception and throughout the chapter the author has tried to present the context in which sport psychology as a sport science can be used as a tool to benefit players, coaches and teams, both in training and competition. The psychological skills and strategies presented above have been selected for their wide applicability and their effectiveness in helping players deal with relevant issues. Unfortunately, today the majority of applied interventions are still taking place in the final hour (Donohue et al., 2004), when coaches and teams are already in critical situations, crisis or having to urgently solve acute problems. It would be more beneficial for teams and players to engage early in mental preparation in order to develop the psychological skills needed to perform at their best (Holliday et al., 2008). Nevertheless, players and coaches should always remember that the physical, technical and tactical aspects of their preparation are still representing the core pillars of their sporting performance, as no team has ever won a game only by mental preparation alone.

References

American Psychological Association. (2017) *Defining the practice of sport and performance psychology*, online, available at: www.apadivisions.org/division-47/about/resources/defining.pdf (accessed on 27th September 2017).
Aoyagi, M. W., Portenga, S. T., Poczwardowski, A., Cohen, A. B., & Statler, T. (2012) Reflections and directions: The profession of sport psychology past, present, and future. *Professional Psychology: Research and Practice*, 43(1), 32.
Bandura, A. (1977) Self-efficacy: Toward a unifying theory of behavioural change. *Psychological Review*, 84(2), 191.
Beilock, S. L., & Carr, T. H. (2001) On the fragility of skilled performance: what governs choking under pressure? *Journal of Experimental Psychology: General*, 130(4), 701–725.
The British Association of Sport and Exercise Sciences, online, available at: www.bases.org.uk/ (accessed on 19th September 2017).
Brown, C. H., Gould, D., & Foster, S. (2005) A framework for developing contextual intelligence (CI). *The Sport Psychologist*, 19(1), 51–62.
Brown, D., & Burke, K. (2003) Fundamental skills of the complete basketball player. In K. Burke, & D. Brown (Eds.) *Sport Psychology Library: Basketball. The Winning Edge Is Mental* (pp. 9–35). Auburn Hills, MI: Data Reproductions Corporation.

Burke, K. L. (2006). Using sport psychology to improve basketball performance. In J. Dosil (Ed.) *The Sport Psychologist's Handbook: A Guide for Sport-Specific Performance Enhancement* (pp. 121–137). West Sussex, England: Wiley.

Burton, D. (1989) Winning isn't everything: Examining the impact of performance goals on collegiate swimmers' cognitions and performance. *The Sport Psychologist*, 3(2), 105–132.

Burton, D., & Raedeke, T. D. (2008) *Sport psychology for coaches*. Campaign, IL: Human Kinetics.

Clough, P., Earle, K., Perry, J. L., & Crust, L. (2012) Comment on "Progressing measurement in mental toughness: A case example of the Mental Toughness Questionnaire 48" by Gucciardi, Hanton, and Mallett (2012), *Sport, Exercise, and Performance Psychology*, 1(4), 283–287.

Connaughton, D., Hanton, S., & Jones, G. (2010) The development and maintenance of mental toughness in the world's best performers. *The Sport Psychologist*, 24, 168–193.

Cruickshank, A., Giblin, S., & Collins, D. (2015) Mental skills training in sprinting. In G. Platt (Ed.) *The science of sport: Sprinting* (pp. 153–164). Ramsbury, Wiltshire: Crowood Press.

Crust, L., & Azadi, K. (2010) Mental toughness and athletes' use of psychological strategies. *European Journal of Sport Science*, 10(1), 43–51.

Donohue, B., Dickens, Y., Lancer, K., Covassin, T., Hash, A., Miller, A., & Genet, J. (2004) Improving athletes' perspectives of sport psychology consultation: A controlled evaluation of two interview methods. *Behaviour Modification*, 28(2), 182–193.

Driska, A. P., Kamphoff, C., & Mork Armentrout, S. (2012) Elite swimming coaches' perceptions of mental toughness, *The Sport Psychologist*, 26, 186–206.

European Federation of Sport Psychology. (1995) *Position statement: Definition of sport psychology*, online, available at: www.fepsac.com/activities/position_statements/ (accessed on 23rd September 2017).

Fournier, J. F., Calmels, C., Durand-Bush, N., & Salmela, J. H. (2005) Effects of a season-long PST program on gymnastic performance and on psychological skill development. *International Journal of Sport and Exercise Psychology*, 3(1), 59–78.

Gould, D., Dieffenbach, K., & Moffett, A. (2002) Psychological characteristics and their development in Olympic champions. *Journal of Applied Sport Psychology*, 14(3), 172–204.

Gould, D., Eklund, R. C., & Jackson, S. A. (1992) 1988 US Olympic wrestling excellence: II. Thoughts and affect occurring during competition. *The Sport Psychologist*, 6(4), 383–402.

Greenglass, E., Schwarzer, R., Jakubiec, D., Fiksenbaum, L., & Taubert, S. (1999) The proactive coping inventory (PCI): A multidimensional research instrument. In *20th International Conference of the Stress and Anxiety Research Society (STAR), Cracow, Poland* (Vol. 12, p. 14).

Gucciardi, D., Hanton, S., & Mallett, C. (2012) Progressing measurement in mental toughness: a case example of the Mental Toughness Questionnaire 48. *Sport, Exercise and Performance Psychology*, 1, 194–214.

Hall, C. R. (2001) Imagery in sport and exercise. *Handbook of Sport Psychology*, 2, 529–549.

Hall, C. R., Rodgers, W. M., & Barr, K. A. (1990) The use of imagery by athletes in selected sports. *The Sport Psychologist*, 4(1), 1–10.

Hardy, J. (2006) Speaking clearly: A critical review of the self-talk literature. *Psychology of Sport and Exercise*, 7, 81–97.

Hardy, J., Jones, J. G., & Gould, D. (1996) *Understanding psychological preparation for sport: Theory and practice of elite performers*, Chichester, UK: John Wiley.

Hatzigeorgiadis, A., Zourbanos, N., Galanis, E., & Theodorakis, Y. (2011). Self-talk and sports performance: A meta-analysis. *Perspectives on Psychological Science*, 6(4), 348–356.

Henschen, K., & Cook, D. (2003) Working with professional basketball players. *The Psychology of Team Sports*, 143–160.

Holliday, B., Burton, D., Sun, G., Hammermeister, J., Naylor, S., & Freigang, D. (2008) Building the better mental training mousetrap: Is periodization a more systematic approach to promoting performance excellence? *Journal of Applied Sport Psychology*, 20(2), 199–219.

Holmes, P. S., & Collins, D. J. (2001) The PETTLEP approach to motor imagery: A functional equivalence model for sport psychologists. *Journal of Applied Sport Psychology*, 13(1), 60–83.
Jackson, R. C., & Baker, J. S. (2001) Routines, rituals, and rugby: Case study of a world class goal kicker. *The Sport Psychologist*, 15(1), 48–65.
Jones, G., Hanton, S., & Connaughton, D. (2002) What is this thing called mental toughness? An investigation of Elite sport performers, *Journal of Applied Psychology*, 14, 205–2208.
Jones, G., Hanton, S., & Connaughton, D. (2007) A framework of mental toughness in the world's best performers. *Sport Psychologist*, 21, 243–264.
Kendall, G., Hrycaiko, D., Martin, G. L., & Kendall, T. (1990) The effects of an imagery rehearsal, relaxation, and self-talk package on basketball game performance. *Journal of Sport and Exercise Psychology*, 12(2), 157–166.
Kosslyn, S. M., Ganis, G., & Thompson, W. L. (2001) Neural foundations of imagery. *Nature Reviews. Neuroscience*, 2(9), 635.
Landin, D. (1994) The role of verbal cues in skill learning. *Quest*, 46(3), 299–313.
Lang, P. J. (1979) A bio-informational theory of emotional imagery. *Psychophysiology*, 16(6), 495–512.
Lavallee, D., Kremer, J., Moran, A. P., & Williams, M. (2004) *Sport psychology: contemporary themes*. Basingstoke, UK: Palgrave Macmillan.
Lidor, R., Blumenstein, B., & Tenenbaum, G. (2007) Psychological aspects of training in European basketball: conceptualization, periodization, and planning. *The Sport Psychologist*, 21(3), 353–367.
Locke, E. A., & Latham, G. P. (2002) Building a practically useful theory of goal setting and task motivation: A 35-year odyssey. *American Psychologist*, 57(9), 705.
Lonsdale, C., & Tam, J. T. (2008) On the temporal and behavioural consistency of pre-performance routines: An intra-individual analysis of elite basketball players' free throw shooting accuracy. *Journal of Sports Sciences*, 26(3), 259–266.
MacIntyre, T. E., & Moran, A. P. (2007) A qualitative investigation of imagery use and meta-imagery processes among elite canoe-slalom competitors. *Journal of Imagery Research in Sport and Physical Activity*, 2(1).
Mahoney, M. J., & Avener, M. (1977) Psychology of the elite athlete: An exploratory study. *Cognitive Therapy and Research*, 1(2), 135–141.
Mahoney, M. J., Gabriel, T. L., & Perkins, T. S. (1987) Psychological skills and exceptional athletic performance. *The Sport Psychologist*, 1, 181–199.
Mallett, C. J., & Hanrahan, S. J. (1997) Race modeling: An effective cognitive strategy for the 100 m sprinter? *The Sport Psychologist*, 11(1), 72–85.
Martens, R. (1987) *Coaches guide to sport psychology: A publication for the American Coaching Effectiveness Program: Level 2 sport science curriculum*. Campaign, IL: Human Kinetics.
Martin, K. A., Moritz, S. E., & Hall, C. R. (1999) Imagery use in sport: A literature review and applied model. *The Sport Psychologist*, 13(3), 245–268.
Meichenbaum, D. (1977) Cognitive behaviour modification. *Cognitive Behaviour Therapy*, 6(4), 185–192.
Mesagno, C., & Mullane-Grant, T. (2010). A comparison of different pre-performance routines as possible choking interventions. *Journal of Applied Sport Psychology*, 22(3), 343–360.
Meyers, A. W., Whelan, J. P., & Murphy, S. M. (1996) Cognitive behavioural strategies in athletic performance enhancement. *Progress in Behavior Modification*, 30, 137–164.
Moran, P. A. (1996) *The psychology of concentration in sport performance*. East Sussex, UK: Psychology Press Publishers.
Morris, T., Spittle, M., & Watt, A. P. (2005) *Imagery in sport*. Campaign, IL: Human Kinetics.
Murphy, S. M., & Martin, K. A. (2002) The use of imagery in sport. In T. S. Horn (Ed.) *Advances in sport psychology* (pp. 405–439). Champaign, IL: Human Kinetics.

Orlick, T., & Partington, J. (1988) Mental links to excellence. *The Sport Psychologist*, 2(2), 105–130.

Paivio, A. (1985) Cognitive and motivational functions of imagery in human performance. *Canadian Journal of Applied Sport Science*, 10, 22–28.

Schippers, M. C., & Van Lange, P. A. (2006) The psychological benefits of superstitious rituals in top sport: A study among top sportspersons. *Journal of Applied Social Psychology*, 36(10), 2532–2553.

Singer, R. N. (2000) Performance and human factors: Considerations about cognition and attention for self-paced and externally-paced events. *Ergonomics*, 43(10), 1661–1680.

Sordoni, C., Hall, C., & Forwell, L. (2000) The use of imagery by athletes during injury rehabilitation. *Journal of Sport Rehabilitation*, 9(4), 329–338.

Theodorakis, Y., Croni, A., Laparidis, C., Bebetsos, E., & Douma, E. (2001) Self-talk in a basketball shooting task. *Perceptual and Motor Skills*, 92, 309–315.

Theodorakis, Y., Hatzigeorgiadis, A., & Chroni, S. (2008) Self-talk: It works, but how? Development and preliminary validation of the functions of self-talk questionnaire. *Measurement in Physical Education and Exercise Science*, 12(1), 10–30.

Tod, D., Hardy, J., & Oliver, E. (2011) Effects of self-talk: A systematic review. *Journal of Sport and Exercise Psychology*, 33(5), 666–687.

Van Gundy, J. (2017) *Additional Quotes: USA 85, Puerto Rico 78*, online, available at: www.usab.com/news-events/news/2017/11/wcq-men-game-1-pur-quotes.aspx (accessed on 6th December 2017).

Vealey, R. S. (1994) Current status and prominent issues in sport psychology interventions. *Medicine & Science in Sports & Exercise*, 26(4), 495–502.

Weinberg, R. S., Butt, J., & Culp, B. (2011) Coaches' views of mental toughness and how it is built. *International Journal of Sport and Exercise Psychology*, 9(2), 156–172.

Weinberg, R. S., & Comar, W. (1994) The effectiveness of psychological interventions in competitive sport. *Sports Medicine*, 18(6), 406–418.

Weinberg, R. S., & Gould, D. (2015) *Foundations of sport and exercise psychology*, Sixth Edition. Campaign, IL: Human Kinetics.

White, A., & Hardy, L. (1995) Use of different imagery perspectives on the learning and performance of different motor skills. *British Journal of Psychology*, 86(2), 169–180.

Williams, J. M., & Krane, V. (2015) *Applied sport psychology: Personal growth to peak performance*, Seventh Edition. New York: McGraw-Hill.

Wulf, G., & Prinz, W. (2001) Directing attention to movement effects enhances learning: A review. *Psychonomic Bulletin & Review*, 8(4), 648–660.

Wulf, G., & Su, J. (2007) An external focus of attention enhances golf shot accuracy in beginners and experts. *Research Quarterly for Exercise and Sport*, 78(4), 384–389.

5
WHEELCHAIR BASKETBALL

Miles Thompson and Haj Bhania

5.1 Introduction

In this section, references to 'the game or sport' will mean wheelchair basketball and the 'running game' (also referred to as the able bodied (a/b) game) will be referred to as such.

Wheelchair basketball was started and developed in the USA around 1946, following World War II, by injured war personnel. These veterans were former running game players who continued playing the game, using their wheelchairs which were adapted, along with changes to the rules to enable them to play the game. A national league tournament was played in the USA in the late 1940s and introduced to the UK at the International Stoke Mandeville Games in 1955. This was considered to be the birth of the Paralympic Movement, with the first Paralympic Games held in Rome in 1960 where wheelchair basketball was one of the sports (IWBF, 2017).

The word 'Paralympic' derives from the Greek preposition 'para' (beside or alongside) and the word 'Olympic'. Its meaning is that Paralympics are the parallel games to the Olympics and illustrates how the two movements exist side-by-side (IPC, 2017a).

The game is now governed by international rules and played according to the International Wheelchair Basketball Federation (IWBF) rules adapted from FIBA, the running game rules. The governing body of the sport worldwide is the IWBF. They delegate to and oversee four regional Zones: Asia Oceania, Africa, Europe and Americas. Each of these organisations are responsible for the sport in their 'Zones' when it comes to rules, classification, officials and player transfers, and enable national governing bodies (NGB) to run their own leagues. There is a process for qualification to major events such as World Championships and Paralympics, and these are simplified as follows:

- In every odd year (i.e. 2017, 2019, 2021) each Zone will hold a qualifying tournament. In Europe, this will be the European Championships and hosted, following a bid process, by one of the countries in the Zone.

- Each Zone has a number of 'Divisions'. Europe has Division A (12 teams), B and C. Only teams from Division A can progress to the major competitions through a qualifying process.
- Each Zone will have between two and seven qualifying places determined as below, and qualifying teams will be entitled to represent and compete at the major tournaments.
- In even years of 4-year intervals (2018, 2022, etc.) the IWBF, through a bid process, will oversee the World Championships, a 12-team competition. In 2010, these were held in Birmingham, UK.
- The host country will automatically qualify for that tournament and must be from the top tier of their Zone.
- At the World Championships, the top seven placed teams will achieve a qualification place for their Zone at the Paralympic games with one place reserved for the host and one each of the remaining four places allocated to each Zone.
- In 2019, the Zones will again arrange their Zonal tournaments to qualify for the Paralympic Games in 2020 and in 2023 for the 2024 Paralympic Games.
- There is a seeding process when draws are made at each of these events. The competitions are usually two pools of six teams with quarter, semi and final games.
- In effect, there is a major competition each year; either Zonal or international and NGBs will have a preparation programme each year.

At the Paralympic games, the International Paralympics Committee (IPC) is the governing body, and the IWBF is responsible for organizing and delivering the sport within the IPC's regulations.

5.2 Basic rules and offensive skills/actions: players' classification

The basic rules of the game are the same as the running game – a brief outline of the major rules is provided below:

- Court dimensions, basket height, key way, foul and three point lines are all the same.
- Playing time of 4 periods of 10 minutes; 5 minutes overtime if the game is tied after this.
- During game time a team will have 5 seconds to inbound, 8 seconds back court, 24 seconds shot clock, 3 seconds in the key, 14 seconds reset on rebound or foul, 2 time-outs during first half and 3 during second half (2 in last 2 minutes), stopping the clock the last 2 minutes.
- If a player 'tips over' (falls to the ground in the chair) and is considered to be interfering with play or is injured or at risk of injury from other players, the game will be stopped. If it is a defensive player, the shot clock is reset to 14 seconds (if already under 14 seconds). If it is an offensive player, the shot clock is not reset.
- Subject to the classification conditions (see below), there are 12 team players, 5 players on the court, with substitutions as required.

- Any wheel contact with the court boundaries with the ball is considered out of bounds, and any player going off court during a phase of play must re-enter the court at the point of exit so as not to gain any advantage by entering at another point, even if accidentally.
- If the score is tied at the end of playing time, the match will be continued with an extra period of 5 minutes or with as many such periods of 5 minutes as are necessary to break the tie.

Scoring

Points scored accrue the same value as the running game: 1 point for a free throw, 2 points from within the 3 points arc and 3 points for outside the arc. The modification to this is that the front castors (front wheels) of the wheelchair can cross the free throw and 3 point lines without penalty and be awarded the same points. The back or big wheels should not contact the lines in the act of shooting until the ball contacts the ring on a free throw.

Dribbling

A player must have the ability to move the wheelchair (push/pull/pivot) and simultaneously dribble the ball. A player can pick up or carry the ball (with the hand under the ball) and/or place the ball on their lap and allowed to take two pushes before they must dribble again, pass or shoot. This action can be repeated continuously. There is no double dribble rule, but a traveling violation applies if the player takes more than two pushes in possession of the ball without dribbling (a wheel pull is counted as a push). While in possession of the ball, players' feet must not touch the playing surface, which is a technical foul, and if a player falls over (tips out), that is considered a turnover violation. Play will be stopped if a player falling over whilst not in possession of the ball is considered to be in the area of play and the safety of that player and others is a concern.

Fouls

Fouls in the game are similar to the running game: charge, block, push, holding, contact, shooting fouls, technical (in addition, feet on the floor in possession of the ball, lifting out of the chair), unsportsmanlike. The player and wheelchair are considered as one. An offensive player is not permitted to enter the defensive key on an inbounds play until the in-bounder is in possession of the ball from the official.

Picking, screening, curling (more technical specific skills in the game)

The *pick and roll* actions in a game are similar to the running game except that the picker is entitled to 'hold' the pick as long as required in that phase of play or in continuation play. The picker can move to improve their position against the picked player provided they retain legal position. The picker (or player picked for) can roll to basket with or without the ball to create a 2-on-1 situation, except the defence will employ switching tactics to deny the offence.

Screening involves a player establishing position, usually at the side of the key, between the two defensive players with the second offensive player sitting either directly behind the screen or in space, with or without the ball. When that player has the ball and is a shooting threat, one of the defensive players will have to make a decision to go to the shooter, which creates the pick and roll game, or the shooter can use the screen as a mismatch to shoot the ball if the defenders hesitate or do not go out. The screener can move and improve their position, provided they maintain legal position and can cut to basket if a space is created.

Curls are usually created off the ball. Players will usually set up a screen as above with a forward in the screen making the defenders maintain position with a guard or low point player (see the classification below) behind. The guard will go high or low in a continuous action, forcing the defenders to maintain or switch position. If the defenders are slow to react or do not maintain position and the guard beats one of the defenders to get into the key or draws the player away, the forward will either follow the guard to the basket to create a close mismatch shot off a pass or drive against the mismatch defender to get to the basket.

Pick back (man out)

A specific tactic used in the game is the 'Pick back/back pick'. One or more offensive players can pick up one or more defensive players full court and keep them in the offensive back court, provided they maintain legal position, while the other offensive players transition to the basket. The offence tactic may be to have a guard target a defensive forward player to create a mismatch in the front court or an offensive forward (and guard) may pick back any defensive player, and they can play a trail offence using a curl or mismatch offence. In this type of offence, the defence will be reactive and the offence will exploit any space or mismatch created by the help defence. Some teams will have set plays for a pick back and others will execute in transition. The purpose of a pick back is more to disrupt the defence than to create a numerical advantage.

Player classification (IWBF rules 2014)

Classification – an overview

Wheelchair basketball classification is based on the players' functional capacity to complete the skills necessary to play – pushing, pivoting, shooting, rebounding, dribbling, passing and catching. It is not an assessment of a player's level of skill, but merely their functional capacity to complete the task. In particular, the trunk movement and stability observed during these actual basketball situations form the basis for the assignment of a player to a particular class.

Under the International Wheelchair Basketball Federation's (IWBF's) classification system, players are permitted to take part in wheelchair basketball if they are unable to run, pivot, or jump at a speed and with the control, safety, stability, and endurance of a non-disabled player, and have a permanent physical disability in the lower limb that can be objectively verified by acknowledged medical or paramedical investigations such as measurement, X-ray, CT (computerised tomography), MRI (magnetic resonance imaging) and other forms of scans.

Volume of action

The critical aspect that is considered when deciding on classification is a player's 'volume of action', which is defined as:

> the limit to which a player can move voluntarily in any direction and, with control, move to the upright seated position, without holding the wheelchair for support or to aid the movement. The volume of action includes all directions and describes the position of the ball when held in both hands.

Volume of action is affected mostly by strength, the range of movement and coordination in the hands, arms, trunk and legs.

Classification process

The process of classification has evolved significantly over the past 12 years. No longer is it necessary to individually examine each player in a medical room, debating about the relative grades of single muscles and making subjective assessments of the balance attributes of a player before assigning them to a given class.

Players are now classified on the basketball court, with all of the strapping that they will use and in their playing wheelchair in a training situation before a tournament starts. This enables the classifier to assess each player as they will be when taking part in actual competition. From this initial observation, a player is assigned a class with which they will begin the tournament. The player is then observed in an actual competition game, at which time their classification will be confirmed or modified if the classification panel feels it is necessary. Only a new player who has not been previously internationally classified needs to undergo this process. Players holding an international card do not need a re-classification at each tournament they attend.

The classes

Players are put into categories from 1 to 4.5, and the more functional the athlete, the higher the number. If classifiers have difficulties putting a player in a particular category because the player does not seem to fit exactly into a given class but shows attributes of two or more, then the classifier has the option of allocating a half-point

TABLE 5.1 IWBF classification system – 2004 Classification Commission

Class	Characteristics
1.0	Little or no trunk movement in any plane. Balance in both forward and sideways directions is significantly impaired, and players rely on their arms to return them to the upright position when unbalanced. No active trunk rotation.
2.0	Some partially controlled trunk movement in the forward direction, but no controlled sideways movement. Has upper trunk rotation but poor lower trunk rotation.
3.0	Good trunk movement in the forward direction to the floor and up again without arm support. Has good trunk rotation but no controlled sideways movement.
4.0	Normal trunk movement but has difficulty with controlled sideways movement to one side, usually due to limitations in one lower limb.
4.5	Normal trunk movement in all directions and able to reach the side with no limitations.

Adapted from IWBF, 2014.

that results in classifications of 1.5, 2.5, 3.5 or 4.5 – see Table 5.1 for details. Each class has characteristics unique to that class and which are evident in each of the basketball skills observed as part of the classification process.

Minimal disability

Minimal disability is the term given to people who may have damaged knees, back, hips, ankles and so on that cannot be repaired by an operation or physiotherapy. This results in them not being able to participate in running sport any more. Minimal disability players would be classified as 4.5. To be classified a player must have had two operations and extensive physiotherapy, and injuries can include damage to the back, ankles, hips, knees and feet. All injuries have to be verified by documented evidence and must be approved by the Great Britain Wheelchair Basketball Association (GBWBA) and IWBF.

Classification review

IWBF provides procedures for NOWB's to request a review of one of their players' international classification both during and outside of a tournament, and a request can also be made by an NOWB for the review of the classification of a player from another nation.

'Points' on court

Under IWBF rules, the classification points of the five players on court when added together must be 14 (or less) in international play, and if this total is exceeded then a bench technical foul is incurred. Governing bodies determine what points total is permissible on court in their domestic competitions.

5.3 The sports wheelchair: player positional play

The sports wheelchair (setup)

As the wheelchair and player are considered as one, elite and international players will have custom made playing sports chairs. These will be specific to the player's classification, function and ability and personal preferences to maximise performance and mobility. The chair must also meet IWBF regulations that are specific as to dimensions and seat height relating to classifications and some aspects of design. All chairs must be within these regulations during competitions and can be inspected by officials prior to or during games; opposing coaches can also request 'a chair check'. Any infringement of the regulations during a game will result in the player concerned being disqualified from that game and further infringement resulting is a tournament disqualification.

Players will have usually tried and played in a number of chairs as they develop and will know their optimum setup. Players will consider speed, height, manoeuvrability, range of motion and any one of these could affect another – a player may prefer to sit higher or maximum allowable height which could affect speed and mobility or sit lower for more efficient stop/start and change of direction actions that are essential in the game. Setup features will include wheel camber angle, seat height, chair width, seat angle/dump, horizontal rear-wheel position, backrest height, centre of gravity and frame length. Chair setup is also relevant to playing position. A forward (3.0–4.5) will want to sit at maximum height to counter opposition forwards in defence and create mismatches in offence.

Players are entitled to use strapping as required. Depending on classification, strapping could include waist, pelvis, lap, knee, lower leg/s, feet and this helps stabilise the player and make them one with the chair. This is also a requirement for safety and balance with the game now played at a higher intensity with greater physicality, speed and contact. Regulations require strapping to be padded or covered to avoid injury to others.

Positional play

As in the running game and many team sports, playing positions can be determined by size, ability, technical and skill sets. A centre will play around the basket to create mismatches off the above picking, screening, curl, pick back offence actions or simple transition; a point guard will handle and create on ball screens and also be a scoring threat and identified shooters will create on ball or play in space for an open shot against switching or rotating defences and/or use the protection of a screen.

In the modern game, the forwards or high classification players dominate the sport as the main scorers and creators and, in most teams, are also the main ball handlers. With team classification of five players at 14 points, most teams will typically use lineups as below or variations of these:

> 4.5, 4.5, 3.0, 1.0, 1.0 / 4.5, 4.0, 3.0, 1.5, 1.0 / 4.0, 4.0, 4.0, 1.0, 1.0 / 4.0, 3.0, 3.0, 3.0, 1.0,

with the low classification players working for the high classification players to create the best scoring options.

Games stats over the last 10–15 years will show how the game has become more forwards dominated with the higher classification players playing more average minutes per game, taking more shots and scoring more points, including the majority of 3 point attempts and free throws, creating more assists and higher efficiency ratings. All teams are developing their forwards into all-round players, driven initially in national league structures. However, lower classification players are having to and are becoming more skilled in more of the technical areas of the game, picking, screening and curling, some ball handling and shooting, and are essential to a team functioning and executing its systems of play.

5.4 Preparation for competition

Preparing for tournaments

Major tournaments are planned and known in advance with the European Championships between 1–2 years ahead, the World Championships between 3–4 years and the Paralympics 5–7 years in advance. This gives the coaches and individual players a preparation period to develop their skills to challenge for selection and teams to develop their styles and systems of play. In preparing for a tournament over a 12 month period, a typical preparation calendar planned in advance for a GB Team will contain the activities included in Table 5.2.

This process will apply whether preparing for a European or World Championships or for the Paralympic Games. The difference is the former are sports specific events in that they are basketball only, whereas the Paralympics are multi-sport. It is possible to prepare for the former with smaller tournaments but less so with the Paralympics, as there are no other multi-sport competitive events. During the preparation process there are a number of other factors to be considered, as it is detailed in Table 5.3.

An example of the Training and Game Schedule for the 2017 European Championships is presented as part of Appendix 5.1. This shows arrival dates, 2 days of training and classification checks, one training session on the main competition court, all other training sessions on non-competition courts, 9 days of competition (eight games) with one non-competition day between the pool games and the start of the crossover games.

Appendix 5.2 contains the Competition Schedule from the Rio Paralympic Games. With the greater travel distance and change of time zones and climate, the teams will usually arrive 7–10 days before the start and acclimatise at a holding camp before moving to the Paralympic Village 4–5 days before the games for training and classification. The teams will have the opportunity to train on the main competition's courts and arrange practice games against teams if required. These have to be sanctioned by the IWBF.

Knowing these schedules in advance enables teams to prepare their programme and plan for specific games. With budget limitations, time and availability of teams,

TABLE 5.2 Preparation calendar over a 12 month period for a GB team

Month	Activity
September	Players begin pre-season league preparation for their respective club teams.
	The GB programme is centralized, and all UK based GB identified players will expect to be training daily in the central programme.
	A fully planned programme is delivered from individual skills sets sessions to shooting sets, small group work and team training.
	Players based in Europe at professional clubs will have located there.
October–March	Daily training programme continues.
	Monitoring of European players' games and performances.
	Whole team training camp, all GB players and select GB Juniors required to attend.
	Physical and fitness testing and nutrition and medical screenings of all players (testing).
	Competitions programme being planned.
December	Training camp to include select GB Junior team players and testing.
	First part of the selection process to reduce the overall squad as we prepare for the next major tournament.
March	Selection camp for the first of the preparation tournaments abroad at Easter.
	Players in Europe are on break during this time.
	16 players selected and likely to form the squad for the remaining preparation programme.
	Competitions programme likely to be confirmed and finalised.
April	Players involved in European Club Cup competitions, including GB league teams and reduced GB programme commitment.
	Daily training programme continues and testing.
May	End of league season except European Club Leagues playoff.
	Players have a short break and required to return to the GB Central programme for the summer to prepare for the major competition.
	Periodised testing continues.
	Selection process continues and likely now to be working with the 16 player squad from which the 12 team members and 4 reserves will be selected.
June–July	Training programme continues and will have a full competitions preparation programme.
	Will be working specifically with individuals and small groups on refining.
	Will be working specifically on line-ups and playing units and refining.
	Periodised testing will be on refining.
	The competition performances and outcomes determine the on-going preparation programme and enforcing or enhancing the systems and changes required.
	Much of this will be reviewed from detailed video and stats analysis.
August	Final preparation process with a 2 week training programme, possible competitions.
	Short break before travelling to competition.
August–September	Post tournament review, individuals and team.
	Review, evolve and repeat 12 month preparation programme.

Source: Author's own elaboration.

TABLE 5.3 Factors to consider during the preparation process

Factors to consider during the preparation process for a competition

Anti-doping	All players will be subject to regular drug testing. Reinforcing the anti-doping regulations and ensuring an anti-doping workshop is delivered is vital.
Staff	Important to ensure all staff have been involved in some or all of the preparation period, are clear on their roles and responsibilities and supported in delivering these, have a good level of experience and that their rest and recovery is managed.
Coaches	Planning and preparing the programme, selecting the right team, managing expectations of event, travel, in competition training, game planning, managing staff and players.
Physio	Managing individual players, injury and illness planning, recording and reporting, dealing with players and the team's prehab/rehab.
Team manager	This is an extensive role from planning the daily schedule to support on the bench to kit washing to dealing with the event organisers. Important to ensure the team manager is respected by all and not taken for granted.
Analyst	Will have worked with the team and staff in the preparation and know how they work and what is required. The analyst will be responsible for ensuring footage of all identified games is available when required and has been tagged or clipped for delivery at video review or preview sessions. The analyst could be in the sports hall for many hours and important to ensure their wellbeing and that coaches or support staff are able to take on some game videoing if required.
Mechanic	An essential role and someone able to undertake on the spot minor repairs and replacements (wheels, tyres, straps) and have checked local repair shops in advance in case any major chair repairs are required, frame cracks, welding and replacements. The mechanic will carry an extensive range of tools and supplies, tyres, inner tubes, push rims, castors, nuts/bolt and pump.
Media	The team will usually have a media specialist who will deal with social media, promotion, publicity, external media requests and any adverse of inappropriate matters arising. In an era of instant and widespread social media, an experienced staff member able to manage and control this will be able to maintain the positive and factual messages and deflect any matters that could affect individuals and the team's preparation.

Source: Author's own elaboration.

it is not possible to replicate a full games programme and play nine matches over a 10 day period against 5–6 different teams. To prepare, some teams will arrange consecutive competitions and host a 4–5 team competition, and then travel to another event and play further games against different teams. These are preparation games with the focus on process and performance to practice and refine line-ups, units and playing style and more outcome based the nearer the competition.

An example training session with offensive emphasis can be seen in Table 5.4. Sessions are planned between 1 hr 30 m to 2 hrs and comprise a warm-up, shooting

TABLE 5.4 Example of a training session with offensive emphasis

9:30 a.m.–11:30 a.m.	2 Courts		
9:30 a.m.–9:50 a.m.	Warm-up Lay-ups	Full court give and go as above	
9:50 a.m.–10:10 a.m.	Shooting sets	As above	
	Groups of 3–4, 2 balls		
10:10 a.m.–10:20 a.m.	2v2 quarter court play	D plays flat and wide, trapping area	Keep ball moving to deny D maintaining position
	Separation and ball movement	O split, engage both D, pass and exchange, made D switch, create space to pick or cut	Various actions
10:20 a.m.–10:30 a.m.	2v2 quarter court play	Creating pick and roll game with reduced movement, Ball with scorer to draw D, use skills from shooting sets	Various actions
	Picking and space to shoot		Picker and screening maintain position, seal and pick
		Create pick and hold or split	Create space with ball
10:30 a.m.–10:40 a.m.	2v2 quarter court play	Create screen for mismatch or open shot	Invert G/F;
	Screening actions and post shot	Developing screen – position	Pass to cutter if defence jumps
		Use moves from shooting sets	
	Quarter or half court or full court sections depending on ball	Establish keyway position	Split the D, create mismatch, deny ball pressure.
		High/low separation	Go high/low with ball to create space and picks.
	S1 – screening actions and post shot	2-man actions	Pass and cut to basket or back for ball.
	S2 – picking and space to shoot	Setting screens	Specific screens and screening
	S3 – separation and ball movement	Pick and roll game	Separate to make D jump then pick or split post.
		Court sections and actions	Make D react.
			Ball to scorer and act.
			Front court and quarter court actions.
10:40 a.m.–11:00 a.m.	5v5 Cut Throat or Transition – 1/2/3 scores	Transition actions starting with inbounder	Defence will know the offence.
	Offensive sets	Early positional play into 2/3 man game	Quick ball, cross and pick, game realistic.
	Defensive intensity – any D	Quarter and half court actions and play	Collapse D early to deny high line.
11:00 a.m.–11:10 a.m.	Cool down & stretch		

Source: author's own elaboration.

sets at some stage during the session, small and whole group sets and detailed breakdown sets. The defence is set up to play in a way an opposition team may play and to practice sets, styles and systems against that. The defence must be aggressive and high tempo and must play beyond game intensity so that the offence must execute effectively to achieve expectations. Sessions are short and intense, reviewed through coaching or video analysis and repeated with adjustments at the next session either that day or the next day. In addition, times will be allocated each day for players to undertake individual shooting sessions, either coached or independent. Coaches will also allocate shooting sessions for identified players where they want to work with that player on shooting specifics which may be technical, tactical or game relevant. Most of the technical shooting coaching is undertaken during the league season and players expected to work on these independently.

5.5 Defence

'Defence wins championships' is one of the oldest anecdotes in sports

The late shot clock violation that cements the big wins, the 40 minutes of defensive hell allowing for lopsided wins or counterbalances an off night defensively, and the suffocating press that is the ingredient of difference in the unthinkable comeback. Defence hardly gets romanticised like its offensive counterpart. In sports, highlight reels contain the action of the shot, not the unwavering, constant of a defence communicating, dictating and winning possessions with physicality and mental alertness.

The legendary coach John Wooden once said, 'The worst thing about new books is they keep us from reading the old ones'. Within wheelchair basketball, the stimulus of the modern game is the increasing accuracy and depth of the 3-point shot. Defences need to defend more space as legitimate 3-point threats increase around the globe. More than ever, defences need to remain true to key defensive principles. These principles are:

Stop chair;
Communicate;
Identify;
Get off contact.

If there are defensive short-comings they are within one of these four defensive principles. As a coach, recognising where the issue lies is the initial step in any defensive fix.

Wheelchair basketball and defending

The most obvious difference between wheelchair basketball and the running game is the lack of lateral movement within the wheelchair game. Playing the game in a chair means hundreds and hundreds of turns within the course of a fixture.

Understanding this, and understanding that the best defence is played with hands on wheels, maintaining wheel position and a constant, communicative dialogue with your teammates, will greatly improve the outcome of the game.

Lack of lateral movement means having your back to the offence at times. This is not ideal (at all). Offences are taught to pick the 'Big Numbers' (defensive player's backs) in an attempt to play within numerical advantages, executing pick and rolls around the rim.

Quarter turns, checking shoulder and shadows

A good offensive player working within a reliable system will be consistently looking to get defensive players' back to his teammate for a potential pick and roll. This is why it is important that defenders work in groups of two or three.

The worst thing a defender in a wheelchair can do is spin circles and defend within 360 degrees. Superior defence is played in 90 degree confines or *quarter turns*. Quarter turns allow vision between attacker and needed teammate. Often, higher classification players look to find lower classification athletes (see Classification table above) in speed mismatches. Lower class players need to dictate, or overplay the high class athlete towards their teammate and help defence. This can only happen when both defending players play in quarter turns. Over rotating, or not rotating enough, will ultimately put defenders at a significant disadvantage. This is called defending at *zero or showing foot-plate*; in other words, a recipe for breakaway baskets, or easy pick and rolls at the rim.

What is vital in defending within *quarter turns* is the fundamental tool of *checking shoulders*. When transitioning back defensively it is essential to check shoulders and have 'basketball conversations' with your teammates. Checking shoulders (glancing back left/right) allows players to know where priority threats are, where help can come from and permits the collective, defensive five to compete in *quarter turns*. Remember, the defence does not want to show its front end, or show its fifth wheel (anti-tip caster wheel in rear of chair). This is called defending at zero and disallows the important defensive elements of dictating, and too often isolates defender against 1-on-1 moves in the post.

Checking shoulders and defending in *quarter turns* leads to the execution of *shadows* and the implementation of shadow lines.

Shadows are a defensive drill that easily translates into action on court. Shadow drills are run 1-on-1, up to 5-on-5. The goal within shadow drills is to keep the offensive opponent between defender and basket. It is important to 'size up' your opponent and defend accordingly. If defender has superior chair skills she/he will look to stop chair, check shoulders and potentially help low-point teammates. If defender is facing superior speed, she/he will 'sag' and communicate help in stopping opponent's chair, with potential help from high-point teammate.

> 1-on-1 shadow drills are best run with like for like chair skills. When running 2-on-2 or 3-on-3 shadow drills the interesting dynamic of classification and help defence are in play.

Boundaries are best in shadows drills:

> 2-on-2. Near lane-line to side-line. Offence starts at baseline and works with (or without) ball to centre court. Defence objective is to eliminate picking angles (working in quarter turns). This is called 'staying flat'.
> 3-on-3. Far lane-line to side-line. Offence works with ball. Same objectives.

Again, the four defensive principles mentioned before must be accounted for to successfully defend in shadows. Each of these four defensive principles will be discussed below (stop chair; communicate; identify; get off contact).

Stopping chair

In the full court

Superior defences stop a chair no matter classification, size or speed. A chair in motion is far more a threat than a chair immobilized. Often a full court shadow, or press off a make/miss is defined how well the group can initially *stop chair*.

High point athletes need to stop chair immediately within the transition to defence, before identifying either a 'sag' to a low/mid-point teammate in attempt of 'getting flat'.

Low and mid-point athletes also need to stop chair within transition to defence. If they are able to do so the likelihood of an eight second count increase dramatically, and thus a defensive turnover is created.

Under full court pressure teams consistently look to get their biggest target across the time line as their long outlet. Within that dynamic the defensive scheme would be to play the 1-on-1 outlet across the time-line whilst maintaining the 4-on-4 outlet before half-court.

There are times when full court shadows can create pressurized turnovers. There are other times when the shadows can be a bit more 'saggy' and conservative in the strategy of eating shot clock and disallowing offenses to get into their sets.

In the half court

Stopping chair in the half court is twofold:

1. Within a 'base' or 'tea cup' defensive scheme (a straight or bent line eliminating picking angles within 3 point arc and free throw line), the desired goal is to stop chair and funnel opponents to a strategic weakness.
2. If the offence works itself through the first line of defence (quite common), creating outlets and dives, the goal is to stop chair when the ball has been swung to perimeter.
   a. The perimeter opponent is a scoring threat and defence needs to stop her/his chair eliminating a quality scoring opportunity.

b. The perimeter opponent is not a scoring threat and defensive strategy is to make weaker player make decision under distress. *Stopping Chair* makes this more difficult.

The key in *stopping chair* is the understanding that it is only the beginning of the defensive process. Speed players quickly need to understand if they need to help or not, whilst mid and low point athletes must comprehend the match up in front of them and either 1) 'take it on' or 2) appreciate the match up and communicate help.

Communicate

The difference between fair and good, or good and great defence, is the level of effective communication. Athletes new to elite sport often think they are communicating when in fact there are varying levels of yelling. Effective communication is a dialogue that asks and answers questions in real time. A few examples are provided for a better understanding.

Example 1 – Player A screams at player B: 'Pick.' Not knowing where the pick is coming from, player A turns towards her/his teammate's voice and runs into pick. Offence executes pick and roll, or a defensive foul is called.

Example 2 – Player A identifies priority and chats it through with teammate. Player B tells player A she is jumping early. She asks players A: 'Are you in?' 'Yes. Go,' is the answer from player A. Player B: 'I'm out. I've got chair (stopped).' Player A: 'You're good. Stay out. I'll bump picker.' Offence attempts to pick Player B. Player A: 'Pick coming. Turn left. Fight under.' Player B: 'Got it. Stay flat with me. I'm in. You're out . . .'.

The second example can be exhausting but also exhausts opponents. It also significantly decreases the likelihood of getting 'picked out.' The more detail-oriented on-court conversations can be, the more opponents will be forced to shoot contested, low percentage shots.

Identify

A few effective questions will be needed during defensive play – examples include:

Where is the priority? Who is on priority? What is that match up like? Where is low priority? Can I sag off her/him?

The ability to *identify* high and low priority is the needed succession with the *defensive* principles. Once we *identify*, the defence can switch and match-up like for like. Once we *identify*, the defence can play to individual tendencies in chair mechanics and shot. Identifying is an advanced form of communication and needs to happen early with defensive possessions.

In the full court

One of the keys in wheelchair basketball is the ability to defend together and not get 'back picked'. Back picks are when the offence obtains a numerical advantage by *stopping chair* and disallowing the defensive player to engage. The offensive player keeps her/himself between the opponent and basket. This allows the offence to 'play in numbers' (5-on-4 or 5-on-3).

Another form of *identifying* is the strategy of eliminating back picking as an essential offensive strategy. To do so, the defensive 5 must *identify* the offensive crosses and picks that permit the offensive team to play in numbers and in transition.

When 'getting back together', defensive players must *identify* early, *check shoulders and get flat* with one another before accelerating to 'base' or half-court defence. The more that teams can defend 5-on-5 by identifying and 'getting back together', the greater the percentage of 'getting stops' and winning games.

In the half court

A common and effective defensive, half court tool, in wheelchair basketball is the 'triple switch'. In order to 'triple switch' effectively teams must *identify* early where threats are.

When watching wheelchair basketball in the half court you will often hear team defences *communicating* 'power'. 'Power' is the identification of a scoring threat on one of the wings.

When in a 'power' defence, there is the understanding that the offence's 2-man game (dive and outlet) is likely to shoot and score if allowed to play 2-on-2. In turn, the defence identifies and brings middle help. Now the offence is playing 2-on-3 and more than likely will need to swing or skip the ball to the middle or opposite wing. The defence recovers with the initial jump relocating to the middle, and the ball is now away from the greatest threat.

The 'triple switch' is perhaps the most commonly used defensive tool in all of wheelchair basketball. Offences have specific strategies to exploit weak-side, and lack of defensive numbers, but when teams *identify* threats early the 'triple switch' is still a valid, denying defensive tool.

Get Off Contact

Without lateral movement in the wheelchair game, and the countless amounts of chairs turning, getting 'stuck on contact' is a defensive liability while also an offensive strategy.

Offensive players look to dig front ends into defender's spokes. This can open a lane to the basket, or allow the offence to play within a numerical advantage. There is nothing more frustrating within team defence to play a solid defensive possession only to get 'stuck on contact' late in the shot clock, and give up an easy look. The ability to *get off contact* demands quick and active hands, and a technique that keeps the opposition's front end out of defender's spokes.

Quick and active hands

The movement of hands within a confined space needs to be greater than the power of a mass into defence's spokes, or front end. The ability to 'hop' one's chair also is a needed tool in avoiding or *getting off contact*. Offences will typically attempt to find contact in transition, as well as their two-man, half court games.

Technique

'Taking it in the tyre' and not the spokes is a needed strategy in *getting off contact*. Mid and low-point players often are unable to 'hop' their chair and the 'taking it in the tyre' technique is prevalent amongst this population. Higher point athletes will also use this strategy as it not only eliminates getting 'stuck on contact' but also allows a propulsion from the impact from the offensive player. This propulsion can be beneficial within the key ingredient of *stopping chair*.

It is important to remember that vision/checking shoulders and communication are important components in *getting off contact*. Defences need to know that opponents look to single out low-point players as likely candidates to get 'stuck on contact'. It is within this dynamic that vision and communication are a central factor.

Overview

Defending in a game of wheelchair basketball is much the same as the running game in that:

Every defensive possession must have its own pulse and full investment to be consistently successful.
Defences that play with a superior level of physicality are more apt to perform.
Communication is an absolute mandate in switches, slides and identification of priorities.
Defences need to be technique driven, and when coupled with next level quickness have the capacity to be diabolical and daunting.

Within a wheelchair basketball fixture there is nothing more frustrating than a defence that has the ability to defend in both the full and half court, consistently has the ability to **stop chair**, **communicates** with a dialogue that is succinct, **identifies** early its threats and has the ability to **get off contact**. Of course there are many and numerous details still to account for when playing defence, including:

Boxing out and rebounding;
Defending opponents caster;
Getting to opponents shooting hand;
Defensive reads in relation to space.

But like coach John Wooden said, 'The worst thing about new books is they keep us from reading the old ones'. If coaches and athletes are able to understand, build and perform what is discussed here there will be a defensive foundation that is the framework for defensive success within the great game of wheelchair basketball.

5.6 Summary

Wheelchair basketball has developed over the last 20 years to become a faster, more physical, intensive sport. This requires players to be fitter, faster and stronger and also have skills sets to play and perform at the highest level. Sports science and sports medicine are crucial in developing players to perform internationally. This includes a consistent but classification specific S&C programme, physio screening and monitoring, nutrition guidance and monitoring and a full, effective testing programme in all of these areas. Other areas that have become essential are chair setup and maintenance; performance analysis and regular and consistent video sessions and feedback to the players; performance lifestyle to support the players work, education, basketball, life balances.

The sport has also seen increases and improvements in individual players and in teams' performances in areas of:

percentage scoring, now averaging between 48–52%;
number of assists per game 16–24;
offensive rebounds;
higher individual free throws percentages;
number of average shots taken per game;
increased average scores per game – 10 years ago, 65 points would be a winning score whereas now, that is an average score;
more scorers on the floor.

One of the most obvious developments in the game is the 3 point shot in terms of numbers taken, number of players able to shoot that consistently and the increased percentages. With the game now available on various platforms internationally, coaches, players and NGBs have up-to-date access to international events and many league games. These are regularly analysed, players and teams strengths, and threats identified and training practices planned and adapted to counter these. Coaches, players and teams will also look to develop their own skills sets and systems to continue to evolve. A system of play, whether set play, motion or read and react based, will be quickly identified and teams will work on ways to counter that and produce their own system that fits their team that others may struggle to defend. This therefore evolves year by year. Higher intensity defence will continue to add pressure to the offence and that seems to be a focus area for all teams. However, as in the running game, using a system of set plays, motion or read and react with ball movement, purposeful player movement and spacing to extend the defence will enable the offence to execute effectively.

The *What It Takes to Win* model has been developed with all these areas considered. The five all-encompassing aspects of the game that need to be trained, performed and executed at the highest level to be successful are identified in priority order as shooting and scoring; speed and chair skills; defensive fundamentals; ball handling and passing; tactics and games sense. As in all sports today, the game relies

APPENDIX 5.1 Training and game schedule for the 2017 European Championships Tenerife (Spain)

Men		Women
Group A	**Group B**	**Group C**
ESP M	GBR M	ESP W
NED M	TUR M	GBR W
ITA M	GER M	NED W
POL M	ISR M	GER W
SUI M	SWE M	TUR W
FRA M	LTU M	FRA W

Game schedule European Championships 2017

Training Schedule European Championship 2017

		Time	TRAIN 1	Time	TRAIN 2	Time	COURT 1	Time	COURT 2
Mon 19 June 2017	Arrival Men								
Tue 20 June 2017	Arrival Women Training and classification Men	9.30	POL M	10.00	SWE M	10.00	NED M	10.00	GBR M
		11.30	FRA M	12.00	LTU M	12.00	ITA M	12.00	GER M
		13.30	SUI M	14.00	ISR M	14.00	ESP M	14.00	TUR M
		15.30	NED M	16.00	GBR M	16.00	POL M		SWE M
		17.30	ITA M	18.00	GER M	18.00	FRA M		LTU M
		19.30	ESP M	20.00	TUR M	20.00	SUI M		ISR M
Wed 21 June 2017	Training and classification Men and Women	Time	TRAIN 1	Time	TRAIN 2	Time	COURT 1	Time	COURT 2
		9.30	GBR M	10.00	SUI M	10.00	TUR W★		ESP W★
		10.30	SWE M	11.00	ESP M	12.00	FRA W★		NED W★
		11.30	GER M	12.00	NED M	14.00	GER W★		GBR W★
		12.30	LTU M	13.00	POL M				
		13.30	TUR M	14.00	ITA M				
		14.30	ISR M	15.00	FRA M				

★Classification

(*Continued*)

APPENDIX 5.1 (Continued)

Game schedule European Championships 2017 / Training Schedule European Championship 2017

Wed 21 June 2017 — Time 17.00 **Opening ceremony** — COURT 1

Thu 22 June 2017

Time	Game	COURT 1	Time	Game	COURT 2	Time	TRAIN 1	Time	TRAIN 2
13.15	ECM 2	NED M – POL M	14.15	ECM 3	GBR M – SWE M	9.30	NED W	10.00	GER M
15.30	ECW 2	NED W – FRA W	16.30	ECM 4	GER M – LTU M	10.30	FRA W	11.00	LTU M
17.45	ECW 3	GBR W – GER W	18.45	ECM 5	TUR M – ISR M	11.30	GBR W	12.00	TUR M
20.00	ECM 6	ITA M – FRA M				12.30	GER W	13.00	ISR M
						13.30	ITA M	14.00	ESP W
						14.30	FRA M	15.00	TUR W
						15.30	ESP M	16.00	GBR M
						16.30	SUI M	17.00	SWE M
						17.30	NED M	18.00	
						18.30	POL M	19.00	
						19.30		20.00	

Fri 23 June 2017

Time	Game	COURT 1	Time	Game	COURT 2	Time	TRAIN 1	Time	TRAIN 2
10.00	ECW 4	GER W – ESP W	11.00	ECM 7	SUI M – ITA M	9.30	ISR M	10.00	FRA W
12.15	ECM 8	LTU M – TUR M	13.15	ECM 9	POL M – ESP M	10.30	GBR M	11.00	GBR W
15.30	ECM 10	ISR M – GBR M	16.30	ECW 5	FRA W – GBR W	11.30	TUR W	12.00	FRA M
17.45	ECW 6	TUR W – NED W	18.45	ECM 11	FRA M – NED M	12.30	NED W	13.00	NED M
20.00	ECM 12	SWE M – GER M				13.30	SWE M	14.00	SUI M
						14.30	GER M	15.00	ITA M
						15.30	GER W	16.00	POL M
						16.30	ESP W	17.00	ESP M
						17.30	LTU M	18.00	
						18.30	TUR M	19.00	
						19.30		20.00	

Sat 24 June 2017

Time	Game	COURT 1	Time	Game	COURT 2	Time	TRAIN 1	Time	TRAIN 2
10.00	ECW 7	GBR W – NED W	11.00	ECM 13	ISR M – SWE M	9.30	ESP W	10.00	TUR M
12.15	ECM 14	ESP M – FRA M	13.15	ECW 8	GER W – TUR W	10.30	FRA W	11.00	GER M

Sun 25 June 2017	Time	Game	COURT 1	Time	Game	COURT 2	Time	TRAIN 1	Time	TRAIN 2
	10.00	ECM 19	TUR M – SWE M	11.00	ECM 20	NED M – SUI M	9.30	GBR W	10.00	NED W
	12.15	ECW 10	FRA W – GER W	13.15	ECM 21	FRA M – POL M	10.30	TUR W	11.00	ESP W
	15.30	ECW 11	GBR W – TUR W	16.30	ECW 12	NED W – ESP W	11.30	LTU M	12.00	ITA M
	17.45	ECM 22	LTU M – ISR M	18.45	ECM 23	ITA M – ESP M	12.30	ISR M	13.00	ESP M
	20.00	ECM 24	GER M – GBR M				13.30	GER M	14.00	NED M
							14.30	GBR M	15.00	SUI M
							15.30	TUR M	16.00	FRA M
							16.30	SWE M	17.00	POL M
							17.30	FRA W	18.00	
							18.30	GER W	19.00	
							19.30		20.00	

Mon 26 June 2017	Time	Game	COURT 1	Time	Game	COURT 2	Time	TRAIN 1	Time	TRAIN 2
	10.00	ECW 13	TUR W – FRA W	11.00	ECM 25	ISR M – GER M	9.30	ESP M	10.00	GBR M
	12.15	ECM 26	POL M – ITA M	13.15	ECM 27	SWE M – LTU M	10.30	NED M	11.00	TUR M
	15.30	ECM 28	ESP M – NED M	16.30	ECM 29	GBR M – TUR M	11.30	SUI M	12.00	ESP W
	17.45	ECM 30	SUI M – FRA M	18.45	ECW 14	ESP W – GBR W	12.30	FRA M	13.00	GBR W
	20.00	ECW 15	GER W – NED W				13.30	GER W	14.00	ISR M
							14.30	NED W	15.00	GER M
							15.30	TUR W	16.00	SWE M
							16.30	FRA W	17.00	LTU M
							17.30	POL M	18.00	
							18.30	ITA M	19.00	
							19.30		20.00	

Additional entries:
- 15.30 ECW 9 ESP W – FRA W   16.30 ECM 15 TUR M – GER M   11.30 NED M   12.00 GBR M
- 17.45 ECM 16 NED M – ITA M   18.45 ECM 17 GBR M – LTU M   12.30 ITA M   13.00 LTU M
- 20.00 ECM 18 POL M – SUI M   13.30 POL M   14.00 ISR M
-   14.30 SUI M   15.00 SWE M
-   15.30 GBR W   16.00 GER W
-   16.30 NED W   17.00 TUR W
-   17.30 ESP M   18.00
-   18.30 FRA M   19.00
-   19.30   20.00

(Continued)

APPENDIX 5.1 (Continued)

Game schedule European Championships 2017

Tue	Time	Game	COURT 1	Time	Game	COURT 2
27 June 2017	15.30	ECM 32	CO 1 M	14.30	ECM 31	CO 2 M
	17.45	ECM 34	QF 1 M	16.45	ECM 33	QF 2 M
	20.00	ECM 36	QF 4 M	19.00	ECM 35	QF 3 M

Wed	Time	Game	COURT 1	Time	Game	COURT 2
28 June 2017	15.30	ECM 38	SF 2 M	14.30	ECM 37	SF 1 M
	17.45	ECW 17	SF 1 W	16.45	ECW 16	SF 2 W
	20.00	ECM 40	SF 4 M	19.00	ECM 39	SF 3 M

Training Schedule European Championship 2017

Time	TRAIN 1		Time	TRAIN 2	
9.30	ECM 31	home	10.00	ECM 32	home
10.30	ECM 31	away	11.00	ECM 32	away
11.30	ECM 33	home	12.00	ECM 34	home
12.30	ECM 33	away	13.00	ECM 34	away
13.30	ECM 35	home	14.00	ECM 36	home
14.30	ECM 35	away	15.00	ECM 36	away
15.30	ECW 16	home	16.00	ECW 17	home
16.30	ECW 16	away	17.00	ECW 17	away
17.30	ECW 18	away	18.00		
18.30	ECW 18	home	19.00		

Time	TRAIN 1		Time	TRAIN 2	
9.30	ECM 37	home	10.00	ECM 38	home
10.30	ECM 37	away	11.00	ECM 38	away
11.30	ECW 16	home	12.00	ECW 17	home
12.30	ECW 16	away	13.00	ECW 17	away
13.30	ECM 39	home	14.00	ECM 40	home
14.30	ECM 39	away	15.00	ECM 40	away
15.30	ECM 41	home	16.00	ECM 42	home
16.30	ECM 41	away	17.00	ECM 42	away
17.30	ECW 18	home	18.00		
18.30	ECW 18	away	19.00		

Thu 29 June 2017	Time	Game	COURT 1		Time	Game	COURT 2		Time	TRAIN1		Time	TRAIN 2
	15.30	ECM 41	9-10 M		16.45	ECM 42	11-12 M		9.30	ECM 41 home		10.00	ECM 42 home
	17.45	ECM 43	5-6 M		19.00	ECM 44	7-8 M		10.30	ECM 41 away		11.00	ECM 42 away
	20.00	ECW 18	5-6 W						11.30	ECM 43 home		12.00	ECM 44 home
									12.30	ECM 43 away		13.00	ECM 44 away
									13.30	ECW 18 home		14.00	ECW 19 home
									14.30	ECW 18 away		15.00	ECW 19 away
									15.30	ECM 45 home		16.00	ECW 20 home
									16.30	ECM 45 away		17.00	ECW 20 away
									17.30	ECM 46 home		18.00	
									18.30	ECM 46 away		19.00	

Fri 30 June 2017	Time	Game	COURT 1						Time	TRAIN 1		Time	TRAIN 2
	10.00	ECW 19	3-4 W						9.30	ECW 20 home		10.00	ECM 46 home
	12.30	ECM 45	3-4 M						10.30	ECW 20 away		11.00	ECM 46 away
	16.00	ECW 20	1-2 W										
	18.30	ECM 46	1-2 M										
	21.00		**Closing ceremony**										

Sat 1st July 2017 — Departure ALL

Adapted from IPC, 2017b.

APPENDIX 5.2 Competition schedule from the 2016 Rio Paralympic Games

Men

Date	Time	Home	Away	Venue
08/09/2016	11:45	GBR	ALG	Rio Olympic Arena
08/09/2016	15:15	BRA	USA	Rio Olympic Arena
08/09/2016	17:30	NED	AUS	Rio Olympic Arena
08/09/2016	15:45	TUR	JPN	Carioca Arena 1
09/09/2016	18:00	GER	IRN	Carioca Arena 1
09/09/2016	21:30	ESP	CAN	Carioca Arena 1
09/09/2016	09:30	USA	GER	Rio Olympic Arena
09/09/2016	11:45	IRN	GBR	Rio Olympic Arena
09/09/2016	12:15	AUS	TUR	Carioca Arena 1
09/09/2016	15:45	JPN	ESP	Carioca Arena 1
09/09/2016	18:00	CAN	NED	Carioca Arena 1
09/09/2016	21:00	ALG	BRA	Rio Olympic Arena
10/09/2016	10:00	ESP	TUR	Carioca Arena 1
10/09/2016	15:15	CAN	AUS	Rio Olympic Arena
10/09/2016	15:45	USA	IRN	Carioca Arena 1
10/09/2016	17:30	GER	ALG	Rio Olympic Arena
10/09/2016	21:00	NED	JPN	Rio Olympic Arena
10/09/2016	21:30	GBR	BRA	Carioca Arena 1
11/09/2016	09:30	ESP	AUS	Rio Olympic Arena
11/09/2016	11:45	TUR	NED	Rio Olympic Arena
11/09/2016	12:15	GBR	GER	Carioca Arena 1
11/09/2016	15:15	BRA	IRN	Rio Olympic Arena
11/09/2016	18:00	ALG	USA	Carioca Arena 1
11/09/2016	21:00	JPN	CAN	Rio Olympic Arena

Women

Date	Time	Home	Away	Venue
08/09/2016	09:30	GBR	CAN	Rio Olympic Arena
08/09/2016	10:00	FRA	USA	Carioca Arena 1
08/09/2016	12:15	BRA	ARG	Carioca Arena 1
08/09/2016	21.00 – 22.45	ALG	CHI	Rio Olympic Arena
09/09/2016	10:00	ARG	GBR	Carioca Arena 1
09/09/2016	15:15	GER	BRA	Rio Olympic Arena
09/09/2016	17:30	NED	ALG	Rio Olympic Arena
09/09/2016	21:30	CHI	FRA	Carioca Arena 1
10/09/2016	09:30	CAN	ARG	Rio Olympic Arena
10/09/2016	11:45	GBR	GER	Rio Olympic Arena
10/09/2016	12:15	FRA	NED	Carioca Arena 1
10/09/2016	18:00	USA	CHI	Carioca Arena 1
11/09/2016	10:00	GER	CAN	Carioca Arena 1
11/09/2016	15:45	NED	USA	Carioca Arena 1
11/09/2016	17:30	ALG	FRA	Rio Olympic Arena
11/09/2016	21:30	BRA	GBR	Carioca Arena 1

Date	Time	Teams	Venue	Date	Time	Event	Venue
12/09/2016	13:30	AUS JPN	Carioca Arena 1	12/09/2016	09:00	CHI NED	Carioca Arena 1
12/09/2016	15:45	USA GBR	Carioca Arena 1	12/09/2016	09:30	USA ALG	Rio Olympic Arena
12/09/2016	14:00	IRN ALG	Rio Olympic Arena	12/09/2016	11:15	ARG GER	Carioca Arena 1
12/09/2016	17:15	NED ESP	Rio Olympic Arena	12/09/2016	11:45	CAN BRA	Rio Olympic Arena
12/09/2016	19:30	CAN TUR	Rio Olympic Arena				
12/09/2016	21:45	BRA GER	Rio Olympic Arena				
				13/09/2016	09:30	Women 9–10 Place	Rio Olympic Arena
				13/09/2016	11:45	Women Quarter Finals	Rio Olympic Arena
				13/09/2016	15:15	Women Quarter Finals	Rio Olympic Arena
				13/09/2016	17:30	Women Quarter Finals	Rio Olympic Arena
				13/09/2016	21:00	Women Quarter Finals	Rio Olympic Arena
14/09/2016	09:30	Men's 11–12 Place	Rio Olympic Arena				
14/09/2016	11:45	Mens Quarter Final	Rio Olympic Arena				
14/09/2016	15:15	Mens Quarter Final	Rio Olympic Arena				
14/09/2016	17:30	Mens Quarter Final	Rio Olympic Arena				
14/09/2016	21:00	Mens Quarter Final	Rio Olympic Arena				
15/09/2016	09:30	Men's 9–10 Place	Rio Olympic Arena	15/09/2016	11:45	Women's Semi Final	Rio Olympic Arena
15/09/2016	17:30	Men's Semi Final	Rio Olympic Arena	15/09/2016	15:15	Women's Semi Final	Rio Olympic Arena
15/09/2016	21:00	Men's Semi Final	Rio Olympic Arena				
				16/09/2016	09:30	Women's 7–8 Place	Rio Olympic Arena
				16/09/2016	11:45	Women's Bronze Game	Rio Olympic Arena
				16/09/2016	15:15	Women's 5–6 Place	Rio Olympic Arena
				16/09/2016	17:30	Women's Gold Game	Rio Olympic Arena
				16/09/2016	19:30	Women's Victory Ceremony	Rio Olympic Arena
17/09/2016	15:15	Men's 5–6 Place	Rio Olympic Arena				
17/09/2016	17:30	Men's Gold Game					
17/09/2016	19:30	Men's victory ceremony					

Source: IPC, 2016.

very much on the ability to execute exceptional fundamentals, teams that work in synchronisation on and off the court, technical and tactical game skills, understanding and ability, sports science, technology and the highest standard equipment.

References

IPC (2016) *Wheelchair basketball schedule confirmed for Rio 2016*. Online, available at www.paralympic.org/news/wheelchair-basketball-schedule-confirmed-rio-2016 (accessed on 26th October 2017).

IPC (2017a) *Paralympics – history of the movement*. Online, available at www.paralympic.org/the-ipc/history-of-the-movement (accessed on 25th October 2017).

IPC (2017b) *IWBF announces European championship schedules*. Online, available at www.paralympic.org/news/iwbf-announces-european-championship-schedules (accessed on 26th October 2017).

IWBF (2014) *Official player classification manual*. Online, available at https://iwbf.org/wp-content/uploads/2017/09/CLASSIFICATION-MANUAL-2014-2018-ENGLISH-FINAL.pdf (accessed on 25th October 2017).

IWBF (2017) *Our game/about the sport*. Online, available at https://iwbf.org/the-game/ (accessed on 25th October 2017).

6

WOMEN'S BASKETBALL

Alexandru Radu and Florin Nini

6.1 Introduction

When compared to other team sports that women play (such as women's football, rugby, volleyball and handball), women's basketball has been very popular in countries like the USA, Spain, France and Australia, mainly due to the performances of the respective national teams and of some highly talented individual players. Career opportunities for women players exist also at club level, and full time and part time professional playing opportunities are available around the world in leagues that attract great audiences (and also viable commercial sponsorship opportunities) such as the WNBA (Women's National Basketball Association), Women Euroleague and FIBA EuroCup Women. The demands (physical, psychological, etc.) and standards for elite players have increased in recent years and this fact led to researchers to be interested in various aspects of the women's game with the same level of interest as for the men's game.

This chapter will address specific considerations for female players and will provide an overview of research relevant to standards and demands of the women's game. Additionally, it will bring in discussion the position of women head coaches and assistant coaches (in both the women's game as well as in the men's game).

6.2 Training aspects specific to female junior and senior players

Since 1953 when the first FIBA World Championship for Women took place in Chile (FIBA, 2017a), women's basketball has been under constant scrutiny. For example, various aspects related to the women's game were investigated and research focused not only on physical aspects and motor abilities (Erculj et al., 2009, 2010) but also on sources of anxiety for national team level and first division level players

(Guillen and Sanchez, 2009), on gender bias and under-representation of women coaches in both the women's and men's game (Walker and Sartore-Baldwin, 2013), on the effect the ankle support (ankle braces) has during basketball specific tasks and the relationship to injuries (Klem et al., 2016) and on impact of gender on the perceived ability of women to coach men's basketball (Walker et al., 2011).

Physical characteristics

According to Karpowicz (2006), the height structure and mass determines and impacts on the playing performance for both male and female basketball players. This might be why these two aspects (height and weight) have been explored extensively and are well documented in literature. For example, Erculj et al. (2009) analysed motor abilities of European top-quality young female basketball players (who were part of FIBA International Camp organised in Slovenia for Under 15 female players – with players selected from 27 European countries). In terms of height, they indicated that guards have on average 167.43 ± 5.70 cm, forwards have 174.09 ± 3.79 cm, while centers are 182.93 ± 3.69 cm tall. With regards to body mass, they reported figures of 59.32 ± 6.00 kg for guards, 61.79 ± 4.67 kg for forwards and 69.05 ± 7.18 kg for centers.

Similarly, Kilinic (2008) looked at a women's basketball team competing at University level and reported heights of 1.74 ± 0.05 m for control group and 1.73 ± 0.05 m for experiment group. With regards to body weight, the University players in the control group part of this study had between 61.3 ± 3.96 kg and 60.6 ± 4.17 kg, while the experiment group players were slightly lighter at 60.3 ± 4.30 kg and 59.2 ± 4.43 kg. Additionally, the percentage of body fat values were presented and these were at 12.5 ± 1.0 (pre-test) and 11.9 ± 1.1 (post-test) for the control group and 12.4 ± 1.7 (pre-test) and 11.2 ± 1.4 (post-test) for the experiment group.

In Australia, Scanlan et al. (2012) reported heights of 174.2 ± 6.9 cm and weights of 72.9 ± 14.2 kg for state level Australian women players. Also, same authors indicated that players covered total distances of 5215 ± 314 m and presented a mean heart rate response of 162 ± 3 beats±min^{-1} (82.4 ± 1.3% of maximum heart rate) for live game time and of 136 ± 6 beats±min^{-1} (68.6 ± 3.1% of maximum heart rate) for total time during the 8 competitive matches which were analysed.

The highest level of play was the focus for Carter et al. (2005) who investigated female players who took part in World Basketball Championship for Women in 1994 and found that mean values for height were 1.72 ± 0.06 m for guards, 1.81 ± 0.06 m for forwards and 1.90 ± 0.06 m for centers. Additionally, body mass figures were 66.1 ± 6.2 kg for guards (from 64 guards looked at), 73.3 ± 5.9 kg for forwards (from 57 players playing this position) and 82.6 ± 8.2 kg for centers (out of 47 investigated). Interestingly, 20 years later, at the World Championship for Women in 2014 in Turkey, the values for height were higher to the ones presented by Carter et al. (2005): average height for guards was 174.82 ± 5.70 cm (for the 81 players playing this position), for forwards was 184.94 ± 5.64 cm (78 players) and for centers was 192.45 ± 5.03 cm (33 players; FIBA, 2017b).

Recently, Karpowicz and colleagues (2015) looked at 169 young Polish female players (15.5 ± 0.5 years old) over a 8-year period of time (between 2006 and 2013), trying to identify the level of motor skills. Using the International Physical Fitness test (IPFT), they found different tendencies and changes in the structure and levels of motor effects amongst this target group. In terms of height and weight, they presented values of 173.5 ± 5.8 cm for height and of 60.2 ± 7.9 kg for weight. Table 6.1 summarises the values presented by various authors for these important components of performance in women's basketball (height, weight, percentage of body fat).

TABLE 6.1 Height, weight and percentage of body fat in women's basketball at junior and senior level

Study	Players	Height	Weight	Body fat percentage
Erculj et al. (2009)	U15 elite players	Guards: 167.43 ± 5.70 cm Forwards: 174.09 ± 3.79 cm Centers: 182.93 ± 3.69 cm	Guards: 59.32 ± 6.00 kg Forwards: 61.79 ± 4.67 kg Centers: 69.05 ± 7.18 kg	Not reported
Kilinic (2008)	University players	1.74 ± 0.05 m for control group; 1.73 ± 0.05 m for experiment group.	Control group: 61.3 ± 3.96 kg and 60.6 ± 4.17 kg; Experiment group: 60.3 ± 4.30 kg and 59.2 ± 4.43 kg.	Control group: 12.5 ± 1.0 (pre-test) and 11.9 ± 1.1 (post-test). Experiment group 12.4 ± 1.7 (pre-test) and 11.2 ± 1.4 (post-test).
Carter et al. (2005)	World Championship 1994	Guards: 1.72 ± 0.06 m Forwards: 1.81 ± 0.06 m Centers: 1.90 ± 0.06 m.	Guards: 66.1 ± 6.2 kg Forwards: 73.3 ± 5.9 kg Centers: 82.6 ± 8.2 kg.	Not reported
Karpowicz et al. (2015)	15 years old Polish players	173.5 ± 5.8 cm	60.2 ± 7.9 kg	Not reported
Scanlan et al. (2012)	Australian state level	174.2 ± 6.9 cm	72.9 ± 14.2 kg	Not reported
Author own elaboration with data from FIBA (2017b)	World Championship 2014	Guards: 174.82 ± 5.70 cm Forwards: 184.94 ± 5.64 cm Centers: 192.45 ± 5.03 cm	Not reported	Not reported

Training load/training and game frequency

Vencurik and Nykodym (2015) and Scanlan et al. (2012) are amongst the researchers who indicated that female basketball players are exposed to high physiological demands as part of the training and the competitive opportunities they are engaged with. Physical load can be analysed by looking at internal and external indicators (Vencurik and Nykodym, 2015) and quite frequently these are expressed by the heart rate (HR) and the blood lactate concentration for internal indicators and by assessing the distance covered and speed characteristics (sometimes using time-motion analysis) for the external ones. As part of this section, reference will be made mainly to the HR characteristics that have been presented in previous research.

Questions such as "How long shall we train our athletes?" and "How much/what intensity shall we train?" are usually being asked by coaches. Knowing the characteristics of the game and the physical requirements experienced in competitive situations will enable coaches to create and implement appropriate training programmes which in turn will improve players' overall physical capabilities. Training volume and load intensity are just two of the most common variables which coaches need to manipulate during the pre-competition and competition stage of a season so that the body adapts to the performance levels required (Issurin, 2009). By evaluating 25 Spanish players (of national and international standard), Rodriguez-Alonso et al. (2003) analysed the physiological demands of match-play and reported a mean heart rate of 176 ± 7 beats$\pm$min^{-1} (91.2% of maximum heart rate) in the national players and 185 ± 4 beats$\pm$min^{-1} (94.4% of maximum) in international players. Several years later, Matthew and Delextrat (2009) reported slightly lower figures for the players they investigated – mean heart rate was 165 ± 9 beats $\pm$ min^{-1} (89.1% of maximum heart rate) for total time and 170 ± 8 beats $\pm$ min^{-1} (92.5% of maximum heart rate) for live time during the games. The differences between the figures reported in these studies can be explained by the fact that Matthew and Delextrat (2009) looked at university level players competing in England compared to the Spanish researchers who looked at national and international level players. This idea (higher standard players recording higher heart rates) is supported by Krustrup et al. (2005) amongst others, while Scanlan et al. (2012) agree that playing styles and physical characteristics of players differ between countries.

While the above data is relevant to intensities during game time, to the authors' knowledge there are not too many studies that investigated the situation in training. Examples of player's heart rate response to the intensity of a training session are provided in Figures 6.1, 6.2 and 6.3 and come from the authors' direct involvement in coaching a women's national team during the preparation stage before a European Championship (Women Eurobasket 2015). As it can be observed, the player in Figure 6.1 (in this case a guard) spent 42.32 minutes in the red zone (zone 5) and 24 minutes in the orange zone (zone 4) out of the total time of 110 minutes for that particular session (total time in the training session including water breaks, demonstration and explanation of the drills, corrections, etc.). This equates to 60% of the session (66.32 minutes) which was spent at these intensities (hard intensity

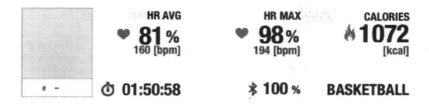

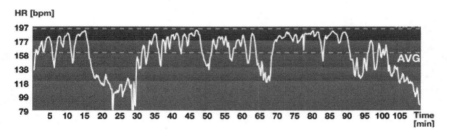

FIGURE 6.1 Heart rate and time spent in various effort zones during training for a guard

and maximum intensity). Similarly, the player in Figure 6.2 (a forward) spent 40.42 minutes in the red zone (zone 5) and 31.16 minutes in the orange zone (zone 4) – this is the equivalent of 65% of the session time was spent at high intensities (71.58 minutes from the total session time). Lastly, Figure 6.3 provides details for a centre who recorded 28.41 minutes in the red zone (zone 5) and 18.03 minutes in orange zone (zone 4) which leads to a total time of 46.44 minutes (42%) from the total session time at these high intensities.

One initial aspect which needs clarification is the fact that the specific training session which is discussed as an example was designed by the coaching staff to be a hard session (high intensity) session. The similarities with regards to the players'

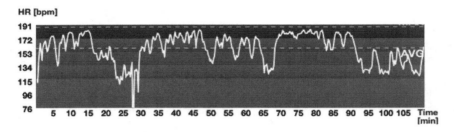

FIGURE 6.2 Heart rate and time spent in various effort zones during training for a forward

involvement and response in the sessions are obvious in the graphs provided with the only exception being the centre player. Analysing the graphs, it can be noted the fact that the centre spent 21 minutes of the session at a very low intensity and 14.32 minutes at a low intensity (towards the final part of the session) – the reason why coaches decided to reduce the intensity in her case was to protect this player from any injury which could have been caused by the fact that she joined the national team camp after a heavy game load with her club at the end of the regular season.

These type of indicators (heart rate) can act as a check point mechanism for coaches who can use objective info in the planning and also in the evaluation stages of their training sessions. The last aspect to be clarified is related to the 5 training

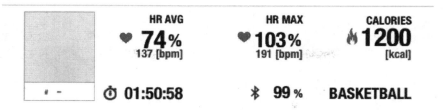

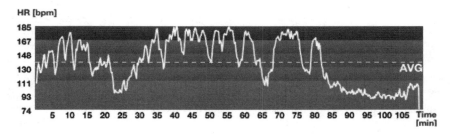

FIGURE 6.3 Heart rate and time spent in various effort zones during training for a centre

zones. Each zone corresponds to a different intensity level, with zone 1 (coloured grey on the graph) being very light effort (intensity), zone 2 (blue zone) being light effort, zone 3 (green) being moderate effort while zone 4 (orange) and zone 5 (red) are hard and maximum intensity, respectively.

With regards to the volume of training some details are presented in literature for both junior and senior female players (different levels of ability). For example, Karpowicz et al. (2015) reported 8 hours training volume per week and 40 games over the season for the young Polish players (15 years old). Kilinic (2008) discussed the intensive combined training programme of a university women's team who trained four times per week during a 10-week training period (in the preparation phase of a season, before the competition started/before the official games started). Looking at this programme from the quantitative point of view, the 2.5 months of training comprised of 38 training days, 62 separate training sessions, 5 preparation matches, 2 medical examinations and 25 rest days (the duration of a training session was 2 hours which led to an overall total of 124 hours of training).

A women's university team was also investigated by Matthew and Delextrat (2009) – the players involved in their study were training 3 times per week (Monday, Tuesday, Friday and a game on Wednesday) and each session lasted 120 minutes (which leads to a 6 hours training volume per week). According to Scanlan et al. (2012) state level players in Australia were engaged in a 8 week pre-season conditioning programme and training.

At elite level, the women's Brazilian National Team spent 12-weeks training and preparing for the official competition (FIBA Americas) as reported by Nunes et al. (2014). Interestingly, this whole preparation phase included 2 overloading and 2 tapering phases: the first overloading phase lasted 3 weeks during weeks 4–6, followed by 1-week tapering phase in week 7, and then the second overloading phase in weeks 8–10 followed by the second tapering phase which was 2 weeks long in weeks 11 and 12. Nunes and his colleagues also reported that the team won the official competition fact which seems to suggest that an appropriate balance between greater training volume (overload) and reduced training volume (tapering) leads to successful performances. Ziv and Lidor (2009) agree with previous point by saying that the right combination of volume and intensity in training as well as rest periods enables the team to achieve peak performance.

To illustrate the number of training sessions per week, an example of a weekly training plan that follows the 2:2:1 model (2 training sessions per day, followed by 2 training sessions in the next day and one training session on the third day) for a national team during the preparation phase ahead of official competition has been provided in Table 6.2.

With regards to game load/game frequency, Table 6.3 provides an indication of the number of games played by three elite level players (randomly selected) during one season (2016–2017). As it can be seen, women players experience a high number of games per season at both club level (domestic league and inter-club competitions) and national team level.

Injuries

Zelisko et al. (1982) reported higher injury rates amongst female professional players compared to males counterparts and indicated that women sustained 60% more injuries to knee and ankles than men did. This view is supported by Klem et al. (2016) and by McCarthy et al. (2013) amongst others who argued that women consistently demonstrate a higher incidence of ankle and knee injuries when compared to male players. According to Tonino (2004, p. 75), the risk of knee injury is greater for female player than men "because of anatomical differences between the sexes". He added that women are two to eight times more likely than men to experience an ACL (anterior cruciate ligament) injury.

TABLE 6.2 Weekly training plan for a national team (senior women) during preparation period

Day / time	Monday 20/04/15	Tuesday 21/04/15	Wednesday 22/04/15	Thursday 23/04/15	Friday 24/04/15	Saturday 25/04/15	Sunday 26/04/15
A.M.	Players arrival	11:30–13:00 Basketball and Testing	11:30–13:00 Weights and Basketball	OFF	10:00 a.m. Blood testing 12:00–13:00 Weights	11:30–13:00 Basketball	11:00–12:30 Recovery
P.M.	Team meeting	18:30–20:30 Testing	18:30–20:30 Basketball	18:30–20:30 Basketball	18:30–20:00 Recovery*	18:30–20:30 Basketball	OFF

*Recovery: Swimming pool, sauna, massage.
Source: adapted from Radu and Nini, 2015.

TABLE 6.3 Game load for elite female basketball players

Name of player (and country)	Club(s) played for during 2016–2017 season (between June 2016-September 2017)	Domestic League (number of games and minutes played /average per game)	Women Euroleague (number of games and minutes played /average per game)	National Team (number of games and minutes played /average per game)	Total number of games (2016–2017 season)
Emma Masserman (Belgium)	UMMC Ekaterinburgh (Russia) and Washington Mystics (USA)	PBL League (Russia) = 20 games (23.1 minutes per game); and WNBA (USA) = 27 games (29.2 minutes per game).	18 games played (20.9 minutes per game)	6 games at Eurobasket 2017 (32.8 minutes per game)	71
Sandrine Gruda (France)	Fenerbahce Istanbul (Turkey) and Los Angeles Sparks (USA)	KBSL League (Turkey) = 25 games (29.6 minutes per game); and WNBA (USA) = 8 games (3.6 minutes per game)	18 games played (25.7 minutes per game)	11 games at Olympic Games in Rio (in June and August 2016) (21.9 minutes per game)	62
Laia Palau (Spain)	USK Prague (Czech Republic)	ZBL League (Czech Republic) = 27 games (20.5 minutes per game)	19 games played (31.8 minutes per game)	6 games at Eurobasket 2017 (20.5 minutes per game)	52

Source: own elaboration with data from Eurobasket.com, 2017.

In their study, Klem et al. (2016) investigated the use of hinged ankle brace and lace-up ankle brace support mechanism with 20 semi-elite players and found that "the hinged ankle brace significantly reduced ankle inversion" (p. 685). Similar finding was reported by Kristianslund et al. (2011) who argued that ankle braces reduce the risk of injury by targeting excessive ankle inversion (which is considered by many as the primary mechanism for ankle sprains and are the most common type of ankle injuries in basketball; Cumps et al., 2007).

Teaching jump-landing techniques (Nagano et al., 2011) while also strengthening muscles that protect the knee (Tonino, 2004) and wearing protective equipment such as ankle braces (Klem et al., 2016) are a few ways which both coaches and players can use in order to prevent (and reduce) these type of injuries. In the same vein, an 8-week Sports Injury Prevention Training Program (SIPTP) has been proposed by Lim et al. (2009; containing detailed six parts/components: warm up, stretching, strengthening exercises, plyometrics, agility exercises and warm down), and this kind of programme was shown to improve the strengths and flexibility of female basketball players that play at a competitive level.

Menstrual cycle

The general view at the moment is that limited information exists in relation to how menstruation affects women's athletic performance (Tsuneura et al., 2013). In a football context, Scott and Anderson (2013) agree that there is "scarce information" (p. 254) in relation to this topic and highlight the inconsistent findings from various reports. In their study, Kishali et al. (2006) stated that performance was the same during menstruation for 62% of the athletes investigated, while 21.2% of these athletes stated that their performance got worse. The same authors reported data about athletes who had a painful menstruation (36.9% of the athletes), while an ever higher percentage (63.1%) said the pain actually decreased during competition.

As for basketball context, anecdotal evidence coming from Romanian-based author's experience and direct involvement in coaching elite women players/teams at both the club level (national championship top division and Women Euroleague) and the national team level seem to suggest that players' state during menstruation is being affected by the interpersonal and social relations on and off the court – the higher the team cohesion, the higher chances to go through this monthly period of time with more success, with an enhanced concentration capacity and generally with a "stick together" attitude. Interestingly, personal reflections from the same author (based on discussions with elite level players) suggest that women players experience menstrual synchrony. Previous research supports this idea – for example, Arden et al. (1999) reported that 80% of the 95 UK-based women who took part in their study believed synchrony occurs while 70% of the same sample stated that they had "personal experience of menstrual synchrony" (p. 259). Furthermore, 29 participants even said that the synchrony was a pleasant, "positive experience" (p. 261). As defined by Arden et al. (1999), menstrual synchrony "occurs when two or more women, who spend time with each other, have their periods at approximately the same time" (p. 257).

Despite these findings, some authors such as Yang and Schank (2006) who investigated Chinese women living in dorms and Ziomkiewicz (2006) whose sample was made out of Polish college age women living in student dormitories, suggested no meaningful relation between synchrony and menstrual related variables. However, the findings from these two particular studies need to be treated with caution because they come from studies who did not involve sport participants (athletes, players, etc.).

Friendship, time living together (e.g. as part of the pre-season training camps) and common activities (i.e. basketball matches, training, common meals time, recovery, etc.) all will determine the frequency of interaction between women's basketball players. All the above is important information for coaches as they have the capacity to modify the intensity and change/adapt the content of training on a monthly basis alongside establishing sport nutrition programs (diet) for their women players to compensate for the loss of nutrients during menstruation – for example, it is known that women athletes lose an additional 0.5 mg of iron per day during menstruation (Holschen, 2004).

6.3 Women as coaches

Despite the fact that women's basketball is gaining popularity and this popularity is at an all-time high (Pendleton, 2001), Luther (2017) highlights the fact that the percentage of women coaches has dropped in USA (at both collegiate and professional level). On the same note, Burke and Hallinan (2006) observed that while the number of active female athletes has increased, there has been "a substantial reduction in the number of female coaches and administrators" (p. 19).

Analysing the situation at NCAA level, Acosta and Carpenter (2014) portray a very clear image in numbers: while in 1972 90% of women teams were coached by women, in 2014 this percentage dropped to only 43%. A more recent finding comes from Saliba (2017), who investigated the number of women coaching in NCAA Division 1 women's basketball teams and reported that this number has decreased from 221 to 196 in the last 6 years (a 11% decrease). Interestingly, for the same division and for the same period of time, the number of male coaches has gone up with 33% (from 114 to 152).

The situation is fairly similar in Europe – to support this point, a quick overview of all the head coaches who coached at FIBA Eurobasket Women 2017 (FIBA, 2017c) reveals that only 2 out of 16 participating teams have women as head coaches (Valerie Garnier of France and Nataliya Trafimava of Belarus). Some other notable exceptions that prove the rule include Becky Hammon and Nancy Lieberman, who are both assistant coaches in the NBA, one of the most prestigious leagues around the world: Becky is currently coaching at San Antonio Spurs (Wright, 2016) while Nancy is with Sacramento Kings (NBA, 2015). Walker (2016) pointed the fact that Becky Hammon was the first woman to be hired as an assistant coach "in any of the big four (i.e. MLB, NBA, NFL, NHL) US professional sports leagues" (p. 115).

Trying to provide an interpretation and a possible answer to the lack of female coaches in men's basketball, Walker and Sartore-Baldwin (2013) used terms such as "hypermasculine, gender exclusive and resistant to change" (p. 303) when analysing men's basketball at NCAA Division I level. On the same note, Walker (2016) spoke about marginalisation, double standards and discrimination when describing this situation and considered it to be "an anomaly" (p. 111).

Women in coaching positions is a hot topic for debate and has been the focus of investigation for several authors including Cunningham and Sagas (2002), Burke and Hallinan (2006) and Borland and Bruening (2010), to name just a few. Despite the fact that there is a large consensus that woman are underrepresented, a press release from WBCA (Women's basketball Coaches Association) in USA provides further clarification with regards to the number of female coaches in NCAA Division 1. For example, females make up 2/3 of all NCAA Division 1 women's basketball head coach roles and 2/3 of NCAA Division 1 women's basketball associate head coaches (WBCA, 2009). Furthermore, Lapchick (2014) highlights the fact that 68% of assistant coaches in WNBA in 2014 (the equivalent of NBA for women) are women, and this number, according to the author, is the highest percentage of assistant coaching positions held by women in the history of WNBA. However, in 2015 his number went down to 45% (Lapchick and Nelson, 2015). In Europe, a quick look at Women Euroleague (which is considered by many the best league for professional women players around Europe) for the 2017–2018 season reveals that there are only 2 women in a head coach position (Marina Maljkovic of Galatasaray SK and Natalia Hejkova of ZVVZ USK Praha) and 4 women as Assistant Coaches out of 43 coaches who are working with the 16 teams taking part (Euroleague Women/FIBA, 2017; Galatasaray SK, 2017).

In time, great steps have been taken by various organisations to address the gender imbalance and the barriers that prevented women to access coaching positions in the so-called "boys club" as Walker and Bopp (2011) referred to it or in the "boys network" as Lovett and Lowry (1994) stated. A perfect example in this sense is "*So you want to be a coach*" workshop, which was put in place by WBCA in 2003 (WBCA, 2009), and the results of such actions (158 of the 278 female participants are working in women's basketball) are encouraging and give further hope that one day things will change and an equal playing field will be created. To echo this point, a similar idea was presented by Walker et al. (2011), who argue that stakeholders (such as people in the administration of athletic departments, coaches, student-athletes, etc.) need to take "proactive measures" (p. 172) to ensure women receive a fair opportunity. Quite clearly, breaking down barriers is required (Walker, 2016) alongside additional research for this topic (Wells, 2016).

6.4 Summary

It is well documented and generally agreed upon that a training programme for elite players should be made out of three inter-related stages: preparation, competition and transition (Bompa, 1999; Matveyev, 1981). When planning for a new season, coaches working with female players need to take this into account and create individualised training according to player position on court (Vencurik and Nykodym, 2015) and to individual player unique characteristics (Ziv and Lidor, 2009). A systematic analysis of various data similar to the one presented as part of this chapter and of info coming from different sources (medical support staff, strength and conditioning staff, performance analysis personnel, etc.) should be undertaken and this, together with personal field observations and daily notes, must inform the content of the training programmes (Ziv and Lidor, 2009). Also, coaches need to be aware of the fact that the female sports person in general (and female player in particular) has certain issues which have to be addressed/considered and that "the differences in physical and physiological characteristics affect performance and risk of injury" (Holschen, 2004, p. 852). In this way the coach will have a degree of control over the so many variables he/she is trying to coordinate, which in turn will lead to improved quality of training and increase the chances of success.

As basketball is part of our culture, coaching is central to the development of players and teams. Despite the (rather small) improvements in recent years, women coaches deserve a similar attention to the one given to men coaches, and more steps need to be taken in order to re-address the imbalance which exists at the moment.

References

Acosta, V. and Carpenter, L. (2014) *Women in intercollegiate sport: A longitudinal, national study – thirty seven year update 1977–2014*, online, available at: www.acostacarpenter.org/2014%20Status%20of%20Women%20in%20Intercollegiate%20Sport%20-37%20Year%20Update%20-%201977-2014%20.pdf (accessed on 2nd November 2017).

Arden, M., Dye, L. and Walker, A. (1999) Menstrual synchrony: Awareness and subjective experiences. *Journal of Reproductive and Infant Psychology*, Volume 17, Issue 3, pp. 255–265.

Bompa, T. (1999) *Periodization: Theory and methodology of training* (4th edition). Champaign, IL: Human Kinetics.

Borland and Bruening (2010) Navigating barriers: A qualitative examination of the under-representation of Black females as head coaches in collegiate basketball. *Sport Management Review*, Volume 13, Issue 4, pp. 407–420.

Burke, M. and Hallinan, C. (2006) Women's leadership in junior girls' basketball in Victoria: Foucault, feminism and disciplining women coaches. *Sport in Society*, Volume 9, Issue 1, pp. 19–31.

Carter, J., Ackland, T., Kerr, D. and Stapff, A. (2005) Somatotype and size of elite female basketball players. *Journal of Sports Sciences*, Volume 23, Issue 10, pp. 1057–1063.

Cumps, E., Verhagen, E. and Meeusen, R. (2007) Prospective epidemiological study of basketball injuries during one competitive season: Ankle sprains and overuse knee injuries. *Journal of Sports Science & Medicine*, Volume 6, Issue 2, pp. 204–211.

Cunningham, G. and Sagas, M. (2002) The differential effects of human capital for male and female Division I basketball coaches. *Research Quarterly for Exercise and Sport*, Volume 73, Issue 4, pp. 489–495.

Erculj, F., Blas, M. and Bracic, M. (2010) Physical demands on young elite European female basketball players with special reference to speed, agility, explosive strength and take-off power. *Journal of Strength and Conditioning Research*, Volume 24, Issue 11, pp. 2970–2978.

Erculj, F., Blas, M., Coh, M. and Bracic, M. (2009) Differences in motor abilities of various types of European young elite female basketball players. *Kinesiology*, Volume 41, Issue 2, pp. 203–211.

Eurobasket.com. (2017) *Women player profiles*, online, available at: www.eurobasket.com/women (accessed on 18th November 2017).

Euroleague Women/FIBA. (2017) online, available at: www.fiba.basketball/euroleague women/17-18 (accessed on 7th November 2017).

FIBA. (2017a) *1953 world championship for women*, online, available at: www.fiba.basketball/pages/eng/fa/event/p/sid/2917/tid/328/_/1953_World_Championship_for_Women_/index.html (accessed on 29th October 2017).

FIBA. (2017b) *2014 FIBA world championship for women*, online, available at: https://archive.fiba.com/pages/eng/fa/event/p/sid/6242/_/2014_FIBA_World_Championship_for_Women/index.html (accessed on 29th October 2017).

FIBA (2017c) *Eurobasket women 2017 final standings*, online, available at: www.fiba.basketball/eurobasketwomen/2017 (accessed 6th October 2017).

Galatasaray, S. K. (2017) online, available at: www.galatasaray.org/pl/kadin-basketbol-idarive-teknik-kadro/14 (accessed on 7th November 2017).

Guillen, F. and Sanchez, R. (2009) Competitive anxiety in expert female athletes: sources and intensity of anxiety in national team and first division Spanish basketball players. *Perceptual and Motor Skills*, Issue 109, pp. 407–419.

Holschen, J. (2004) The female athlete. *Southern Medical Journal*, Volume 97, Issue 9, pp. 852–858.

Issurin, V. (2009) Generalised training effects induced by athletic preparation: A review. *Journal Sports Med Phys Fitness*, Volume 49, pp. 333–345.

Karpowicz, K. (2006) Interrelation of selected factors determining the effectiveness of training in young basketball players. *Human Movement*, Volume 7, pp. 130–146.

Karpowicz, K., Karpowicz, M. and Strzelczyk, R. (2015) Structure of physical fitness among young female basketball players (trends of changes in 2006–2013). *Journal of Strength and Conditioning Research*, Volume 29, Issue 10, pp. 2745–2757.

Kilinic, F. (2008) An intensive combined training program modulates physical, physiological, biomotoric and technical parameters in women's basketball. *Journal of Strength and Conditioning Research*, Volume 22, Issue 6, pp. 1769–1778.

Kishali, N., Imamoglu, O., Katkat, D., Atan, T. and Akyol, P. (2006) Effects of menstrual cycle on sports performance. *International Journal of Neuroscience*, Volume 116, Issue 12, pp. 1549–1563.

Klem, N. R., Wild, C., Williams, S. and NG, L. (2016) Effect of external ankle support on ankle and knee biomechanics during the cutting manoeuvre in basketball players. *The American Journal of Sports Medicine*, Volume 45, Number 3, pp. 685–691.

Kristianslund, E., Bahr, R. and Krosshaug, T. (2011) Kinematics and kinetics of an accidental lateral ankle sprain. *Journal of Biomechanics*, Volume 44, Issue 14, pp. 2576–2578.

Krustrup, P., Mohr, M. and Ellingsgaard, H. (2005) Physical demands during an elite female soccer game: Importance of training status. *Medicine and Science in Sports and Exercise*, Volume 37, pp. 1242–1248.

Lapchick, R. (2014) *The 2014 women's national basketball association racial and gender report card*, online, available at: www.tidesport.org/wnba-rgrc.html (accessed on 7th November 2017).

Lapchick, R. and Nelson, N. (2015) *The 2015 women's national basketball association racial and gender report card*, online, available at: http://nebula.wsimg.com/28d57b7b134d9c22a277d36d8ce5d35d?AccessKeyId=DAC3A56D8FB782449D2A&disposition=0&alloworigin=1 (accessed on 7th November 2017).

Lim, B. O., Lee, Y., Kim, J., An, K. and Kwon, Y. (2009) Effect of Sports Injury Prevention Training on the biomechanical risk factors of anterior cruciate ligament injury in high school female basketball players. *The American Journal of Sports Medicine*, Volume 37, Issue 9, pp. 1728–1734.

Lovett, D. and Lowry, C. (1994) Good old boys and good old girls clubs: myth or reality? *Journal of Sport Management*, Issue 8, pp. 27–35.

Luther, J. (2017) *What women's basketball coaching shows about sexism in sports*. In Teen Vogue, available at: www.teenvogue.com/story/womens-basketball-coaches-sexism (accessed on 7th October 2017).

Matthew, D. and Delextrat, A. (2009) Heart rate, blood lactate concentration and time-motion analysis of female basketball players during competition. *Journal of Sport Sciences*, Volume 27, Issue 8, pp. 813–821.

Matveyev, L. (1981) *Fundamentals of sports training*. Moscow: Progress.

McCarthy, M., Voos, J., Nguyen, J., Callahan, L. and Hannafin, J. (2013) Injury profile in elite female basketball athletes at the Women's National Basketball Association combine. *American Journal of Sports and Medicine*, Volume 43, Issue 3, pp. 645–651.

Nagano, Y., Miki, H., Tsuda, K., Shimizu, Y. and Fukubayashi, T. (2011) Prevention of anterior cruciate ligament injuries in female basketball players in Japan: an intervention study over four seasons. *British Journal of Sports Medicine*, Volume 45, Issue 4, p. 365.

NBA (2015) *San Antonio Spurs 2017–2018 Pre-season guide*, available at: www.nba.com/spurs/2017-18-preseason-media-guide (accessed on 7th October 2017).

Nunes, J., Moreira, A., Crewther, B., Nosaka, K., Viveiros, L. and Aoki, M. (2014) Monitoring training load, recovery-stress state, immune-endocrine responses and physical performance in elite female basketball players during a periodised training program. *Journal of Strength and Conditioning Research*. Volume 28, Issue 10, pp. 2973–2980.

Pendleton, S. (2001) Motivating female athletes for success in basketball. *Coach and Athletic Director*, Volume 70, Issue 7.

Radu, A. and Nini, F. (2015) *Report – analysis of National Team activity during preparation stage for Women Eurobasket 2015 (training and friendly games)*. Internal document – Romanian Basketball Federation.

Rodriguez-Alonso, M., Fernandez-Garcia, B., Perez-Landaluce, J. and Terrados, N. (2003) Blood lactate and heart rate during national and international women's basketball. *Journal of Sports Medicine and Physical Fitness*, Volume 43, pp. 432–436.

Saliba, L. (2017) *Female head women's basketball coaches in NCAA on the decline*, The Red & Black, 25th April 2017, available at: www.redandblack.com/sports/female-head-womens-basketball-coaches-in-ncaa-on-the/article_34e21388-29c2-11e7-a5ad-c7589fe72cce.html (accessed on 6th November 2017).

Scanlan, A., Dascombe, B., Reaburn, P. and Dalbo, V. (2012) The physiological and activity demands experienced by Australian female basketball players during competition, *Journal of Science and Medicine in Sport*, Volume 15, pp. 341–347.

Scott, D. and Anderson, H. (2013) *Women's soccer* (Chapter 13), In Williams, A. (editor) *Science and soccer: Developing elite performers* (3rd edition). Abingdon: Routledge.

Tonino, P. (2004) Female basketball players at greater risk for knee injury, in *PT: Magazine of Physical Therapy*, Issue: 1st October 2004, p. 75.

Tsuneura, A., Sugiyama, E. and Yasuda, N. (2013) Evaluation of athletic performance level based on free throw shooting during menstrual cycle phase. *Journal of Science and Medicine in Sport*, Volume 16, Supplement 1, p. 70.

Vencurik, T. and Nykodym, J. (2015) The intensity of load experienced by female basketball players during competitive games. *International Journal of Medical, Health, Biomedical, Bioengineering and Pharmaceutical Engineering*, Volume 9, Issue 7, pp. 565–568.

Walker, N. (2016) *Cross-gender coaching: Women coaching men* (Chapter 7). In LaVoi, N. (editor) *Women in sports coaching*. Abingdon: Routledge.

Walker, N. and Bopp, T. (2011) The underrepresentation of women in the male dominated sport workplace: perspective of female coaches. *Journal of Workplace Rights*, Volume 15, Issue 1, pp. 47–64.

Walker, N., Bopp, T. and Sagas, M. (2011) Gender bias in the perception of women as collegiate men's basketball coaches. *Journal for the Study of Sports and Athletes in Education*, Volume 5, Issue 2, pp. 157–176.

Walker, N. and Sartore-Baldwin, M. (2013) Hegemonic masculinity and the institutionalised bias toward women in men's collegiate basketball: what do men think? *Journal of Sport Management*, Issue 27, pp. 303–315.

WBCA. (2009) *WBCA Research shows diversification of women's basketball coaches*. Press release from WBCA, available at: https://wbca.org/about/press-releases/wbca-research-shows-diversification-womens-basketball-coaches (accessed on 31st October 2017).

Wells, J. (2016) *Female assistant coaches: Planting seeds and growing roots* (Chapter 9). In La Voi (editor) *Women in sports coaching*. Abingdon: Routledge.

Wright, M. (2016) *Q&A with Becky Hammon: "Incredible honor from an incredible organisation"*, at ESPN.com, available at: www.espn.com/wnba/story/_/id/16428931/qa-san-antonio-spurs-assistant-coach-becky-hammon (accessed on 7th October 2017).

Yang, Z. and Schank, J. (2006) Women do not synchronize their menstrual cycle. *Human Nature*, Volume 17, Issue 4, pp. 433–447.

Zelisko, J., Noble, H. and Porter, M. (1982) A comparison of men's and women's professional basketball injuries. *American Journal of Sports and Medicine*, Volume 10, Issue 5, pp. 297–299.

Ziomkiewicz, A. (2006) Menstrual synchrony: fat or artifact? *Human Nature*, Volume 17, Issue 4, pp. 419–432.

Ziv, G. and Lidor, R. (2009) Physical attributes, physiological characteristics, on-court performances and nutritional strategies of female and male basketball players. *Sports Medicine*, Volume 39, Issue 7, pp. 547–568.

7
MEDICAL ISSUES IN BASKETBALL

Darren Cooper

7.1 Introduction

Basketball from a graduate sports therapist's (GST) perspective is a constant challenge with a wide range of factors to consider at all times when trying to prevent, treat and rehabilitate players. In England, the British Basketball League (BBL) has an intensive season with players competing in a minimum of 33 games per season, with up to two games a week, either on consecutive days or with a day's rest in-between. As a result, this presents a broad array of challenges that you would not encounter with other elite/professional athletes who typically only peak for a few events a year. When players become injured, this typically manifests itself in cumulative chronic injuries that require extensive in-season management and treatment to maximise athletic performance throughout the rest of the competitive schedule.

7.2 Common injuries in basketball: injury prevention and treatment

Basketball, in general, is synonymous with lateral ankle sprains and jumper's knee/patellofemoral dysfunction (Drakos, Domb, Starkey, Callahan, & Allen, 2010; Starkey, 2000); however, players experience one of the largest range of injuries seen in any sport due to the athleticism involving all parts of the body, the speed/intensity of the game and the firm surface it is played on. Although the game is non-contact from a rules perspective, a considerable amount of contact injuries are experienced throughout the course of a season. These range from minor abrasions through to traumatic head injuries from swinging limbs or falling from a height head first, each of which I have witnessed on more than one occasion. Despite the considerable range of injuries, some of which are impossible to prevent, the most common that I have encountered, in order, relate to tendons/tendon-bone interface, ankles and ligament injuries in general.

Tendons versus tendon-bone interface

Tendon injuries are notoriously difficult to classify as the underlying pathology and mechanisms that lead to tendon injuries are still not fully understood (Riley, 2008). As a result, all tendon injuries in this chapter will be referred to as *tendinopathies* (Sharma & Maffulli, 2005). To further complicate aspects, the vast majority of tendinopathies encountered within basketball around the knee or ankle tend to involve the tendon-bone interface as well, and at times it is difficult to differentiate between them. These injuries are extremely well-known by basketball players, and it is commonly known as jumper's knee, which whilst accurate in terms of mechanism of injury is a little too vague for a therapist.

Tendon-bone interface

The most common injury associated with this classification of injury within basketball players is Osgood-Schlatters Syndrome (OSS). OSS typically affects those who are skeletally immature, as the quadriceps develop at a faster rate than the player's bone density, resulting in a traction apophasis of the quadriceps tendon from the tibia characterised by an overly prominent tuberosity. The other less common version of this injury is Sinding-Larsen-Johansson syndrome (SLJS), where the quadriceps tendon is this time pulled from the distal pole of the patella, resulting in a fin-like bony formation in the area which is just as painful as OSS. Generally, the main advice from healthcare professionals is rest; however, this is rarely adhered to by young athletes, and they push through regardless, often with the use of non-steroidal anti-inflammatories despite the potential for gastrointestinal distress. Modifications to activities of daily living (ADLs) result in some of the most significant improvements to everyday life, and these include walking up and down stairs backwards, raising the height of chairs and ensuring items they need daily are at an appropriate height so they do not have to bend down to pick them up. Secondly, it is worth reviewing the player's diet (with a nutritionist if need be) to ensure they are getting enough calcium and protein on board in combination with sufficient vitamin D from natural or supplementary sources. Finally, the advice of rest is partially contrary to the healing method that most therapists would base their treatment and rehabilitation protocol on – that being Wolf's law. For those that are not familiar with Wolf's law, this is the theory that states that bone density is related to loading and if you do not load a bone (with varying types of stress; i.e. compression, torsion, rotation and shear forces), the osteocytes will remove excess tissue, resulting in a weaker bone overall. Therefore, it is important to load injured structures in a controlled way, and this is why those that fractured bones in their feet are now given walking boots instead of being put in plaster casts and being non-weight bearing on crutches for 4–6 weeks. The process of loading is where a GST is vital in the rehabilitation process, as they will find ways to load the bones in a progressive way, up to the extreme amount of loading that is applied rapidly when jumping or landing.

The vast majority of basketballers survive this period of their playing career with the minimal problem, pain or dysfunction; however, this is all dependent on what level they reach or the amount of time they dedicate to playing throughout this time frame. Those that play at a higher level or invest a large amount of time into training often encounter the largest number of complications as a result of the structural changes that are slowly developing. Currently there are no appropriate studies to the author's knowledge that have investigated the correlation between training and depth/prominence of tibial tuberosity/distal pole; however, it would be reasonable to assume that there is a positive correlation between them. This then theoretically results in biomechanical changes to the function of the tibiofemoral (knee) joint that I shall now explain: the patella is a syndesmosis bone; it functions as a pulley for the quadriceps/quadriceps tendon that it is encapsulated within. As the tendon is slowly changing its relative position due to either OSS or SLJS, the neuromuscular control of the quadriceps and the proprioceptors in the knee joint have to constantly relearn how to function as the axis of rotation and the direction of force will change. Although these changes are going to be very small in terms of degrees and millimetres, they will have a cumulative effect on the function of the joint, the timing of muscle contractions and the stability of the joint. Numerous players have reported sensations of instability and giving way whilst experiencing OSS or SLJS, and whilst this could be due to any swelling in the joint or a plethora of other factors, it is something that is biomechanically logical, given how the skeletal structure is being modified through these syndromes. As the beginning of this section stated, tendon injuries are notoriously hard to classify due to the fact that the underlying pathology and mechanisms are unknown; this I believe is a further factor that compounds the incidence of tendon injuries and leads to recurring tendon injuries as the athlete's skeletal structure and biomechanical function changes throughout their time playing sport.

Tendons

Tendon injuries can take many different guises within basketball, the most common would have to be due to rapid loading as a result of the explosive and dynamic nature of the sport. In basketball, there is a distinct likelihood that musculotendinous units will have to adapt to unpredictable loads due to landing in different positions (on another player's foot, for example, resulting in a far more forceful contraction than anticipated to maintain body position) or to some the most random incidents I have seen whereby the elbow is hyper-extended during an exuberant dunk and the biceps tendon is unable to cope with the rapid contraction to prevent excessive hyper-extension.

Predominantly, however, most of the tendon injuries are chronic in nature (whilst players will experience acute tendon injuries such as those stated above which, if not treated and rehabilitated properly, will lead to a chronic injury) and are due to cumulative macro or micro traumas that are not treated or rehabilitated properly at the time as they are not severe enough to produce an inflammatory response and/

or pain for the player to report them. When players do report said injuries, it is often at a point in the season when 'traditional' treatment is not appropriate/feasible, and as such the therapist has to manage the problem as best they can throughout the remainder of the season.

Traditional tendon treatment

'Traditional' tendon treatment involves the prescription of eccentric exercises with progressive resistance, each repetition is performed over a prolonged period, generally 10 times for up to 3 sets, over a 4- to 6-week period (Murtaugh & Ihm, 2013; van der Plas et al., 2011). This treatment regime has proven to be successful countless times within literature, with a vast variety of athletes from differing sports benefiting from the protocol. Personally, I have used this approach in sportsmen and women participating in rock climbing (finger flexor tendon injury) through to ultra-distance runners (Achilles tendon injury) demonstrating that it is a versatile approach for strength and endurance athletes alike. The approach is optimised when all other training and competition variables can be controlled to ensure progressive loading is applied, allowing the tendon to strengthen and adapt appropriately.

It is possible to modify or customise the exercise to suit differing injuries and sports, or to apply a greater amount of load to the tendon. A prime example of this that is wholly relevant to basketball players is the work of Jonsson and Alfredson (2005) with the quadriceps tendon, whereby athletes will perform eccentric squats on a 30° decline board. The purpose of this board is the enable anterior translation of the femur over the tibia, elongating the quadriceps tendon, thereby placing greater controlled and progressive loads onto the structure. Obviously, this approach requires custom-built equipment and free weights; however, not all tendon injuries require as much specific equipment. Finger/thumb tendon injuries can be treated with a roll of zinc oxide tape, a bag and some water in the early stages. Using water in a bag that is taped to the distal aspect of the injured digit allows for full range movement when positioned correctly and a very simple way to progress or regress the amount of load applied to the nearest millilitre.

As a result, the principles of the 'traditional' regime are incredibly versatile when applied appropriately or imaginatively in a variety of settings; however, within a basketball season (unless it is over a natural planned or unplanned break), time is major compounding factor to the approach and alternative strategies to managing tendon injuries need to be implemented.

Tendon management

As a mechanism to manage tendon injuries, Cook and Purdam (2014) introduced the role of isometric exercises as a way to mitigate the pain and initiate the healing within tendon injuries in-season. Rio et al. (2015) recommended a loading protocol using a leg extension machine in a gym with 70% of 1 RM being held at 60° for 45 seconds, five times with 2 minutes recovery between sets. Whilst this was entirely feasible after training sessions and after home games (due to the proximity of the weights room), many away teams would not either: have a weights room on site or would be as accommodating, so an adaptation was required as the regime provided encouraging results initially with a couple of players. As a result, through experimentation and imagination we modified the traditional wall sit so that the player's leg was held at 30°, they performed the exercise with one leg only as the loading felt similar. Ideally, we would have quantified the load via electromyography (EMG); however, this was not feasible due to a multitude of reasons, so a subjective assessment by the athletes was taken as the best marker. The approach proved to be very successful with the athletes in mitigating their pain to the extent that some of them started performing the exercises before warm-ups and games. Interestingly, one of the players thought back to when they used to play basketball elsewhere as a child, and at the end of every training session, they were made to hold wall sits for prolonged durations. Was this coach ahead of the curve or was it meant to solely be strengthening the quadriceps? Something we will never know!

Ankles

Now despite basketball being synonymous with lateral ankle sprains (LAS), I cannot classify ankle injuries into this specific category. Whilst the majority of initial ankle injuries that basketball players encounter will be LASs to the anterior talofibular ligament (AFTL) or calcaneo fibular ligament (CFL), the ligaments will become lax, as the initial injury will predispose them to further injuries, as the integrity of the bone to bone interface will be compromised. As a result, subsequent LAS injurious mechanisms will start affecting and injuring other structures in and around the area. This is boring out through a multitude of conversations with players about their history of ankle injuries, with one of the most common answers when questioned about the number of injuries being: "I've lost count of a number of times I've rolled my ankles"! Furthermore, you can witness a classic LAS mechanism occur on the court, the player hobbles for a minute or so but then returns to playing normally. After the game, they may have a bit of swelling but no distinct pain, and they do not feel the need to seek any treatment for it, as they know it will resolve overnight. This creates a plethora of problems for the therapists working with the teams as players almost treat them as part of the game, they do not typically fear them and they know (as long as it is a minor sprain) that it will not keep them from training or playing. As a result, player education and screening (despite the recent critical review by Bahr, 2016) is vital, and getting them to buy into injury prevention programmes is key. Although they may not fear LASs, there is the potential for syndesmotic injuries, tendon crush injuries, other ligament sprains/ruptures and bone injuries to occur once the range that was normally constrained by the intact or even slightly lax lateral ligaments is exceeded.

Screening and player education

As a team, until now we have applied a simple approach to screening and player education with the use of an isokinetic dynamometer. Obviously, these are not pieces of equipment that are available to every team, but they do provide a good insight into the function of a joint and the contractile and non-contractile elements of the area. Whilst there is a vast range of ways to screen for ankle injuries, functional methods are greatly supported and the Star Excursion Balance test is a good example of one of these methods – see Gribble, Hertel, and Plisky (2012) for a review. Due to prior experience and the precision with which data collection can be collected from the *gold standard for laboratory studies*, we have favoured isokinetic testing and acknowledge its limitations regarding the non-functional or sport specific setup alluded to by Terrier, Rose-Dulcina, Toschi, and Forestier (2014). An isokinetic dynamometer is able to record data that you cannot obtain from any other setting. Whilst concentric and eccentric strength is important, power and time to peak torque are some of the most useful metrics that it collects, as these can, in our opinion, be used to judge who may or may not experience an ankle injury. Time to peak (eccentric) torque is one of our key indicators, as if this is not at a quantity that we are happy with, we are not confident that they are able to utilise their evertor muscles in a protective way.

Secondly, the players respond to the use of an isokinetic dynamometer far better than other functional tests, as it is an impressive piece of kit! It provides objective data that they can work on and the vast majority of them strive to make improvements in all areas, so when the opportunity arises for a way to potentially reduce injury risk that is reasonably straightforward, most grasp the opportunity firmly and make the retest a competitive thing within themselves and among others.

Syndesmotic injuries

Now there is an ongoing debate around ankle injuries and the influence that shoes (mainly heel stiffness and collar height) have on the prevention of injuries and the type of injuries that players encounter. Regarding the prevention of injuries, Liu, Wu, and Lam (2017) have conducted an effective study concluding that collar height could have a larger impact on lateral stability than heel stiffness, with no significant difference found for performance variables. This finding supports the use of a higher collar height to improve ankle stability during sidestep cutting movements. Anecdotally, players that I have worked with have found that higher collars do affect their performance (in terms of agility) and 'weigh them down', as the shoes are naturally heavier. The first aspect is in agreement with some previous research cited by Liu et al. (2017) but not their findings relating to performance, the latter point, however, is certainly more psychological than performance-based and links to an aspect below regarding hydration. Regardless, players build up an argument for or against particular shoe types, styles and even brands (typically due to who they sponsor in the NBA). An interesting argument that several players referred to (in different seasons and from different backgrounds) was that they felt that low collar heights enabled 'the foot to roll' during a lateral sprain mechanism, whereas a higher collar secured the foot more but resulted in high ankle sprains or syndesmosis injuries at certain times. Now I have to stress that this is purely anecdotal and there is no evidence to support either view in basketball; however, syndesmosis injuries are more prevalent in sports where athletes have to wear a stiff boot or skate (Dubin, Comeau, McClelland, Dubin, & Ferrel, 2011). Given the body has clear kinetic chains throughout, it started to be resonant with me and made me evaluate the anatomy and biomechanics of the area. The theoretical conclusion that we arrived at was that the higher collars would be useful at preventing minor LASs but during a larger more forceful event, minimising the amount of movement through the mid-tarsal and subtalar joint could result in rotational loads about the anterior-posterior axis or longitudinal axis being applied to the talocrural joint (a hinge joint, that traditionally only moves in one plane and axis [mediolateral]), causing a high ankle sprain or syndesmosis injury. Unfortunately, there is no ethical way to test this theory, and each year I canvas opinion from the players on their shoe choice making no reference to this theory in any way.

Tendon crush/stretch injuries

Quite often this is one of the most overlooked, undertreated or under-rehabilitated injuries following an ankle sprain of any description, as it is seen as a consequence rather than an injury. If we look at the biomechanics of the most common lateral sprain injury as an example, during inversion and plantar flexion the peroneal tendons and supporting fascial structures will be stretched around the talus and calcaneus and the tibialis posterior tendon, and fascial structures will be crushed between the calcaneus and the medial malleolus. Both of these mechanisms of injuries result in a very distinct bruising pattern along the path of each tendon, on their respective sides. Despite the very obvious signs and symptoms, the treatment and rehabilitation of this part of the ankle sprain are usually neglected as attention is given to the ligament involved. The reasons as to why are not clear; however, the potential consequences are far-reaching as both the peroneals and tibialis posterior are responsible for a large proportion of ankle stability. By not treating these tendons and fascial structures alongside the ligament injury, therapists will potentially elongate the rehabilitation of the player, as these could progress to chronic injuries or at least impede the player regaining strength, power and proprioceptive control of their ankle. Given peroneal strength is quite often reduced in basketball players from repeated ankle injuries, this can have a further compounding effect on their prevalence for injury in a vicious circle. As a result, it is imperative that the GST treats and rehabilitates every sign and symptom that they observe as soon as possible, as a single MOI can result in a multitude of injuries to differing structures.

Other ligament sprains/ruptures

The ankle has a large number of ligaments due to the number of bones within the foot, quite often most of these are overlooked or simply unknown by most therapists, as they are not generally taught, studied or even injured. The latter is quite often the reason as to why they are unknown, as even if they are taught they may slip from memory due to the rarity that they are encountered. During an LAS, the position of the foot is key to determining the involvement of other ligaments, dorsiflexion and inversion typically involve the posterior talofibular ligament, neutral and inversion the calcaneofibular ligament and plantar-flexion and inversion typically the anterior talofibular ligament; however, the latter can also bring the midtarsal and tarsometatarsal joints into play. The mid-tarsal and tarsometatarsal joints hold the cuboid, navicular, cuneiforms and metatarsals in place, and all of these are susceptible to injury depending on how the foot is positioned when landing, what they land on and the footwear they are wearing at the time of landing. Of these, the cuboid and the fourth and fifth metatarsals are the most lateral structures and therefore most likely to roll under the foot during a LAS. This is further exacerbated and therefore possibly more commonly seen with basketball players due to previous LASs, as the subtalar joint will most likely be laxer resulting in a larger range of inversion and increased likelihood of these structures rolling under the foot.

Assessing these structures can be quite difficult as the ligaments on the dorsum of the foot are under multiple tendons and fascial structures and the plantar fascia covers those on the plantar surface. As a result, the player may complain of pain and discomfort over the cuboid or metatarsals during functional activities that are difficult to replicate during a clinical assessment. Sometimes manual manipulation of the joints can reveal its location, but quite often the area is diffuse due to the multiple ligaments involved, particularly around the cuboid. An injury in the metatarsal region can quite often be mistaken for a minor fracture since the prevalence of metatarsal fractures increased in the previous decade.

Bone injuries

Bone injuries in basketball have many guises from complete fractures through to bruising; the extent of the injury is generally related to the specific location. As a result, we will deal with bruised bones first; the most common location for this to occur is the greater trochanter of the femur (as long as the bursa is not injured) that can experience multiple impacts from falls resulting in distinct bruising and tenderness. This is generally why padded undershorts are worn by many players to try and prevent this type of bone injury; the ramifications of the bruising can be quite severe as the gluteal muscles insert into this bony location affecting the majority of the player's movements.

Many other forms of bruising are the result of bone on bone collisions between different players body parts and as such are relatively minor in comparison to that seen with the greater trochanter. The only exception to this is when a body part, such as the kneecap or olecranon process (point of elbow) impacts another bone on a player. The former has the most injurious capacity especially when contact is made between a kneecap and the fibula, which is a non-weight bearing bone that is by far and away the most fragile in the lower limb. Although the fibula is non-weight-bearing, it has a vital role as an origin for muscles in the shank, as a result a fracture to this bone can have a significant impact.

Another player on player collisions or player on equipment (i.e. hoop or backboard) can result in fractures, particularly when digits or the upper extremity go from being in an open kinetic chain to a closed kinetic chain in a traumatic manner when grasped or caught by another player's apparel. The consequence of many of these collisions, in addition to the fracture, is extensive muscle bruising or contusions, which can mask the fracture to some extent if it is not complete or extensive enough to cause high levels of pain.

7.3 Rehabilitation after injuries

Rehabilitation, post injurious event, is extremely time sensitive within basketball due to numerous factors – namely the next league, cup, trophy or playoff game and the time of year. The latter is relevant as playing well in particular games or competitions can have a big effect on their contract negotiations for the following year. As a result, the most commonly asked question that every therapist will be asked is 'When can I return to play?'. Therefore, one of the largest aspects of the rehabilitation process is managing expectations through player education and goal setting.

Player education is exceptionally important as it ensures they understand the magnitude of the injury, its implications and what will be required of them throughout the rehabilitation process.

Educating them with the anatomy of an injured structure, its function and how the body will naturally compensate (and thereby potentially challenge or compromise other structures) is always the key starting point. The magnitude of the injury is often difficult to convey. A fracture is self-limiting and very easy for them to understand; however, other injuries require more specific approaches such as utilising an ultrasound machine to provide a pictorial representation of the injured site or, when appropriate, an isokinetic analysis to fully convey the deficits in and around a particular joint. The latter two examples are always favourable but not always feasible, as they provide an objective measure which players and GSTs can use to strictly monitor progress.

Once the player has a full grasp of the implications of the injury, a timeline can be initiated, although as with other factors, this is very much an individual process as players have differing rates of healing and no two injuries are ever identical. Breaking the timeline into small achievable goals is of paramount importance to aid with rehabilitation compliance. The GST also needs to ensure they adopt a 'whole athlete approach' and modify all the appropriate factors (nutrition is one of the most crucial) and minimise the negative consequences of an injury where possible on certain factors such as cardiovascular fitness and strength in the region or contralateral limb.

Managing a player's progress through these goals then becomes the next biggest challenge, as they quite often will start to set goals for themselves due to external influences (i.e. upcoming games, finals or even media pressure). All too often a player will 'try' something to 'test' themselves and regress their rehabilitation; it is therefore vital that the GST gains their professional trust – a factor that is incredibly complex and multifaceted.

Once a player progresses through the rehabilitation stages, the question of returning to play becomes a challenging one, as the demands of the game are difficult to replicate in a late/pre-discharge phase safely. As a result, the GST will need to devise appropriate strategies to test and load the player so that they return to play at the same level or, ideally, higher when they are ready. The latter is always seen as particularly challenging; however, with some basketball players, it is something that is achievable if you have their professional trust and practice what you preach.

7.4 Means of recovery for basketball players

Recovery is one of the most important factors an athlete can control to influence their training and performance. Sleep is the most natural form of recovery, however, that is not always feasible when training sessions end during the day! Therefore, the timing and application of other strategies are paramount from a recovery perspective be it: using compression garments; massage; hydrotherapy; cryo/thermotherapy; nutrition and hydration, some of which will be discussed below.

Sleep

Sleep is paramount for training and athletic performance; there is a multitude of factors that affect sleep, such as mattress firmness/size, bed frame, pillow quantity and firmness, duvet tog, temperature, humidity, ambient noise and so on. Whilst most of these are relatively easy to control and manipulate (even with the height of some players!), certain modern factors that are now 'integral' to modern life (on-demand video streaming services) and in particular a basketball player's 'social media' are beginning to encroach on the most natural form of recovery and need to be considered by a GST.

During restorative sleep, physical healing, mental and emotional recuperation takes place in specific phases; however, the quantity and quality of sleep are under threat in modern life due to the use of handheld devices. The use of handheld light-emitting devices is coming under ever increasing scrutiny, and Chang, Aeschbach, Duffy and Czeisler (2015) identify that the use of these devices before bedtime increases the time it takes to fall asleep by suppressing the sleep-inducing hormone melatonin, delays the circadian clock, decreases the quantity of REM (rapid-eye movement) sleep and reduces alertness the morning after.

Furthermore, the use of handheld devices for social media places a cognitive load on the athlete and a cumulative (generally unappreciated) physical load due to the positions some athletes hold/view them in for prolonged periods of time.

On-demand video streaming services, either via a smart TV or a tablet, will generally have a minimal impact in terms of cognitive load but they can account for lots of tension and stiffness in player's lumbar, thoracic and cervical regions due to poor posture and view positions for prolonged periods of time, as they watch 'just one more' episode.

Whilst athletes have a responsibility to maintain their own welfare when it comes to sleep, the modern influence is ever-encroaching, with a large cross-section (encompassing basketball players) of the population becoming addicted to handheld devices and on-demand video streaming services. As a result, the role of sleep, as a key recovery parameter, needs to be brought back into the limelight with players to ensure all aspects are addressed to maximise the quality and quantity of sleep.

Compression garments

Whilst this is a reasonably well-researched area in terms of general sporting performance (running in particular), with big brands investing heavily in research and development, it is particularly under-researched in basketball (Calleja-González et al., 2015).

Given basketball is a high-intensity, intermittent game research applied to this area is directly applicable. Pruscino, Halson, and Hargreaves (2013) conducted a study examining the effects of graduated compression on recovery after intermittent exercise with field hockey players. The participants conducted an intermittent exercise regime and then wore graduated compression garments for 24 hours. After this time period, participants reported feeling 'better recovered' and earlier exercise readiness; however, all blood markers and physical tests revealed little to no difference. A study by Duffield, Cannon and King (2010) examining the effects of compression garments following high-intensity sprint and plyometric exercise noted highly comparable findings. None of the physical tests resulted in any significant differences; however, the level of perceived muscle soreness was reduced and therefore the benefits of compression garments may aid with the athlete's perception of their recovery. In the final study worth noting, Aulkner, Leadon and Aren (2013) mirrored the findings of the other studies above, although they noted that the perception of exertion when wearing compression garments was reduced, which could lead to a positive training and/or performance effect.

As a result, the efficacy of compression garments is contentious in the literature as the sample above indicates; however, the psychological benefits and perceptions of compression garments would warrant their usage. This ambiguity is seen across players, as some actively use compression garments when playing and for recovery, yet others do not feel it has any worthwhile benefit. From a GSTs perspective, they are an item that could potentially only have a beneficial effect, even if that is purely psychological. It is certainly an item that would warrant further attention, particularly their usage when returning from away games when players have restricted movement opportunities.

Hydration

Now this is a very tricky subject from a GSTs/Sports Scientists perspective, as we are fully aware of the necessity to be hydrated from a performance perspective;

however, something that I have encountered many times is the phenomenon that players do not want to be fully hydrated prior to a game, as it will 'weigh them down'. Now, this was not something I expected to hear at all, but it is something that I have heard consistently across seasons despite the clear-cut evidence (see Cheuvront and Kenefick [2014] for a full breakdown) that being dehydrated by even a small percentage will have an effect on all performance variables. Highlighting that some players could cut some body fat and hydrate instead to be the same weight has not been well received on a variety of occasions; others have taken it on board and seen performance gains.

Throughout a game, the high intensity and the temperatures of an indoor sport mean that players are sweating extensively throughout the game to such an extent that they require towels to help mop up the perspiration. By the end of the game, I shudder to think how much water and electrolytes players lose throughout the game and strongly encourage them to drink extensively until they reach an appropriate colour on a pee chart. However, as most games in England do not finish until around 21:00, with players not getting home until around 22:00 on a good night, they have limited time to hydrate appropriately and this is an area for future investigation.

7.5 Summary

In summary, the role of a GST is varied when working with a basketball team addressing the various medical issues. The text above is only a small snapshot of the variety that is encountered; the nature of the game means you can experience quite possibly every injury over the course of a few seasons. The players and the playing schedule present unique challenges that, whilst comparable to other sports, are unique in many ways, and as such working with a basketball team is very rewarding and yields a wide range of experiences.

References

Aulkner, J. A. A. F., Leadon, D. A. G., & Aren, J. A. M. C. L. (2013) Effect of lower-limb compression clothing on 400-m sprint performance. *Journal of Strength and Conditioning Research, 27*(3), 669–676.

Bahr, R. (2016) Why screening tests to predict injury do not work – and probably never will . . .: a critical review. *British Journal of Sports Medicine, 50*, 776–780. https://doi.org/10.1136/bjsports-2016-096388

Calleja-González, J., Terrados, N., Mielgo-Ayuso, J., Delextrat, A., Jukic, I., Vaquera, A., . . . Ostojic, S. M. (2015) Evidence based post exercise recovery strategies in basketball. *The Physician and Sportsmedicine, 0*(0), 1–5. https://doi.org/10.1080/00913847.2016.1102033

Chang, A-M., Aeschbach, D., Duffy, J. F., & Czeisler, C. A. (2015) Evening use of light-emitting eReaders negatively affects sleep, circadian timing, and next-morning alertness. *Proceedings of the National Academy of Sciences, 112*(4), 1232–1237. https://doi.org/10.1073/pnas.1418490112

Cheuvront, S. N., & Kenefick, R. W. (2014) Dehydration: Physiology, assessment, and performance effects. *Comprehensive Physiology, 4*(1), 257–285. https://doi.org/10.1002/cphy.c130017

Cook, J. L., & Purdam, C. R. (2014) The challenge of managing tendinopathy in competing athletes. *British Journal of Sports Medicine, 48*(7), 506–509. https://doi.org/10.1136/bjsports-2012-092078

Drakos, M. C., Domb, B., Starkey, C., Callahan, L., & Allen, A. (2010) Injury in the national basketball association: A 17-year overview. *Sports Health, 2*(4), 284–290. https://doi.org/10.1177/1941738109357303

Dubin, J. C., Comeau, D., McClelland, R. I., Dubin, R. A., & Ferrel, E. (2011) Lateral and syndesmotic ankle sprain injuries: A narrative literature review. *Journal of Chiropractic Medicine, 10*(3), 204–219. https://doi.org/10.1016/j.jcm.2011.02.001

Duffield, R., Cannon, J., & King, M. (2010) The effects of compression garments on recovery of muscle performance following high-intensity sprint and plyometric exercise. *Journal of Science and Medicine in Sport, 13*(1), 136–140. https://doi.org/10.1016/j.jsams.2008.10.006

Gribble, P. A., Hertel, J., & Plisky, P. (2012) Using the star excursion balance test to assess dynamic postural-control deficits and outcomes in lower extremity injury: A literature and systematic review. *Journal of Athletic Training, 47*(3), 339–357. https://doi.org/10.4085/1062-6050-47.3.08

Jonsson, P., & Alfredson, H. (2005) Superior results with eccentric compared to concentric quadriceps training in patients with jumper's knee: A prospective randomised study. *British Journal of Sports Medicine, 39*(11), 847–850. https://doi.org/10.1136/bjsm.2005.018630

Liu, H., Wu, Z., & Lam, W-K. (2017) Collar height and heel counter-stiffness for ankle stability and athletic performance in basketball. *Research in Sports Medicine, 25*(2), 209–218. https://doi.org/10.1080/15438627.2017.1282352

Murtaugh, B., & Ihm, J. M. (2013) Eccentric training for the treatment of tendinopathies. *Current Sports Medicine Reports, 12*(3), 175–182. https://doi.org/10.1249/JSR.0b013e3182933761 [doi]

Pruscino, C. L., Halson, S., & Hargreaves, M. (2013) Effects of compression garments on recovery following intermittent exercise. *European Journal of Applied Physiology, 113*(6), 1585–1596. https://doi.org/10.1007/s00421-012-2576-5

Riley, G. (2008) Tendinopathy – from basic science to treatment. *Nature Clinical Practice: Rheumatology, 4*(2), 82–89. https://doi.org/10.1038/ncprheum0700

Rio, E., Kidgell, D., Purdam, C., Gaida, J., Moseley, G. L., Pearce, A. J., & Cook, J. (2015) Isometric exercise induces analgesia and reduces inhibition in patellar tendinopathy. *British Journal of Sports Medicine,* 1–8. https://doi.org/10.1136/bjsports-2014-094386

Sharma, P., & Maffulli, N. (2005) Basic biology of tendon injury and healing. *The Surgeon, 3*(5), 309–316. https://doi.org/10.1016/S1479-666X(05)80109-X

Starkey, C. (2000) Injuries and illnesses in the national basketball association: A 10-year perspective. *Journal of Athletic Training, 35*(2), 161–167. www.pubmedcentral.nih.gov/articlerender.fcgi?artid=1323413&tool=pmcentrez&rendertype=abstract

Terrier, R., Rose-Dulcina, K., Toschi, B., & Forestier, N. (2014) Impaired control of weight bearing ankle inversion in subjects with chronic ankle instability. *Clinical Biomechanics, 29*(4), 439–443. https://doi.org/10.1016/j.clinbiomech.2014.01.005

van der Plas, A., de Jonge, S., de Vos, R. J., van der Heide, H. J. L., Verhaar, J. A. N., Weir, A., & Tol, J. L. (2011) A 5-year follow-up study of Alfredson's heel-drop exercise programme in chronic midportion Achilles tendinopathy. *British Journal of Sports Medicine, 46*(3), 214–218. https://doi.org/10.1136/bjsports-2011-090035

8
COACHING AND BASKETBALL COACH EDUCATION

Alexandru Radu

8.1 Introduction

Coach education (and development) is central to the professionalization of sports coaching (Lyle, 2007), and this is clearly the case in the context of basketball coaching. Robinson (2010) argues that coach development pathways need to exist and, while these pathways are either provided (e.g. by the National Governing Body of a particular sport) or searched and developed by individual coaches for their own benefit, some fundamental questions remain: how do basketball coaches learn to coach? How will a coach get to an elite level and what will help him/her during the process? Richards et al. (2012, p. 411) state that "coaches are continually trying to develop both their declarative knowledge (knowing what to do) and their procedural knowledge (knowing when and how things should be done)". On a similar note, Robinson (2010) suggests that "the coach should engage in 'horizontal learning' and attend NGB workshops, courses, coaching conferences, and keep up to date" (p. 171).

Despite these facts, questions such as "Where do I get the knowledge from?", "How do I do it?" and "What is the best learning opportunity for the stage where I am now?" still need to be answered. As Nash and McQuade (2014) point out, research investigating coaches' learning, development and knowledge acquisition remains an area requiring more exploration, particularly with regards to the discussion as to what is the most effective method or combination of tools which will enhance the learning process. This is what this chapter will try to achieve: firstly, to provide an overview of the ways basketball coaches acquire their knowledge and, secondly, to offer practical solutions and ideas which coaches can apply in practice in their attempt to develop future generations of performers. Last but not least, this chapter aims to provide some "food for thought" and encourage other coaches to join the debate.

8.2 Development of basketball coaches

Having as a starting point what Mullem and Croft (2015) identified as formal, non-formal and informal learning situations and also Cushion et al.'s. (2010) and Coombs and Ahmed's (1974) coach learning and development framework (which are presented in Figure 8.1), each of these learning areas will be discussed separately below.

Before the discussion begins, it is useful to point out at this stage that there is no consistency (and no agreement) in the literature with regards to the terminology being used. Nelson et al. (2006) argue that there is a "need for a clear conceptual framework of coach learning" (p. 248). In this respect, various terms – such as learning, education, training, development, coach certification, continuous professional development (CPD), etc. – have been used interchangeably by various researchers including Lyle (2007), Cushion et al. (2003) and Martens (2004), amongst others, when discussing aspects related to how coaches learn and acquire the much needed knowledge.

Obviously, there are some differences between learning and education. As defined by Rogers (2002, p. 45) education is "the process of assisted or guided learning" while learning is "the act or process by which behavioural change, knowledge, skills and attitudes are acquired" (Boyd, 1980, pp. 100–101). Nelson et al. (2006) add that, in the case of learning, the emphasis is transferred to the person in whom the educators expect to see some change. Furthermore, they add that learning can encapsulate all the forms and means by which knowledge is assimilated by the coaches with the aim of informing and supporting their professional practice.

Formal learning

Cushion et al. (2003) agree that, most of the time, new coaches "learn through ongoing interactions" (p. 217) with various actors involved in the learning process

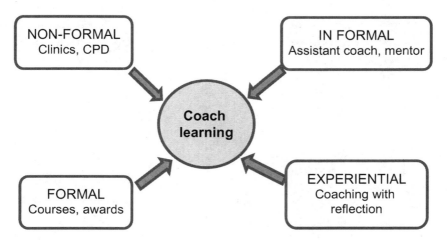

FIGURE 8.1 Learning situations which lead to coach learning and development

Adapted from Cushion et al., 2010; Coombs and Ahmed, 1974; Mullem and Croft, 2015.

(educators, fellow coaches, teachers, team managers, parents, etc.). These interactions take place in a variety of settings and one of the most common settings is the classroom. Coach education programmes are traditionally offered by national governing bodies (NGB) or federations – for example, in England, in the case of basketball, by Basketball England (organisation that offers awards from Level 1 up to Level 4). Alongside these programmes, coaching degrees that are provided by numerous universities also aim at imparting knowledge and at developing practitioners. At a European level, FIBA Europe Coaching Certificate (FECC) proves to be a very popular option for basketball coaches who are nominated by their NGB and who want to raise their level and to learn from experts and top coaches in the field (FIBA, 2017). In other places, such as Canada and the USA, aspiring coaches engage with the National Coaching Certification Program workshops offered by Canada Basketball (Canada Basketball, 2017) and with the USA Basketball Coach Academy which is part of USA Basketball (USA Basketball, 2017) in order to learn the basics of being a coach and to be able to have an impact when working with players of various levels of ability.

According to Lyle (2007, p. 281) and to Coaching Review Panel (1991, p. 33), six essential elements should be present in any coach education programme: sports-specific knowledge; ethics and philosophy; performance-related knowledge; management/vocational skills; teaching/coaching methodology and practical coaching experience. Arguably, as Cushion et al. (2003) discuss, two factors that significantly impact and affect the learning as part of the coach education should also be present on this list: reflection and experience.

In recent years, coach education programmes have been scrutinised and even criticised for various reasons such as lack of consistency, for providing a de-contextualised learning or were seen as a tool box – the work of Cushion et al. (2003), Abraham and Collins (1998) and Jones and Wallace (2005) are relevant examples in this sense. Speaking about education and training, Lyle (2007) noted that they are determined by a mixture of formal and informal provision; he also emphasized the importance of learning and preparation especially in the context of analysing practice.

Cushion et al. (2003) ask the question "How can a single coach education program realistically prepare coaches for so many contexts and a myriad of contextual factors?" (p. 221). They also provide an answer by saying that there is no easy solution. Furthermore, Cushion and co-workers (2010) add that sometimes the theoretical material which is covered as part of various courses is considered to be too abstract and rather distant from everyday practice to be considered worthwhile. The same authors add the idea that courses are guilty of adding too much info into a short space of time.

Despite these facts, the findings of a study that investigated Spanish basketball coaches (coaches of school-aged children) seem to prove that actually this method of learning (formal education) still has value and is seen as beneficial by coaches who engage in this kind of activity: Feu and his colleagues (2009) reported that formal education means (such as federations, universities or other organisations) had the greatest acceptance amongst the coaches who participated in the study. In the same study, this (formal education) was built upon the knowledge which was acquired as part of the playing experiences and was followed by the experiences and innovations as an active coach. The study undertaken by Irwin et al. (2004) supports these findings despite the fact that the sport context is different – coaching courses were seen as a significant way of acquiring knowledge by 36% of the gymnastics coaches who were interviewed.

NGBs and federations are interested in upskilling the workforce (coaches, team managers, etc.). Some federations support this point of view – for example, the Italian Basketball Federation suggested that "an increased emphasis must be placed on training coaches and players" (Little, 2015, p. 22). Speaking about this federation in particular, Little (2015) highlights that regular and high-quality training is now mandatory for coaches, managers and generally people involved in basketball coaching. By merging traditional methods (training that takes place in classrooms and/or arenas which is usually instructor led) with online learning and offering blended learning opportunities, the Italian Federation demonstrated a proactive approach by implementing innovative training strategies (Little, 2015). Little (2015) adds the fact that the learning management system (LMS) in place in Italy helps to manage and monitor 2000 learners throughout the country. Similar to FIBA Europe Coaching Certificate course mentioned before, this system (which runs in Italy) is very useful especially from the point of view that coaches can learn from basketball experts who are sharing their knowledge.

Interestingly, the same idea of basketball coaches using distance learning methods with the help of information and communications technology (ICT) was the purpose of a study conducted by Tsamourtzis et al. (2009) with 60 Greek basketball coaches. Some of the main findings (which support the move towards an online learning environment for basketball coaches) were that the less difficulties and the more attractive the study was, the easier and the faster the effort to engage with the whole distance learning was considered in comparison to traditional learning.

In this context of learning and acquiring knowledge, it is no surprise that various coaching clinics and seminars that take place every year are very well attended by coaches (of different levels and abilities) who want to learn and stay current with all the trends of the modern game. For example, the 2017 NBA Coaching Clinic in London (organised jointly by Basketball England and by NBA) was attended by more than 150 coaches (Basketball England, 2017). Every summer, around 250–300 coaches usually attended the International Coaching Clinic in Lithuania, a clinic which is organised by the Lithuanian Basketball Coaches Association (Masiulis, 2017). Lastly, Mullem and Croft (2015) talk about the clinic organised by the National Association of Basketball Coaches (NABC) during the National Collegiate Athletic Association (NCAA) Men's Final Four, and this attracts coaches from all over USA.

Informal learning

Mullem and Croft (2015) argue that informal learning takes place when coaches learn by actually coaching and working in the field (e.g. coaching as an assistant coach and interacting with the head coach). In other words, they learn through their own practical experience (Trudel and Gilbert, 2006; Gilbert et al., 2009).

Discussing the learning process in informal contexts, Lemyre et al. (2007) highlighted "the importance of others" (p. 192) and the influence they can have on developing knowledge. Similarly, the interaction(s) with other coaches (by sharing ideas, discussing and exchanging opinions) is fundamental to the concept of "communities of practice" (CoP) which Wenger et al. (2002) proposed. Jones (2006) is in agreement when stating that coaching is an interactive profession, and Mullem and Croft (2015) support this by emphasising "the importance of cultivating a network of colleagues" (p. 16) which will help coaches develop. In their research, Gilbert et al. (2009) provide a basketball-related example of a CoP by highlighting how John Wooden, UCLA basketball coach, planned his sessions for 2 hours on an everyday basis and interacted with his coaching staff (so, in essence, forming a CoP within their club).

On the same topic of communities of practice and of developing relationships with other coaches to interact and engage with, Culver and Trudel (2008, as cited in Mullem and Croft, 2015) add two additional concepts: informal knowledge networks (IKN) and networks of practice (NOP). In either situation/scenario, establishing a professional relationship with other coaches is essential. Consequently, the network of coaches acts as a valuable resource in itself (Mullem and Croft, 2015). Culver and Trudel (2008) provided explanations as to what NOP and IKP are. For instance, IKN is made out of groups of people who do not necessarily work within the same organisation but who know each other and are willing to share information and knowledge. According to the same authors, in the case of NOPs, the information is exchanged between coaches who might not know each other and they do not interact on a usual basis.

Observing practices and sessions delivered by other coaches is another useful way of establishing a professional coaching relationship with others (Mullem and Croft, 2015). On this particular point, Meurs (2017) mentions his trip to Spain in order to observe Spanish coaches delivering sessions and considers this whole experience to be an "eye opener" for himself. Observing practices is something that the NBA coach Gregg Popovich did at a particular moment during his career when he spent one season (1985–1986) with University of Kansas head coach Larry Brown (as reported by Monroe, 2014).

In recent years, social networking became the norm during the communication process for various professionals and coaches (basketball coaches included) follow the trend. FitzPatrick (2014) mentions Facebook, Twitter and Instagram as the most popular methods to interact and communicate with players, parents, fellow coaches and so on. Similar findings were reported in a survey conducted by Sports Coach UK with 1000 sport coaches (UK Coaching, 2017): the most popular social media tool for coaches to share thoughts and engage in information exchange is Facebook (with 24.8% of coaches using now this form of communication), followed by Twitter (15.7%%), discussion forums (12.9%) and blogs (7.3%).

Reflection

Personal reflection and inquiry are seen by Gilbert et al. (2009) as a "critical form of professional development" (p. 15), while Knowles et al. (2006) perceive reflection ability as "a form of analysis" (p. 169). Anderson et al. (2004) tried to define reflective practice and argued that reflection is an approach that helps people working in a particular domain (i.e. practitioners, coaches) to explore the decisions they have taken alongside their experiences with the ultimate aim of enhancing their understanding of practice.

A reassessment of personal coaching philosophies and the intention to reflect on them might be a potential way to make sure coaches become involved in the process of reflection as Cushion et al. (2003) suggested. Obviously, it might take several years for this to happen (Schon, 1987) as this is a difficult thing to do (Johns, 1994).

Similar to Knowles et al. (2001), Gilbert and Trudel (2001) argue that there are three main forms of reflection related to the actual time (moment) of reflection: reflection-in-action (coaches' thoughts and decisions that are being taken during the practice); reflection-on-action (analysing what happened, after the practice or game has finished); and retrospective reflection-on-action (immediately or some time after the session is over).

Anderson et al. (2004) discussed the practical aspects (how to reflect) and provided various types of reflection: spontaneous, planned, part of an activity that could be both personal or public, and the whole process can be conversational or documented in writing. This last idea of documenting your thoughts in writing has been supported by Walker (2006), who identified journal writing as a method designed to encourage reflection. In a similar way, writing journals as a method for how to reflect and how to capture reflective practice has been proposed by Knowles et al too (2014) alongside other tools such as creation of a mind map, engagement in reflective conversations and even using recording devices to capture ideas, feelings and opinions.

Reflection has been discussed as part of the informal learning by Koh et al. (2017) and by Nelson et al. (2006). Coaches need to be open and to question their own practice, their activities and those of others. Ultimately, reflection "could provide a bridge" (Nelson and Cushion, 2006, p. 175) that links all the information and knowledge accumulated from various sources such as practice (e.g. from playing experience), theory (time spent as part of coach education courses and/or degrees), direct observations and/or interactions with important others.

Mentoring

The topic of mentoring, mentoring programmes and the role which mentors play during the formative coaching years has been rigorously examined by Lemyre et al. (2007) and Cushion et al. (2003), amongst others. Other researchers such as Koh et al. (2017) analysed what experiences contributed to the development of mentor coaches and their role as mentors in a basketball coach education programme. They found that previous leadership roles and even the playing experience played an important part during the process of developing mentor coaches alongside various informal learning opportunities.

In other sports such as ice hockey, Hockey Canada (the governing body of the sport) identified and implemented a mentoring programme at national level (titled National Coach Mentorship Programme), which was seen as the key to the contribution and future growth of coaching (Hockey Canada, 2017). Football in the UK has seen a similar Coach Mentor Programme run by the Football Association (FA), which benefitted from a major investment in recent years (Football Association, 2017). In the basketball environment, the Women's Basketball Coaches Association (WBCA) from the USA organises the Coach to Coach Mentoring Programme (WBCA, 2017), with the clear aim of "sharing ideas, confront challenges and learn from each other's experiences".

Gilbert and Trudel (2001) agreed that mentoring is happening and coaches see the benefits of such an approach to learning and development. This view is further supported by the participants in a study conducted by Bloom et al. (1995), who reported that mentoring was the most important factor in their development. Despite these facts, Cushion (2006) stated that mentoring is still "unstructured and uneven in terms of quality and outcome" (p. 131). Finding an experienced coach who has the willingness and the time to act as a mentor to younger and less experienced coaches might be sometimes problematic. Apart from this, the outcome of the process (if learning takes place or not) is influenced by the quality of mentor-mentee relationship (Cushion, 2006). That is why, as Cushion et al. (2003) argue, mentoring should be incorporated within formal coach education frameworks, and the organisations that are responsible for providing this kind of educational support and opportunities must be fully supportive throughout the process.

8.3 Coaches role in the development and performance of basketball players

Douglas et al. (2016) together with Cote and Gilbert (2009) highlighted the importance and the key role a coach plays in order for an individual sports person or a team to achieve success and generally to develop sport talent. Coaches work on a daily basis with numerous variables (Lyle, 2007) which they need to control. In order to do so, coaches should to create an environment that will facilitate its own development, which consequently will lead to the development of the players, from the initial selection stage all the way to reaching high performance levels. When it comes to training sessions (the actual practice), the environments created will need to replicate the requirements of the game so that the technical, tactical, physical abilities are all rehearsed and simultaneously integrated (Richards et al., 2009). Player development (from various angles: technical, tactical, etc.) can be facilitated and speeded up by creating an atmosphere in which players are encouraged to engage in reflective practice and learn in an autonomous manner (Richards et al., 2009).

Coach's previous playing experience (alongside previous coaching experience) plays a major part in understanding the phenomenon and the context in which players learn and develop. It also helps developing and shaping an early viewpoint about the game and how it should be managed, a viewpoint which consequently has the potential to transform into their coaching philosophy. Understanding your athletes should be a priority for coaches according to elite basketball coaches who were interviewed as part of the research conducted by Douglas et al. (2016).

Every so often the fundamental question for coaches is *how?* How do we teach? How do we influence our players? How do we make sure that what we teach will be received and will have an impact on our players? Providing an answer and a potential solution, Douglas et al. (2016) proposed the concept of "moving players to action" (MP2A; p. 38). They argue the coach should have the ability to "orchestrate", exactly as a conductor will do with his orchestra, the actions of players and their moves on and off the court, their trust, while being effective in his selected strategies and methods, combined with psychological aspects (such as dealing with various personalities, confidence, goal setting, coping with pressure, etc.) while maximising the time available to them to work with the team. Verbal and non-verbal communication plays an important role too and will facilitate (or impede) the transfer of knowledge from the coach to the athlete.

Planning what is the best way to teach and deliver a topic (Douglas et al., 2016) remains a fundamental aspect of good coaching together with organisational skills. Lastly, passion has to be considered too; this is what usually drives basketball coaches in their quest for success on their journey to elite levels.

8.4 Summary

Cushion et al. (2003) argue that meaningful practical experiences, coaching activities that are supported in a variety of settings and critical reflection are the essential elements of coach education. The same is applicable for basketball coaches who engage in a variety of activities in order to learn and develop.

When access to formal learning opportunities is restricted because of time constraints (e.g. because of competition demands/high number of training sessions and games per season), self-learning (Jimenez et al, 2009) becomes a viable option, and coaches need to be proactive in finding sources that are accessible and useful to them – for example, books, specialised coaching magazines (*FIBA Assist* magazine is a valuable resource in this context), engagement in coaching conversations, regular coaching newsletters, DVDs/videos and so on. Additionally, as we have seen, social media outlets are becoming increasingly important in our everyday life and offer useful and time-effective tools for communication with various stakeholders.

Constant curiosity was identified by expert basketball coaches in Douglas et al.'s study (2016) as a way of acquiring knowledge and permanent development. A continuous "quest for excellence in teaching and learning" (p. 34) was another key finding from the same study, and this clearly signals what coaches need to do in order to improve and get better. With knowledge "constantly being renewed" and becoming rapidly devalued (Raikou and Karalis, 2010, p. 104), there is a clear need for coaches to stay current with all the trends of the modern game and to be aware of existing practice (on the national and international scene). As Foster (2013) indicates, "the day when you stop thinking you can learn as a coach is the day you should pack your bags and move along". He adds that basketball coaches should take any opportunity which comes their way and which involves being around and learning from other coaches. Coaches should transform themselves into lifelong learners (Nater and Gallimore, 2010) if they want to succeed.

At the end of the day, what is important is not only how coaches acquire knowledge but mainly how coaches apply this knowledge in practice (Nash and Collins, 2006). It is hoped that the ideas and practical suggestions presented above as part of this chapter will provide a starting point for future discussions and debates on such a fundamental aspect of coaching process – that of education and further personal development.

References

Abraham, A. and Collins, D. (1998) Examining and extending research in coach development. *Quest*, Vol. 50, pp. 59–79.

Anderson, A., Knowles, Z. and Gilbourne, D. (2004) Reflective practice for sport psychologists: concepts, models, practical implications and thoughts on dissemination. *The Sport Psychologist*, Vol. 18, pp. 188–203.

Basketball England. (2017) *2017 NBA coaching clinic*, online, available at: www.basketballengland.co.uk/coach-and-officials/coaching/2017-nba-coaching-clinic (accessed on 21st November 2017).

Bloom, G., Salmela, J. and Schinke, R. (1995) Expert coaches views on the training of developing coaches. In Vanfraechem, R. and Vanden Auweele, Y. (eds.) *Proceedings of the ninth European congress on sport* (pp. 401–408). Brussels: Free University of Brussels.

Boyd, R. (1980) *Redefining the discipline of adult education*. San Francisco: Jossey-Bass.

Canada Basketball. (2017) *Coaching*, online, available at: www.basketball.ca/en/page/coaching (accessed on 20th November 2017).

Coaching Review Panel. (1991) *Coaching matters: A review of coaching and coach education in the UK*. London: Sports Council.

Coombs, P. and Ahmed, M. (1974) *Attacking rural poverty: How nonformal education can help*. Baltimore: Johns Hopkins University Press.

Cote, J. and Gilbert, W. (2009) An integrative definition of coaching effectiveness and expertise, *International Journal of Coaching and Sports Sciences*, Vol. 4, pp. 307–323.

Culver, D. and Trudel, P. (2008) Clarifying the concept of communities of practice in sport: A response to commentaries. *International Journal of Sports Science and Coaching*, Vol. 3, Issue 1, pp. 29–32.

Cushion, C. (2006) *Mentoring: Harnessing the power of experience*. In Jones, R. (ed.) *The Sports coach as educator: Re-conceptualising sports coaching* (pp. 129–144). London: Routledge.

Cushion, C., Armour, K. and Jones, R. (2003) Coach education and continuing professional development: experience and learning to coach. *Quest*, Vol. 55, Issue 3, pp. 215–230.

Cushion, C., Nelson, L., Armour, K., Lyle, J., Jones, R., Sandford, R. and O'Callaghan, C. (2010) *Coach learning and development: A review of literature. Executive summary*, online, available at: www.ukcoaching.org/sites/default/files/Coach%20Learning%20and%20Development%20(exec%20summ).pdf (accessed on 10th November 2017).

Douglas, S., Smith, M., Vidic, Z. and Stran, M. (2016) Developing coaching expertise: Life histories of expert collegiate wheelchair and standing basketball coaches, *Palaestra*, Vol. 30, Issue 1, pp. 31–42.

Feu, S., Garcia, J., Parejo, I., Canadas, M. and Saez, J. (2009) Educational strategies for the acquisition of professional knowledge by youth basketball coaches. *Revista de Psicologia del Deporte*, Vol. 18, suppl., pp. 325–329.

FIBA. (2017) *FIBA Europe coaching certificate*, online, available at: www.fiba.basketball/coaches/europe-coaching-certificate (accessed on 20th November 2017).

FitzPatrick, A. (2014) *Coaches vary on use of social media*, In Courier News, 1st February 2014, online, available at: www.blythevillecourier.com/story/2047611.html (accessed on 21st November 2017).

Football Association. (2017) *Get extra guidance and support through the FA's coach mentor programme*, online, available at: www.thefa.com/get-involved/coach/coach-mentor-programme (accessed on 23rd November 2017).

Foster, J. (2013) *FIBA U19W – Coaches benefit from clinic in Klaipeda*, online, available at: www.fiba.basketball/pages/eng/fc/news/fibaFamilyNews/p/newsid/57331/arti.html (accessed on 21st November 2017).

Gilbert, W., Gallimore, R. and Trudel, P. (2009) A learning community approach to coach development in youth sport. *Journal of Coach Education*, Vol. 2, Issue 2, pp. 3–23.

Gilbert, W. and Trudel, P. (2001) Learning to coach through experience: reflection in model youth sport coaches. *Journal of Teaching in Physical Education*, Vol. 21, pp. 16–34.

Hockey Canada. (2017) *National coach mentorship program*, online, available at: www.hockeycanada.ca/en-ca/hockey-programs/coaching/mentorship (accessed on 23rd November 2017).

Irwin, G., Hanton, S. and Kerwin, D. (2004) Reflective practice and the origins of elite coaching knowledge. *Reflective Practice*, Vol. 5, Issue 3, pp. 425–442.

Jimenez, S., Lorenzo, A. and Ibanez, S. (2009) Development of expertise in Spanish elite basketball coaches. *Revista Internacional de Ciencias del Deporte*, Vol. 17, Issue 5, pp. 19–32.

Johns, C. (1994) Guided reflection. In Palmer, A., Burns, S. and Bulman, C. (eds.) *Reflective practice in nursing* (pp. 110–130). Oxford: Blackwell Science.

Jones, R. (2006) How can educational concepts inform sports coaching? In Jones, R. (ed.) *The sports coach as educator: Re-conceptualising sports coaching* (pp. 3–13). New York: Routledge.

Jones, R. and Wallace, M. (2005) Another bad day at the training ground: coping with ambiguity in the coaching context. *Sport, Education and Society*, Vol. 10, Issue 1, pp. 119–134.

Knowles, Z., Gilbourne, D., Borrie, A. and Nevill, A. (2001) Developing the reflective sports coach: A study exploring the processes of reflection within a higher education coaching programme. *Reflective Practice*, Vol. 2, pp. 185–207.

Knowles, Z., Gilbourne, D., Cropley, B. and Dugdill, L. (2014) *Reflective practice in the sport and exercise sciences: Contemporary Issues*. Abingdon: Routledge.

Knowles, Z., Tyler, G., Gilbourne, D. and Eubank, M. (2006) Reflecting on reflection: Exploring the practice of sports coaching graduates. *Reflective Practice*, Vol. 7, Issue 2, pp. 163–179.

Koh, K., Ho, X. and Koh, Y. (2017) The developmental experiences of basketball mentor coaches. *International Journal of Sports Science and Coaching*, Vol. 12, Issue 4, pp. 520–531.

Lemyre, F., Trudel, P. and Durand-Bush, N. (2007) How youth-sport coaches learn to coach. *The Sport Psychologist*, Vol. 21, pp. 191–209.

Little, B. (2015) Online training helps basketball federation towards its goals: Coaches and players learn the steps to success. *Human Resource Management International Digest*, Vol. 23, Issue 2, pp. 22–24.

Lyle, J. (2007) *Sports coaching concepts: A framework for coaches' behaviour*. Abingdon: Routledge.

Martens, R. (2004) *Successful coaching* (3rd ed.). Champaign, IL: Human Kinetics.

Masiulis, N. (2017) Personal email communication, 22nd November 2017.

Meurs, P. (2017) *How Estudiantes Madrid shook my idea upon basketball in 2010 (and embarrassed me)*, online, available at: www.pascalmeurs.com/2017/09/how-estudiantes-madrid-shook-my-idea-upon-basketball-in-2010-and-embarassed-me/ (accessed on 20th November 2017).

Monroe, M. (2014) *Relationship building, hard work helped Popovich rise from humble start*. In San Antonio Express News, 20th October 2014, online, available at: www.express news.com/sports/spurs/article/Hard-work-loyalty-5835278.php (accessed on 21st November 2017).

Mullem, P. and Croft, C. (2015) Planning your journey in coaching: building a network for success. *Strategies. A Journal for Physical and Sport Educators*. Vol. 28, Issue 6, pp. 15–22.

Nash, C. and Collins, D. (2006) Tacit knowledge in expert coaching: Science or art? *Quest*, Vol. 58, pp. 464–478.

Nash, C. and McQuade, S. (2014) Mentoring as a coach development tool (pp. 206–222). In *Practical sport coaching*. Edinburgh: Routledge.

Nater, S. and Gallimore, R. (2010) *You haven't taught until they have learned: John Wooden's teaching principles and practices*. Morgantown: Fitness International Technology.

Nelson, L. and Cushion, C. (2006) Reflection in coach education: The case of the national governing body coaching certificate. *The Sport Psychologist*, Vol. 20, pp. 175–183.

Nelson, L., Cushion, C. and Potrac, P. (2006) Formal, nonformal and informal coach learning: A holistic conceptualisation. *International Journal of Sports Science and Coaching*, Vol. 1, Issue 3, pp. 247–259.

Raikou, N. and Karalis, T. (2010) Non-formal and informal education processes of European lifelong learning programmes for higher education. *The International Journal of Interdisciplinary Social Sciences: Annual Review*, Vol. 5, Issue 1, pp. 103–113.

Richards, P., Collins, D. and Mascarenhas, D. (2012) Developing rapid high-pressure team decision-making skills: The integration of slow deliberate reflective learning within the competitive performance environment: A case study of elite netball. *Reflective Practice*, Vol. 13, Issue 3, pp. 407–424.

Richards, P., Mascarenhas, D. and Collins, D. (2009) Implementing reflective practice approaches with elite team athletes: Parameters of success. *Reflective Practice*, Vol. 10, Issue 3, pp. 353–363.

Robinson, P. (2010) *Foundations of sports coaching*. Abingdon: Routledge.

Rogers, A. (2002) *Teaching adults* (3rd ed.). Buckingham: Open University Press.

Schon, D. (1987) *Educating the reflective practitioner*. San Francisco: Jossey-Bass.

Trudel, P. and Gilbert, W. (2006) Coaching and coach education. In Kirk, D., O'Sullivan, M. and McDonald, D. (eds.) *Handbook of physical education* (pp. 531–554), Thousand Oaks: Sage.

Tsamourtzis, E., Pechlivanis, P. and Karipidis, A. (2009) Distance learning and attitudes of Greek basketball coaches. *Revista de Psicologia del Deporte*, Vol. 18, suppl., pp. 421–424.

USA Basketball. (2017) *Coach development*, online, available at: www.usab.com/youth/deve lopment/coach.aspx (accessed on 20th November 2017).

UK Coaching. (2017) *What social media do coaches use to discuss ideas?* online, available at: www.ukcoaching.org/blog/what-social-media-do-coaches-use-discuss-ideas (accessed on 21st November 2017).

Walker, S. (2006) Journal writing as a teaching technique to promote reflection. *Journal of Athletic Training*, Vol. 41, Issue 2, pp. 216–221.

WBCA. (2017) *Become a mentor*, online, available at: https://wbca.org/connect/coach-coach-mentoring-program/become-mentor (accessed on 23rd November 2017).

Wenger, E., McDermott, R. and Snyder, W. (2002) *Cultivating communities of practice*. Boston: Harvard Business School Press.

9
YOUTH BASKETBALL

Rutenis Paulauskas and Alexandru Radu

9.1 Introduction

Basketball is a very popular sport that is played in an organised manner in a variety of settings by men, women, young and old alike in 213 countries around the world (FIBA, 2017). Millions of youngsters dream of becoming professional players and of following the footsteps of star players such as Luka Doncic (Slovenia), Jonas Valanciunas (Lithuania) or Stephen Curry (USA). According to Karpowicz et al. (2015), one of the most important stages in coaching is the training of children and young people. In recent years there has been a growing interest and systematic efforts being undertaken by national federations, governing bodies of the sport and individual clubs to identify, select and work with talented young players – resources are being invested in an attempt to develop the future generations of basketball players. Mohamed et al. (2009) explored the selection of talent, and they argued that this is an ongoing process designed to identify the individuals (or groups of individuals) who demonstrate specific standards of performance. Constant interaction between young players and their coaches (and generally coaches' roles during the coaching process) is seen as the key to continuity in youth sport (Viciana and Mayorga-Vega, 2014). Basketball coaches have used various selection criteria such as assessment of technical and tactical abilities, motor skills, anthropometrical and physiological indicators in their attempts to select the better players (Strumbelj and Erculj, 2014). This chapter will explore the topic of youth basketball in relation to selection and talent identification.

9.2 Selection and identification of young players: stages in the talent identification process

The selection of children to basketball training sessions usually starts when they begin attending educational institutions: school or kindergarten. Selection is a relevant issue of perennial training which helps unfold individual talent and allows the formation of teams involving different capacity players. Williams and Franks (1998) suggest that talent search and development is a four-stage activity process including detection, identification, selection and development. In today's basketball, coaches, scouts and managers often provide subjective information indicating highly aggregated data about technical performance, personality traits, basketball awareness and speed. Talent may not be evident at an early age, but there will be some indicators that enable coaches to identify its presence. These early indicators of talent may provide a basis for predicting those individuals who are more or less likely to succeed at some later stage (Howe et al., 1998). However, basketball players' training would be more effective if the selection of athletes was based on objective pedagogical, medical-physiological, psychological, sociological and other indicators. They should be the basis for the evaluation of genotypic factors, identification of individual skills necessary for the further development of players.

Players' selection involves the ongoing process of identifying players at various stages that demonstrate prerequisite levels of performance for inclusion in a given squad or team. Selection involves choosing the most appropriate individual or group of individuals to carry out the task within a specific context (Borms, 1996).

In different countries, the popularity of basketball and the number of children attending training sessions are rather different. This may partly determine the criteria used in the selection and cause some difficulty in finding talented basketball players. However, in the countries where basketball is popular and where there are high numbers of basketball schools, youth and adult teams, there are also good conditions to unfold talents and carry out their selection. Player selection is subject to various methods which enable not only to identify those characteristics, but also to predict the further development of athletes (Bloom, 1976; Regnier et al., 1993; Williams and Reilly, 2000). According to the specificity of the issues raised, the scientific methods used in the selection of players can be grouped into the categories which are presented in Figure 9.1.

Athletic selection should contribute to meeting the challenge of the selection of promising players who can become highly skilled athletes, and will lead to their development strategy as part of the training system. The long-term athlete training periodization structure became a four-stage model of training: initiation, athletic formation, specialization and high performance (Bompa, 1999; Bompa and Carrera, 2015). It should be noted that the selection is a continuous process (Dragnea, 1999; Radu 2015) and includes the whole long-term training, but with each stage of training essential characteristics start emerging. Therefore, on the basis of long-term periodization, four stages of selection can be distinguished:

1 *Initial selection*: This is part of the initial involvement of all children in basketball training sessions.
2 *Secondary selection*: Children are selected for the school teams and/or club teams.
3 *Main selection*: Players are selected for the national youth teams.
4 *Final selection*: Players are selected for the world's best clubs and national teams.

Each stage is characterized by distinct selection methods and criteria, evaluation accuracy and the assertiveness of conclusions. Several significant features and physical as well as motor skills can be distinguished, and they have already been investigated by numerous authors including Williams and Franks (1998); Bencke et al. (2002); Gabbet (2000); Saenz-Lopez et al. (2005) and Mohamed et al. (2009), amongst others. These features are summarized in Figure 9.2.

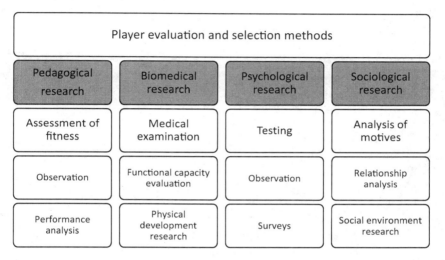

FIGURE 9.1   Basketball players' evaluation and selection methods (authors' own elaboration)

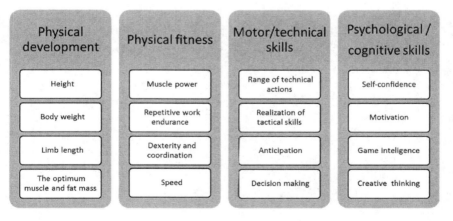

FIGURE 9.2   Characteristic features of basketball players in the course of specialized selection

Adapted from Paulauskas, 2015.

1 Initial selection

According to the Lithuanian basketball training system model, initial selection stage starts for children of about 5–8 years of age (Paulauskas, 2015). The main task of the initial selection stage represents the coordination of children's involvement in basketball – efforts are being made to enthuse and invite as many children as possible to engage in basketball. Everyone who wants to play sports should be admitted to the initial training groups. The main selection criterion at this stage is the children's own desire to play, to compete and to lead; however, school teachers' and parents' observations and recommendations about their children's skills, their height and physical activity are of great importance as well.

Practical activity shows that children's morphological, functional and psychological features identified in the initial selection stage do not accurately predict their further development and evolution. This is often corrected by the individual patterns of development and adaptation phenomena in different periods of life (Philippaerts et al., 2006). However, the data obtained by studying the young basketball players in the initial selection phase could help reveal certain relationships. For example, certain studies (Paulauskas, 2015) examined physique and physical fitness of 6-year-old children (n = 217) who started attending regular basketball training sessions, as well as the height of both parents. The investigation showed that the height of children at this age correlated with their parents' height ($r = 0.294$, $p < 0.001$), as can be observed in Figure 9.3.

According to Malina (1997), human height is determined by heredity by 70%, while the other 30% by nutrition, sport and health condition. It appears that the child's height can be predicted – one of the methods was proposed by researchers such as Khamis and Roche (1994). It is argued that if the child does not have health

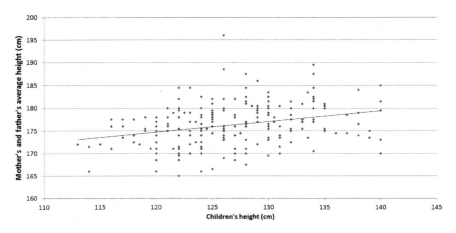

FIGURE 9.3 Correlation between average height of 6-year-old children who started attending basketball training sessions and their parents' average height

Adapted from Paulauskas, 2015

problems, this method is reliable. Standard error of predicted height indicators can be no greater than ±3 cm. Therefore, it can be stated that in the search for taller players in basketball groups, their parents' height should be taken into consideration. Children's physical skills were assessed as well: their jump height, isometric hand grip force and tennis ball throw. Although no inter-correlations between these parameters have been observed, such indicators can serve in assessing the development of basketball players of this age. Table 9.1 presents the percentile scale of Lithuanian 6-year-old children's anthropometric and physical fitness indicators.

2 Secondary selection

This stage starts at about 9–12 years old. The main task of this stage is the identification and selection of talented players for excellence development groups, basketball school or youth club teams. These groups are selected in the course of specialized training, when intensive teaching of the main technical actions (the so-called fundamentals) is happening alongside participation in matches. In the secondary selection phase children's body adaptation to physical loads is observed (noticed), and also adaptation to new movements as well as the acquisition of combinations of these fundamental movements. At this stage, the selection of teams is carried out by the coach who takes into consideration the following features of children's development: health condition, physical development, physical fitness, development and improvement perspectives of motor control and mental qualities.

Manifestation of all these features may be different, so at this age physical fitness may show up more, and then locomotive skills can unfold, and vice versa. In this selection stage, there is a systematic involvement of children into the basketball matches, consistently moving to more serious tasks in the training sessions, and technical specialization signs of players begin to emerge towards the end of this stage: taller players are trained to be the centers, smaller players – point guards. As

TABLE 9.1 Percentile scale of Lithuanian 6-year-old children's (n = 275) body composition and physical fitness assessment

Percentiles (%)	Height (cm)	Body mass (kg)	Jump height (cm)	Static hand grip force (kg)	Tennis ball throw (m)
90	135	35	29	18	16,5
80	132	31	25	15	14,2
70	130	30	23	13	13,1
60	128	29	22	11	12,7
50	126	27	20	10	12
40	124	26	19	9	11,2
30	123	25	17	7	10,2
20	122	24	16	6	9,1
10	119	23	14	4	8

Adapted from Paulauskas, 2015.

part of the selection, coaches usually apply the following methods to collect info/data about their players: performance observation, testing physical fitness, evaluation of physical development and analysis of quantitative game performance indicators.

This selection phase may last up to 5 years. During this period, the strongest players in basketball schools are brought together into teams that participate in schoolchildren's matches. Basketball schools usually have several training groups that compete in matches of different ability levels. Best players are highly motivated, they demonstrate leadership skills, fast decisions in the game and good tactical thinking. The coach evaluates these skills observing the children not only in matches, but also in training sessions. However, the mere subjective information about the player is not sufficient. In the selection process, the objective information is provided by physical and functional fitness tests, using adapted pedagogical tests for basketball players. Physical fitness is usually tested using some (or all) of the following tests:

- Three-quarter-court sprint (20 m) (base line to opposite foul line) test (National Basketball Conditioning Coaches Association, 2007);
- No-step vertical jump test (Bosco et al., 1983);
- Line agility (5 + 10 + 5 m) test (Brittenham, 1998);
- "Square agility" test (Johnson and Nelson, 1986);
- Tennis ball throw test.

Based on a previous study (Paulauskas, 2015), an ordinal scale of somatic, physical fitness and technical fitness indicators for 12-year-old basketball players has been provided in Table 9.2.

At this stage, the main selection criterion is the game performance analysis. The evaluation is based on the points scored, the ratio of made and missed shots, the

TABLE 9.2 Percentile scale of physical development and physical fitness indicators for 12-year-old basketball players (n = 12)

Percentiles %	Height (cm)	Body mass (kg)	Vertical jump height (cm)	20 m run (s)	Square agility (rep.)	Line agility (s)
90	182	73.7	48	3.39	31	5.26
80	175.5	65.2	44	3.4	31	5.3
70	172	64.2	43	3.44	31	5.32
60	170	56.5	42	3.45	30	5.35
50	169	54.7	41	3.57	30	5.43
40	167.5	51	40	3.58	29	5.48
20	166	48.5	39	3.6	28	5.53
30	164	46.6	39	3.61	28	5.56
10	162.5	46.2	36	3.96	27	5.9

Adapted from Paulauskas, 2015.

number of rebounds, turnovers, assists and other objective parameters that reflect the participation in the game.

3 Main selection

This phase begins when the child is about 16–20 years old. The main task is to select the most talented basketball players who can enter the country's youth national teams set up and aspire to play in professional basketball teams.

Screening is usually carried out through expert assessment of the game activities, physical fitness and functional capacity tests (Williams and Reilly, 2000). Players' selection to the teams can be facilitated by the following criteria:

- players' ability to realize their athletic excellence in extreme conditions;
- game awareness together with the ability to use their strengths (skills in which they excel at) in matches;
- ability to endure training and competition loads, and also to quickly recover after them;
- motivation, diligence, perseverance, determination, mobilization, fitness.

Paulauskas (2015) investigated the physical development, physical fitness and functional capacity indicators of the best Lithuanian young basketball players who were selected for the junior national basketball teams. Although top basketball players are characterized by their integral fitness, it is quite difficult to assess this in its complexity. Additional information can be obtained by studying different fitness parameters such as:

1. Somatic physical development indicators
2. Assessment of muscle static strength
3. The muscle power (MP), measuring the jump height and contact time (Bosco et al., 1983)
4. Anaerobic alactic muscle power (AAMP; Margaria et al., 1966)
5. Psychomotor reaction time (PRT; Nelson, 1967)
6. Movement frequency (10 s) measurement; tapping test

Lithuanian U16 junior boys' basketball team players who won fourth place in the European championship, and 18-year-old Lithuanian youth basketball team players (U18) who won second place in the European championship were investigated by Paulauskas (2015) who looked at some of their somatic and physical fitness indicators – these indicators are provided in the ordinal rating scale in Tables 9.3 and 9.4.

4 Final selection

This phase lasts for the entire career as an adult player. It encompasses the selection of players to national teams, club teams, as well as their ratings and the elections of

TABLE 9.3 Assessment scale of Lithuanian cadet basketball team players' (U16) physical development and physical fitness indicators

Percentiles %	Height (cm)	Body mass (kg)	Hand grip strength (kg)	Jump height (cm)	Contact time (mls)	MP (W/kg)	AAMP (W/kg)	PRT (mls)	MF (10 s/ times)
90	204.6	92.2	53.2	69.3	172.1	30.1	17.6	162.6	87.2
80	201.3	88.7	50.0	65.5	187.5	28.8	17.0	167.1	84.2
70	199.1	85.4	47.9	62.9	197.8	28.0	16.6	170.2	82.2
60	196.9	83.1	45.8	60.3	208.1	26.2	16.2	173.3	80.2
50	194.7	80.8	43.7	57.7	218.4	25.4	15.8	176.4	78.2
40	192.5	78.5	41.6	55.1	228.7	24.6	15.4	179.5	76.2
20	190.3	76.2	39.5	52.5	240.0	23.8	15.0	182.6	74.2
30	188.1	73.9	37.4	49.9	250.3	23.0	14.6	185.7	72.2
10	184.8	71.5	34.1	46.1	265.7	21.7	14.0	190.2	69.2

Adapted from Paulauskas, 2015.

TABLE 9.4 Assessment scale of Lithuanian junior basketball team players' (U18) physical development and physical fitness indicators

Percentiles %	Height (cm)	Body mass (kg)	Hand grip strength (kg)	Jump height (cm)	Contact time (mls)	MP (W/kg)	AAMP (W/kg)	PRT (mls)	MF (10 s/ times)
90	204.0	92.5	58	70	173.8	35.10	19.80	164	87
80	202.0	90.0	50	68	189.3	31.37	17.75	169	86
70	198.5	88.0	48	64	199.6	30.39	17.25	173	83
60	197.0	87.0	46	63	209.9	30.29	16.67	180	82
50	194.0	83.0	45	61	220.2	29.51	16.47	184	81
40	193.5	82.5	44	60	230.5	25.78	16.27	190	74
20	192.0	79.5	42	59	240.8	25.00	16.18	192	72
30	190.0	78.5	40	58	251.1	23.33	15.98	196	67
10	188.0	77.7	38	57	266.6	23.14	15.21	198	65

Adapted from Paulauskas, 2015.

the best players based on the concept of the model at a particular moment in time for a particular age group and for a particular position in the team (e.g. the Top 5 / team of the tournament). Basketball player selection for the elite teams is carried out in accordance with the following criteria:

- achievements in game activities and their dynamics in the course of several years;
- robustness of technical and tactical actions and ability to realize them in the maximum competitive conditions;

- high levels of physical fitness and trends of its change (ability to maintain a good physical shape for 2–3 consecutive months or more – players who can do this will perform better and will be more successful);
- ability to learn new techniques and tactical actions and reproduce them in rapidly changing conditions;
- athlete's personality traits and character features.

Selection in the final stage is carried out throughout the whole active professional player's life. The most talented players can be invited to the national team very early. For example, Jonas Valančiūnas (Lithuania) entered the national men's team at the age of 19 (FIBA Europe, 2012) and Arvydas Sabonis (Lithuania) became the world champion in basketball at the age of 17 years (Stankovic, 2013). This shows that when players are invited to represent the highest excellence teams and their national teams, age limit is not a limiting factor. Šarunas Jasikevičius (Lithuania) represented the Lithuanian national team in London Olympic Games, being 36 years old (Stein, 2012). Tim Duncan (USA) announced his retirement at 40 years old, after spending 19 seasons with the San Antonio Spurs in the NBA, winning five championships and giving the team a .710 winning percentage (Lutz, 2016). However, the selection of mature players is reflected by the average age of players involved in a national team. For example, in 2011, the average age (M ± S) of players in the Lithuanian national team at the European Men's Championship in Lithuania was 29.3 ± 4.2 years, and in the same year, in the European Women's Championship, the average age of players in the Lithuanian team was 26.4 ± 4.6 years.

Some authors such as Dragnea (1999) agree that this final selection stage (named by him as *current selection*) is based on the form of a player at a particular moment in time (during the season), and this allows coaches to select players for a particular game or a particular tournament (as it is the case with selection of players from a large squad of 15–16 to the last 12 who could be entered on the scoresheet and consequently play in the game).

It is rather difficult to objectively define model characteristics of competitive activities for players aspiring to the national teams and international level club teams; this, according to Bangsbo (1994), is a complex, integral activity. However, most relevant and sought are individual offensive and defensive skills, and the ability to apply them in the context and for the benefit of the team. Figure 9.4 provides two groups of selection criteria: offensive skills and defensive skills. Applying the method of qualitative analysis, they can be divided into even smaller qualitative units. Skill levels of all basketball players may be very different; thus the coach's competence of combining the players' opportunities to play on the same team is of great importance. In practice, there are cases where a player who is very effective on one team does not fit on a new team when he signs a new contract. It is very important to assess the changing tendencies of competitive achievements, as well as the objective reasons for their improvement or deterioration.

Players in elite men's and women's teams are distinguished by specific physical fitness indicators as well. In basketball, considering the prevalence of high-power

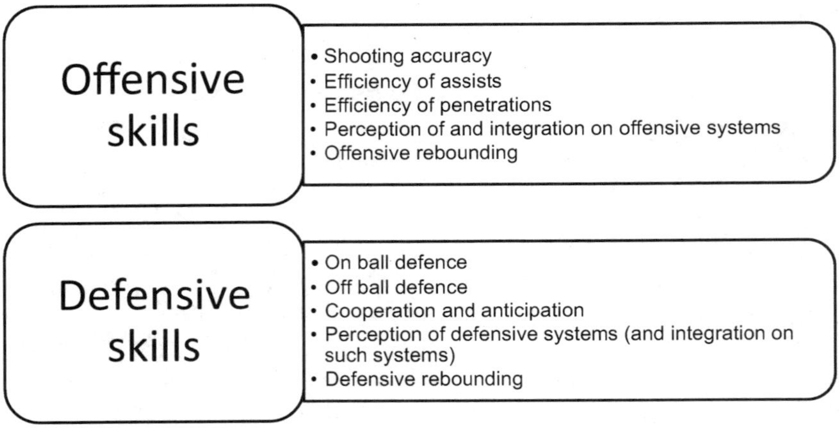

Offensive skills
- Shooting accuracy
- Efficiency of assists
- Efficiency of penetrations
- Perception of and integration on offensive systems
- Offensive rebounding

Defensive skills
- On ball defence
- Off ball defence
- Cooperation and anticipation
- Perception of defensive systems (and integration on such systems)
- Defensive rebounding

FIGURE 9.4 Parameters of competitive activities applied in the selection of players

Adapted from Paulauskas, 2015.

and high-intensity short actions – jumping, running, shooting, changing direction and so on; specific muscle power and ability to repeat the action as many times as required by the game situation are of particular relevance (Drinkwater et al., 2005). Therefore, in the selection process, a significant criterion is muscle power. Also, in the acceleration of considerable powers, anaerobic alactic muscle power (AAMP) and separate forms of speed – psychomotor reaction time (PRT) and movement frequency become important, which partly reflects the central nervous system (CNS) motility functions. Having analysed multiple Lithuanian champions such as players of Vilnius TEO women's basketball team and women's national basketball team, players of Vilnius "Lietuvos Rytas" and Vilnius "Sakalai" men's basketball team, Paulauskas (2015) provided their assessment scale in relation to various indicators such as physical development, physical fitness and functional capacity – details are included in Tables 9.5 and 9.6.

The highest-capacity teams' players often have particularly high physical fitness indicators that are away from the team average by one, two and sometimes even three standard deviations. Most often these are phenomenal athletes with genetically determined physical fitness plots, which is important to observe during the selection process. Paulauskas (2015) found that the women's Euroleague 2010 regular championship top scorer C. L. is considerably different from the team players with regard to her jump height and take-off speed – as can be noticed in Figure 9.5. Her lower limb explosive power was especially great, which was even within two standard deviations away from the average of the team in which she played. Similarly, AAMP and PRT were much higher than the average values of the whole team.

TABLE 9.5 Physical development, physical fitness and functional capacity assessment scale for elite women's basketball players

Percentiles %	Height (cm)	Body mass (kg)	Hand grip strength (kg)	Jump height (cm)	Contact time (mls)	MP (W/kg)	AAMP (W/kg)	PRT (mls)	MF (10 s/times)
90	192.5	83.5	46	55	172.5	26.8	16.6	157	95
80	189.0	82.0	45	51	183.0	25.3	16.1	164	89
70	186.0	76.0	44	49	193.1	23.1	15.2	165	87
60	184.5	75.0	43	47	203.2	22.3	15.0	170	84
50	184.0	72.5	42	46	213.3	21.5	14.5	175	83
40	182.0	68.5	41	45	223.4	20.4	14.1	179	79
20	179.0	67.0	40	44	233.5	19.3	13.4	180	76
30	178.0	62.0	37	42	243.6	18.1	12.9	182	74
10	177.5	61.0	36	38	254.1	17.5	12.1	187	72

Adapted from Paulauskas, 2015.

TABLE 9.6 Physical development, physical fitness and functional capacity assessment scale for elite men's basketball players

Percentiles %	Height (cm)	Body mass (kg)	Hand grip strength (kg)	Jump height (cm)	Contact time (mls)	MP W/kg	AAMP (W/kg)	PRT (mls)	MF (10 s/times)
90	207.5	107.5	80	77	165	31.4	18.3	142	94
80	203	104	74	72	174	30.9	18.2	160	88
70	201	102	69	69	184	28.1	18.0	163	86
60	198	100	66	68	187	27.9	17.9	166	85
50	197	95.4	61	66	197	27.3	17.6	169	83
40	196	92	59	64	208	26.2	17.5	172	82
20	192	90.5	55	63	216	23.7	17.2	174	80
30	189.5	88.2	52	61	223	23.6	16.9	175	77
10	183.5	85.5	50	60	231	21.3	16.1	177	73

Adapted from Paulauskas, 2015.

It was established that the phenomenal Lithuanian basketball player R. Š. (who became European champion in 2003, Euroleague champion in 2007 and 2008, elected Most Valuable Player of Euroleague regular championship in 2008 and bronze medalist at 2000 Olympic Games in Sydney) was distinguished by high physical fitness (Paulauskas, 2015). He was characterized by considerable jump height, lower limb explosive power and anaerobic alactic muscle power. His physical fitness indicators were standardized and provided by the Z-value profiles to demonstrate how they varied from elite basketball team average – details in Figure 9.6.

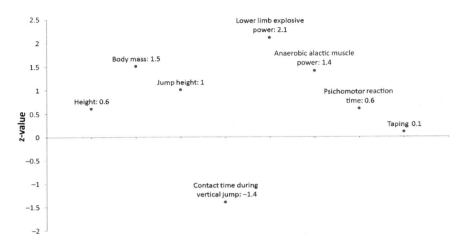

FIGURE 9.5 Standardized indicator profiles of physical development and physical fitness for Women's Euroleague 2010 top scoring player C. L.

Adapted from Paulauskas, 2015.

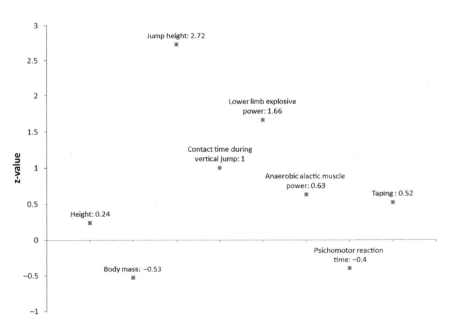

FIGURE 9.6 Standardized indicator profiles of physical development and physical fitness for Men's Euroleague 2008 MVP R. Š.

Adapted from Paulauskas, 2015.

9.3 Potential predictors of talent in basketball/ selection criteria

In the final selection stage, players who enter the strongest teams, clubs and national teams, often have an advantage not only because of their physical skills, but also because of their mental characteristics and personality maturity traits. Figure 9.7 presents personal characteristics of players that help or hinder achieving good results and let them compete with others (adapted from Lickona, 1991; Nelsen, 2006; Martens, 2012). Some traits are genetically predetermined, while others can be changed and improved by athletes themselves. Each of these characteristics will be briefly overviewed below.

> *Will* is conscious regulation of a person's activities and behaviour that helps them overcome obstacles when pursuing a specific goal. Lack of will could lead to shortcomings on the basketball players' development.
> *Reasoning (and reasoning skills)* is a process of cognitive activity associated with the changing situation of the match, given the broad range of choice and rejection options, the ability to make the right decision and act quickly. This feature can often compensate the lack of physical skills (physical ability).
> *Self-confidence* is a positive belief that relates to an individual's trust in his/her own abilities; it also relates to a player's actions and application of his/her skills in order to perform the tasks assigned by the coach, club managers or even by themselves.
> *Perseverance* is the consistent pursuit of the objectives under difficult situations and subjective working conditions.

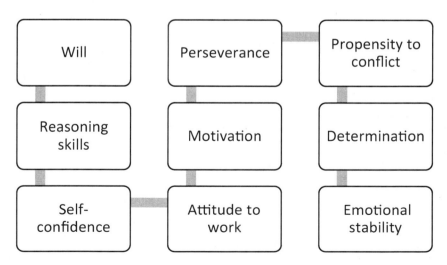

FIGURE 9.7 Athlete's mental characteristics and personality traits of maturity
Adapted from Lickona, 1991; Nelsen, 2006; Martens, 2012.

Motivation is the need to win, to overcome obstacles, to show the power to carry out something that looks very difficult, to be proud of own achievements.

Attitude to work is the real work performance and player's satisfaction or dissatisfaction with their work.

Propensity to conflict is a personality trait which manifests itself in the desire to oppose, argue, be offended, insult and so on. Conflictive personality may be undesirable in a team. Relationship cohesion in a team can be one of the selection criteria.

Determination is a personality trait which manifests itself in the ability to correctly assess the situation, make a decision on time, consistently and persistently implement it.

Emotional stability is the human ability to calmly respond to the changing situation, external stimulation, stress, success and failures.

Basketball players' selection to elite teams and national teams is usually carried out on the basis of the following criteria:

- Comprehensive observation of competitive activities, evaluations by coaches, managers, scouts and experts;
- Recommendations by scientists and medical professionals after physical fitness testing and after examination of the health condition of the players;
- The player's motives and reasons to play and be part of a team which they are invited to;
- Player evaluation in the control matches (friendly games) and the selection camps;
- Statistical game performance analysis and identification of patterns in play;
- Evaluation of the mental traits observing the player in matches and training sessions.

Player selection is a dynamic process requiring continuous improvement. Due to acceleration and longer duration of active participation in sport, selection phase limits may be adjusted. Also, increasing physical fitness of players leads the new assessment requirements. Tactical and intellectual maturity of players is the object of on-going improvement, so the advanced training technologies have to change along with the advancement of the selection of players.

9.4 Summary

The progression from youth to elite sport is "a complex process" (Mohamed et al., 2009, p. 258), and it is almost impossible to measure and assess all the relevant attributes needed for selection that are available to coaches (Strumbelj and Erculj, 2014). Considering such context, there is a clear need to constantly monitor young players through their years of participation mainly because of the fact that they develop at various rates. Apart from this, there is no guarantee that young people who perform well at youth level (at Under 14s, Under 16s and even at Under 18s level) will necessarily do the same when they reach adult age. In order to identify and exploit their strengths and improve their weaknesses, expert and objective assessments of the developmental changes (Vaeyens et al., 2013) coming from the coach's knowledge and experience are required nowadays in youth basketball coaching. As Goncalves et al. (2011, p. 458) stated, the whole process should be "scientifically grounded" and by doing so, the chances to transform the selected young individuals into elite performers will increase.

References

Bangsbo, J. (1994) *Fitness training in football – a scientific approach*. Copenhagen, Denmark: August Krogh Institute, University of Copenhagen.

Bencke, J., Damsgaard, R., Saekmose, A., Jorgensen, P., Jorgesen, K. and Klausen, K. (2002) Anaerobic power and muscle strength characteristics of 11 year old elite and non-elite boys and girls from gymnastics, team handball, tennis and swimming. *Scandinavian Journal of Medicine and Science in Sports*, Vol. 12, pp. 171–178.

Bloom, B. S. (1976) *Human characteristics and school learning*. New York: McGraw-Hill.

Bompa, T. (1999) *Periodization: Theory and methodology of training*, 4th edition. Champaign, IL: Human Kinetics.

Bompa, T. and Carrera, M. (2015) *Conditioning young athletes*. Champaign, IL: Human Kinetics, 21–23.

Borms, J. (1996) *Early identification of athletic talent*. Keynote Address to the International Pre-Olympic Scientific Congress, Dallas, TX.

Bosco, C., Komii, P., Tihanyi, J., Fekete, C. and Apor, P. (1983) Mechanical power test and fiber composition of human leg extensor muscles. *European Journal of Applied Physiology*, Vol. 51, pp. 129–135.

Brittenham, G. (1998) *Complete conditioning for basketball*. Champaign, IL: Human Kinetics.

Dragnea, A. (1999) *Sports training (Antrenamentul sportiv)*. Bucharest: Pedagogical Printing Press.

Drinkwater, E., Hopkins, W., McKenna, M., Hunt, P. and Pyne, D. (2005) Characterizing changes in fitness of basketball players within and between seasons. *International Journal of Performance Analysis in Sport*, Vol. 5, Issue 3, pp. 107–125.

FIBA. (2017) *FIBA family: National federations*, online, available at: www.fiba.basketball/national-federations (accessed on 8th December 2017).

FIBA Europe. (2012) *Valanciunas, young men's player of 2011*, online, available at: www.fibaeurope.com/compID_qMRZdYCZI6EoANOrUf9le2.season_2011.roundID_7526.coid_9WLDWELHJ6UUC8U7g50A93.articleMode_on.html (accessed on 6th December 2017).

Gabbet, T. J. (2000) Physiological and anthropometric characteristics of amateur rugby league players. *British Journal of Sports Medicine*, Vol. 34, pp. 303–307.

Goncalves, C. E., Coelho e Silva, M., Carvalho, H. and Goncalves, A. (2011) Why do they engage in such hard programs? The search for excellence in youth basketball. *Journal of Sports Science and Medicine*, Vol. 10, Issue 3.

Howe, M. J. A., Davidson, J. W. and Sloboda, J. A. (1998) Innate talents: Reality or myth? *Behavioural and Brain Sciences*, Vol. 21, pp. 399–442.

Johnson, B. L. and Nelson, J. K. (1986) *Practical measurements for evaluation in physical education*. Basingstoke, UK: Palgrave Macmillan.

Karpowicz, K., Karpowicz, M. and Strzelczyk, R. (2015) Structure of physical fitness among young female basketball players (trends of changes in 2006–2013). *Journal of Strength and Conditioning Research*, Vol. 29, Issue 10, pp. 2745–2757.

Khamis, H. J. and Roche, A. F. (1994) Predicting adult stature without using skeletal age: The Khamis-Roche Method. *Pediatrics*, Vol. 94, Issue 4, pp. 504–507.

Lickona, T. (1991) *Educating for character*. New York: Bantam Books.

Lutz, T. (2016) Tim Duncan ends brilliant NBA career after 19 seasons with San Antonio Spurs. *The Guardian*, online, available at: www.theguardian.com/sport/2016/jul/11/tim-duncan-retires-san-antonio-spurs-nba (accessed on 6th December 2017).

Malina, R. M. (1997) Prospective and retrospective longitudinal studies of the growth, maturation and fitness of Polish youth active in sport. *International Journal of Sports Medicine*, Vol. 1, pp. 179–185.

Margaria, R., Aghemo, P. and Rovelli, E. (1966) Measurement of muscular power (anaerobic) in man. *Journal of Applied Physiology*, Vol. 21, pp. 1662–1664.

Martens, R. (2012) *Successful coaching*. Champaign, IL: Human Kinetics.

Mohamed, H., Vaeyens, R., Matthys, S., Multael, M., Lefevre, J., Lenior, M. and Philippaerts, R. (2009) Anthropometric and performance measures for the development of a talent detection and identification model in youth handball, *Journal of Sports Sciences*, Vol. 27, Issue 3, pp. 257–266.

National Basketball Conditioning Coaches Association. (2007) *Complete conditioning for basketball*. Foran B. and Pound R. (editors). Champaign, IL: Human Kinetics.

Nelsen, J. (2006) *Positive discipline*. New York: Ballantine Books.

Nelson, F. B. (1967) *Development of a practical performance test combining reaction time speed of movement and choice response*. Unpublished study, Louisiana State University, Boton Rouge.

Paulauskas, R. (2015) *Krepšininkų rengimas: (Training basketball players)*. Monography. Vilnius, Lithuania: Lietuvos Edukologijos Universitetas.

Philippaerts, R., Vaeyens, R., Janssens, M., Van Renterghem, B., Matthys, D., Craen, R., Bourgois, J., Vrijens, J., Beunen, G. and Malina, R. (2006) The relationship between peak height velocity and physical performance in youth soccer player. *Journal of Sports Sciences*, Vol. 24, Issue 3, pp. 221–230.

Radu, A. (2015) *Basketball coaching: Putting theory into practice*. London: Bloomsbury.

Regnier, G., Salmela, J. H. and Russell, S. J. (1993) Talent detection and development in sport. In *A Handbook of Research on Sports Psychology*, edited by R. Singer, M. Murphey and L. K. Tennant, pp. 290–313. New York: Palgrave Macmillan.

Saenz-Lopez, P., Ibanez, S. J., Gimenez, J., Sierra, A. and Sanchez, M. (2005) Multifactor characteristics in the process of development of the male expert basketball player in Spain. *International Journal of Sport Psychology*, Vol. 36, pp. 151–171.

Stankovic, V. (2013) *Arvydas Sabonis, the Lithuanian tsar*, online, available at: www.euroleague.net/features/voices/2012-2013/vladimir-stankovic/i/109445/arvydas-sabonis-the-lit huanian-tsar (accessed on 6th December 2017).

Stein, M. (2012) *Lithuania still causing issues for USA*, online, available at: www.espn.co.uk/olympics/summer/2012/basketball/story/_/id/8233684/2012-olympics-lithuania-causing-issues-team-usa (accessed on 6th December 2017).

Strumbelj, E. and Erculj, F. (2014) Analysis of experts' quantitative assessment of adolescent basketball players and the role of anthropometric and physiological attributes. *Journal of Human Kinetics*, Vol. 42, pp. 267–276.

Vaeyens, R., Coelho e Silva, M., Visscher, C., Philippaerts, R. and Williams, A. (2013) Identifying young players. In *Science and soccer: Developing elite performers*, edited by A. Williams, 3rd edition. Abingdon: Routledge.

Viciana, J. and Mayorga-Vega, D. (2014) Differences between tactical/technical models of coaching and experience on the instructions given by youth soccer coaches during competition. *Journal of Physical Education and Sport*, Vol. 14, Issue 1, Article 1, pp. 3–11.

Williams, A. M. and Franks, A. (1998) Talent identification in soccer. *Sports, Exercise and Injury*, Vol. 4, pp. 159–165.

Williams, A. M. and Reilly, T. (2000) Talent identification and development in soccer. *Journal of Sports Sciences*, Vol. 18, pp. 657–667.

INDEX

Achilles tendon 146
adaptation 7
adaptation principle 7
aerobic capacity 33, 38, 39, 46, 73, 75
aerobic demands 37
aerobic endurance 16, 17
aerobic energy systems 38
aerobic fitness 38
aerobic metabolism 15, 37, 38
aerobic performance 52
agility 20, 28, 33, 35, 40, 43, 44, 46, 51, 75, 136, 172
agility training 20
all round player 108
American Psychological Association (APA) 86
amino acid 75
anabolic window 63
anaemia 68, 69
anaerobic-alactic 16
anaerobic alactic muscle power (AAMP) 173, 176, 177, 178
anaerobic capacity 33, 40
anaerobic exercise 15
anaerobic glycolysis 16
anaerobic glycolytic process 39
anaerobic-lactic 16
anaerobic-lactic endurance 17
anaerobic leg power 41
anaerobic metabolism 15, 38, 39, 75
anaerobic power 33, 40, 75
anaerobic stress 39
anaerobic threshold 16

analyst 110
ankle: ankle braces 136; ankle injury 148; ankle sprain 143, 149; ankle stability 149; ankle weights 12
annual training plan 27, 29, 53; *see also* training
anterior cruciate ligament (ACL) 134
anterior talofibular ligament (ATFL) 147, 150
anthropometric characteristics 34, 46
anthropometric indicators 171
anthropometry 33, 41
anti-doping 110
antioxidant 67, 69, 70, 71
anxiety 87, 96
assist 173, 176
assistant coach 127
attention 92
awareness 87

backcourt 39
back pick 115, 116
backrest height 107
balance 12, 43, 107
ball handling 108
basketball endurance 16
Basketball England 158, 159
basketball fitness 9
basketball specific power 10
bench press 41
β-Carotene 70, 71
β-alanine 75
biomechanics 149

blocking 37, 39, 71
blogs 160
blood: blood glucose level 52; blood lactate 130; blood lactate concentration 39; blood metabolite 38; blood test 69, 135
body composition 33, 34, 46, 52, 55, 67, 171
body fat 34, 35, 46, 58, 59, 129, 154
body fat percentages 36, 128
body mass 34, 42, 53, 74, 128, 171, 172, 174, 177, 178
body mass index 34
body strength 41
body weight 52, 76, 169
bone injuries 150
box-out 36, 40, 41, 90, 117
branched-chain amino acids (BCAA) 67, 72, 73, 76
British Association of Sport and Exercise Science (BASES) 86
British Basketball League (BBL) 143
British Psychological Society (BPS) 86
British Universities and Colleges Sport (BUCS) 2
bruised bones 150

caffeine 64, 66, 67, 73
calcaneo fibular ligament (CFL) 147, 150
calcaneus 149
calcium 58, 60, 144
caloric intake 56, 57, 61, 76
calories 59
Canada Basketball 158
carbohydrate (CHO) 52, 56, 57, 58, 62, 63, 64, 66, 67, 71, 72, 73, 78, 79, 80
cardiovascular fitness 151
carnosine 75
center 4, 34, 38, 39, 42, 43, 44, 46, 53, 107, 128, 129, 131, 132, 133, 171
central nervous system (CNS) 176
centre of gravity 107
chair: chair check 107; chair width 107
checking shoulder 113, 116, 117
choking under pressure 95, 96
class 105
classification: classification checks 108; classification conditions 102; classification points 106; classification process 105, 106; classification review 106; classification system 105, 106
coach: coach certification 157; coach education 156, 158, 162, 163; coach learning 157

coaching: coaching clinic 159; coaching philosophy 161, 163; coaching process 164
collegiate players 41
communication 117
communities of practice 160
competitive period 53, 54
compression garments 152, 153
computerised tomography (CT) 105
concentration 87, 88, 92, 95
concentric strength 148
conditioning 5; conditioning drills 15; physical conditioning 5
confidence 88, 89, 90, 163
continuous professional development (CPD) 157
cool down 111
coordination 3, 43, 105, 169
coping with stress 92
core stability 10
creatine 67, 71, 72, 76
creatin kinasa (CK) 73
curling 108
curls 104

defence 112; on ball defence 176; off ball defence 176
defending at zero 113
defensive principles 115
defensive skills 175, 176
defensive transition 39
dehydration 52, 58, 61
detraining 8
diet 51, 52, 57, 58, 61, 73, 74, 137, 144; balanced diet 70, 72; dietary reference intake (DRI) 60; dietary strategy 62, 64; low fat diet 58; Recommended Dietary Allowance (RDA) 60; unbalanced diet 59
discussion forum 160
double dribble 103
dribbling 36, 103, 104
drill speed 20
drug testing 110
dynamic power 46

eating: eating habits 51; eating plan 51
eccentric strength 148
education 157, 158; formal education 159
electrolytes 58, 64, 154
electromyography (EMG) 147
elite level 156; elite player 40, 41, 42, 43, 45, 55, 70, 94, 95, 127, 129, 143; elite teams 174; elite women players 136
endurance 13, 25, 54, 65, 73, 75, 91, 169

energy 52, 59, 61, 62, 63, 64, 71, 76; energy demands 53; energy expenditure 55; energy intake 58; energy requirements 55; energy stores 51; energy systems 15
ergonutritional aids 71
euhydration 52
Euroleague 56, 57, 176, 177, 178
European Championship 101, 108, 119, 120, 130, 173, 175
explosive weights 28

Facebook 160
fast break 37
fatigue 45, 51, 52, 57, 62, 72, 73
fat mass 53; high fat meal 59
fats 58, 59, 61, 62, 67, 76
fatty acids 38, 74
ferritin 68, 69
FIBA 43, 101
FIBA Americas 134
FIBA Assist Magazine 163
FIBA Eurocup Women 127
FIBA Europe Coaching Certificate (FECC) 158, 159
FIBA International Camp 128
FIBA World Championship for Women 127
fibre 56, 63
fibula 150
fitness status 44
F.I.T.T. principle 7
flexibility 22, 23, 25, 43, 75, 136; dynamic flexibility 23; flexibility training 24; static flexibility 23, 25
Football Association 162
force: explosive force 9; rapid force 9
forward 4, 34, 38, 42, 43, 46, 53, 104, 107, 108, 128, 129, 131, 132
foul 103
fracture 150, 151
frame length 107
free throws 88, 89, 90, 92, 94, 95, 96
frequency 7, 11
friendly games 27
front castors (front wheels) 103
functional capacity 104, 173, 176, 177
fundamentals 171

game: game awareness 173; game frequency 130, 134; game load 134, 135; game planning 110; game schedule 118
general preparatory phase 53, 54
genetic traits 52
getting off contact 116, 117
glucose 52, 63
glycogen 52, 76; glycogen resynthesis 63; glycogen stores 56, 64

goal: action goals 90; goal setting 86, 87, 90, 91, 151, 163; long-term goals 90; outcome goals 90; performance goals 90, 91; process goals 91; short-term goals 90
graduate sports therapist (GST) 143, 149, 151, 152, 153, 154
Great Britain Wheelchair Basketball Association (GBWBA) 106
group cohesion 89
group dynamics 89
guard 34, 36, 38, 39, 42, 43, 46, 53, 104, 128, 129, 130

haemoglobin 68
hand grip 171, 174, 177
handheld devices 152, 153
head coach 127
health 52, 170; health status 29; health supplements 65
heart rate (HR) 37, 38, 130, 131, 132, 133
height 46, 107, 128, 129, 169, 170, 171, 172, 174, 177, 178
help defence 104
high classification player 107, 108, 113, 114, 117
Hockey Canada 162
hormonal responses 38
hydration 52, 60, 61, 62, 64, 148, 152, 153
hydrotherapy 152

imagery 87, 89, 90, 93, 95, 96; arousal imagery 95; mastery imagery 95
immune system 57
immunity 65
individuality 5
individual technique 28
informal knowledge networks (IKN) 160
information and communications technology (ICT) 159
injury 29, 151; chance of injury 24; injury prevention 7, 8, 24, 143, 147, 148; injury prophylaxies 54; knee injury 42; risk of injury 12, 45, 75
in-season 29, 42
inside player 34, 36
Instagram 160
integral fitness 173
integrated training 5, 8, 16, 20, 29; integrated training for drill speed 22; integrated training for plyometrics 12; integrated training for speed reaction 20, 21; integrated training for strength 12
intensity 7, 27, 55, 65, 133, 134, 143; intensity load 55; intensity of training 27, 55; sub-maximum intensity 16

International Paralympic
    Committee (IPC) 102
International Physical Fitness
    Test (IPFT) 129
International Wheelchair Basketball
    Federation (IWBF) 101, 102, 104, 105,
    106, 107, 108
iron 67, 68, 69, 76; iron deficiency 69; iron
    metabolism 68, 69; iron
    supplementation 69
isokinetic analysis 151; isokinetic
    asymmetry 42; isokinetic dynamometer
    147, 148; isokinetic strength 41, 42, 46;
    isokinetic testing 148
isoleucine 72, 73
isometric exercise 146
isometric hand grip 171
isotonic beverages 62; isotonic drinks 61,
    78, 79, 80
Italian Basketball Federation 159

jump 1–3, 36, 37, 39, 42, 73, 177; maximal
    jump 2
jumping 71, 144, 176
junior player 40, 42

kneecap 150

lactate concentrations 39
lactate dehydrogenase (LDH) 73
lactic-acid-tolerance 39
landing 144
lateral ankle sprain (LAS) 147, 149, 150
lay-up 39
leadership 89, 172
learning 92, 156; blended learning 159;
    distance learning 159; formal learning
    157, 158, 163; informal learning 157,
    158, 159, 161, 162; learning management
    system (LMS) 159; learning process 160;
    non-formal learning 157; online learning
    159; self-learning 163; traditional
    learning 159
leucine 72, 73
lifestyle 87
ligament injuries 143
ligament sprains 149
lipid intake 61
lipids 69
Lithuanian Basketball Coaches
    Association 159
load 26, 130, 132, 144, 173
long-term athlete training 168
low classification player 108, 113,
    117
low point player 104, 114

macro-cycle 27
macronutrient 56
magnesium 60
magnetic resonance imaging (MRI) 105
maintenance 55
manoeuvrability 107
man to man defence 38
mass 33, 46, 128
massage 152
maturation 26
maturity traits 179
meal timing 60; post-match meal 63;
    pre-match meal 62
mechanic 110
media 110
medial malleolus 149
medical control 27
medical screening 109, 134
menstrual cycle 136
menstrual synchrony 136
menstruation 137
mental attitude 87; cognitive mental
    imagery 95; mental characteristics 179;
    mental control 171; mental imagery
    93, 94; mental practice 93; mental
    preparation 85, 86, 89, 97; mental
    rehearsal 93; mental skills 85, 87, 88, 89,
    94, 95; mental skills development 87;
    mental strategy 86, 89; mental toughness
    85, 87; mental training 85, 86; mental
    traits 180
mentoring 161
meso-cycle 27, 28
micro-cycle 27, 28, 53
micronutrients 70; micronutrient
    requirements 59
mid-season 56
minerals 60; mineral needs 60; mineral
    supplements 59, 60
minimal disability 106
mismatch offence 104
mobility 107
monounsaturated fatty acids 59, 76
motivation 87, 90, 169, 173, 179, 180
motor control 171
motor skills 167, 169
muscle: muscle bruising 151; muscle
    contraction 40, 72, 145; muscle damage
    70, 71; muscle fatigue 69, 75; muscle
    growth 57; muscle injury 73; muscle mass
    58, 71, 72; muscle power 169, 173, 176;
    muscle recovery 72, 76; muscle repair 57;
    muscle soreness 153; muscle tissue 72
muscular destruction 58
muscular power 10
musculoskeletal mass 53

National Association of Basketball Coaches (NABC) 159
National Basketball Association (NBA) 2, 4, 25, 36, 44, 68, 69, 138, 148, 159, 160, 175
National Coach Mentorship Programme 162
National Collegiate Athletic Association (NCAA) 2, 137, 138, 159
national governing body (NGB) 101, 102, 106, 118, 156, 158, 159, 167
network of colleagues 160
networks of practice (NOP) 160
neuromuscular system 9, 12
nocturnal fasting 56
nutrients 68, 71, 137
nutrition 51, 52, 53, 55, 59, 61, 69, 109, 118, 151, 152, 170
nutritional demands 51; nutritional goals 55; nutritional guide 51; nutritional limiting factors 52; nutritional needs 51, 55; nutritional planning 57, 64; nutritional strategy 55, 57, 62, 64, 66; post-match nutritional strategies 63; pre-match nutritional strategies 60
nutritionist 58, 65, 144

offensive skills 175, 176
offensive transition 39
official games 27
off-season 10, 11, 29
Olympic Games 135, 175, 177
omega 3 fatty acids 59, 73, 74, 76
Osgood-Schlatters Syndrome (OSS) 144, 145
overload 7
over rotating 113
overtraining 41, 69, 71

Paralympic Games 101, 102, 108, 124
participation guidelines 26
passing 39, 104
patellofemoral dysfunction 143
perception 93
performance analysis 118, 139, 172, 180
performance lifestyle 118
perimeter player 34, 36
periodisation 27, 53, 65
personality 175, 179
phosphocreatine (PCr) 38, 76
phosphorus 60
physical: physical ability 3, 9, 17, 25, 26, 27, 29; physical attributes 34; physical characteristics 128; physical conditioning 44; physical development 173, 174, 176, 177, 178; physical disability 105; physical fitness 171, 172, 174, 175, 176, 177, 178, 180; physical load 13, 130, 171; physical preparation 27, 97; physical skills 179; physical training 5, 27, 28; see also training
physio 110
physiological demands 29, 46; physiological testing 44
physiotherapy 106
pick 36, 108
pick and roll 103, 104, 111, 113
pick back (man out) 104
pivoting 104
planning 45, 90, 110, 132, 163
player classification 102, 104, 107; player development 162; player education 151
playing style 110
plyometrics 11, 12, 136; plyometrics volume 11
plyometric training 11, 12
point guard 4, 34, 43, 107, 171
polyunsaturated fatty acids 59, 76
positional play 107, 111
positional players 34
posterior talofibular ligament 150
potassium 60, 64
power 3, 11, 40, 42, 51, 53, 65, 71, 73, 148, 149, 176
power defence 116
power forward 4, 34, 43, 44
power training 28; see also training
preparation: preparation games 110, 134; preparation period 108, 110; preparation phase 134; preparation process 110
pre-performance routine 86, 89, 90, 95, 96, 97
pre-season 10, 11, 27, 29, 41, 42, 55, 64, 71, 91, 109, 134, 137
professional development 161
professional player 42
progression 6
protein 57, 58, 59, 60, 61, 62, 63, 64, 66, 67, 69, 76, 144; animal protein 58; plant protein 58; protein consumption 58; protein powders 60; vegetable protein 58
psychological aspects 27; psychological factors 85; psychological preparation 27, 86, 88, 89; psychological profile 87; psychological skills 86, 87, 88, 97; psychological strategies 89
psychomotor reaction time (PRT) 173, 176

quarter turns 113, 114

range of motion (ROM) 25, 107
range of movement 25, 105
rapid-eye movement (REM) 152
rebound 36, 37, 40, 53, 71, 90, 104, 117, 173; defensive rebound 90, 176; offensive rebound 176
recovery 1, 8, 27, 29, 51, 52, 55, 57, 63, 64, 66, 67, 68, 75, 110, 135, 137, 152, 153; complete recovery 12; hypertonic recovery drink 78, 79, 80; post-exercise recovery 71, 73; post-training recovery 59; recovery meal 67; recovery process 51, 74, 75; recovery time 11, 73
reflection 158, 161, 163; reflection-in-action 161; reflection-on-action 161
reflective practice 161, 162
rehabilitation 151, 152
relaxation 96
reliability 45
resistance test 41
rest 8, 11, 26, 27, 29, 45, 63, 110, 134, 143, 144; rest guidelines 26; rest intervals 12
running: high intensity running 1, 39; running game 101, 102, 103, 107, 112, 117; running sport 106

safety 107
safety considerations 12
scoring 103
screen 40
screening 103, 108, 111, 173
season 27
seat angle 107
seat height 107
selection 109, 162, 167, 168, 169, 171, 172, 174, 175; current selection 175; final selection 168, 173, 175, 179; initial selection 168, 170; main selection 168, 173; secondary selection 168, 171; selection methods 169
self-confidence 87, 169, 179
self-efficacy 92
self-instructions 91, 92
self-talk 86, 87, 89, 90, 91, 92, 95, 96; instructional self-talk 92; motivational self-talk 92; negative self-talk 92; self-talk strategy 92, 93
semi-elite players 136
session plan 28
set plays 104, 118
shadows 113
shooting 28, 39, 104, 108, 176; shooting foul 103; shooting guard 4, 34, 43, 44
shot clock 102
showing foot-plate 113

shuffling 36, 37, 39, 43, 44
Sinding-Larsen-Johansson syndrome (SLJS) 144, 145
skill acquisition 91, 93
sleep 152, 153
small forward 34, 43, 44
small-sided games (SSG) 6
social media 152, 160, 163
social networking 160
sodium 60
specialisation 26, 171
specificity 6, 45
specific preparatory period 53, 54
speed 2, 3, 17, 20, 25, 28, 33, 35, 41, 43, 44, 46, 51, 75, 107, 130, 143, 168, 169; maximal speed 44; speed reaction 20; speed training 20
sport dietitian 55
sport Injury Prevention Training Programme (SIPTP) 136
sport medicine 118
sport nutrition 137
sport psychologist 86, 88
sport psychology 85, 86, 89, 97
Sports Coach UK 160
sports drink 52, 56, 57, 60, 62, 63, 64
sports gel 56, 57, 63
sports science 118
sport supplements 71
sports wheelchair 107
sprinting 2, 37, 43
squat press 40
starchy food 56
Star Excursion Balance 148
stopping chair 114, 115, 117
strength 9, 11, 25, 28, 33, 40, 42, 43, 54, 65, 71, 105, 149; absolute strength 53; dynamic strength 42; explosive strength 9, 11; functional strength 10, 11; maximal strength 10, 40, 91; periodized strength regime 10; phases of strength training 10; specific strength 9, 10, 11; strength and conditioning 46, 91, 118; strengthening exercises 136; strength training 11; sub-maximum strength 9
stretching 22, 23, 111, 136; ballistic stretching 23; dynamic stretching 23, 25; static stretching 23, 24, 25
sub-elite players 41
supplementation 72, 73, 74, 75
supplements 51, 60, 67
switching tactics 104; switching defence 107
syndesmotic injury 148
system of play 108

190 Index

tactical ability 25, 27; tactical concepts 26; tactical skills 9; tactical training 28, 29, 97
talent 179
talent identification 167, 168
talus 149
tapering 134
team: team classification 107; team manager 110; team performance 85
technical ability 25, 27, 88
technical concepts 26
technical foul 103; bench technical foul 106
technical preparation 97
technical skills 9
tendinopathies 144
tendon 143, 145; tendon injuries 144, 146, 149; tibialis posterior tendon 149
test/testing: aerobic capacity test 45; agility test 45; anaerobic capacity test 45; fitness test 91; maximum power test 45; muscular endurance test 45; non-fatiguing test 45; pedagogical test 172; sprint test 45; strength test 45; T-test 35, 43, 44, 45, 46
theoretical-methodical preparation 27
therapist 146
thermotherapy 152
throwing 53
training: endurance training 7, 15; frequency of training 55; maximum intensity training 73; multifactorial training benefit 9; over-training 6, 8; phases of training 27; plyometric training 10, 11; resistance training 7; tactical training 27, 29; technical training 27, 28, 29; training camp 109, 137; training effect 8; training environment 87; training load 8, 29, 130, 173; training periodisation 53; training phase 53, 67; training plans 27, 65; training principles 5; training programme 5, 11, 27, 28, 33, 42, 44, 46, 64, 130, 133, 138, 139; training schedule 52, 118; training season 42; training session 27, 28, 46, 110, 111, 130, 131, 132, 134, 162, 167, 171, 172; training system 168, 170; training volume 64, 130, 133, 134; training week 28
transition 111, 138
transition defence 114
transition phase 27
transitory period 53, 54
travelling violation 103
treatment 143
triple switch 116

trunk movement 106; trunk rotation 106
turnover 103, 114, 173
Twitter 160
type of exercise 7

unit of training 27, 28
university level player 43
unsportsmanlike foul 103
USA Basketball 158

validity 44
valine 72, 73
vertical jump 35, 42, 43, 90, 172
video analysis 112
visualisation 93, 94
vitamin 59, 60; vitamin C (ascorbic acid) 70, 71; vitamin D 65, 67, 68, 76, 144; vitamin D2 (ergocalciferol) 65; vitamin D3 (cholecalciferol) 65; vitamin E (α-tocopherol) 70, 71, 74
volume 27, 65, 134
volume of action 105
VO_2 37, 38
VO_2 max 35, 38, 45, 46, 73

warm down 136
warming up 12, 28, 110, 111, 136
water 52; water deficit 52
weekly training programme 27, 135; weekly training load 28
weight 55, 58, 128, 129
weighted vests 12
wheel camber angle 107; rear-wheel position 107
wheelchair 103, 105
wheelchair basketball 101, 104, 105, 112, 115, 116, 117, 118
windows of opportunity 25
Wingate test 35, 40
wing-span 36, 41
Women Eurobasket 130, 135, 137
Women Euroleague 127, 135, 136, 138
Women's Basketball Coaches Association (WBCA) 138, 162
Women's National Basketball Association (WNBA) 127, 135, 138
World Championships 101, 102, 108, 128, 129

X-ray 105

youth basketball 26, 167, 181
youth sport 167